Classroom Cheat Codes

Transform your teaching today with creative and tactical strategies!

Teaching can be exhilarating when creativity, innovation, and wide-open enthusiasm are cranked up to the max! In *Classroom Cheat Codes*, Todd Finley offers visually engaging and practical strategies designed to energize your instructional approach.

What's Inside?

- **Inspiring Ideas**—Over 1,200 awesome instructional tips, each accompanied by a unique graphic.
- **PD/PLC-Ready Design**—Each chapter includes previews of key strategies, a unique mnemonic device, reflection questions, and a checklist of activities to try.
- **Evidence-Based Insights to Common Problems**—Experts are cited for solutions to *Lesson Starters, How to Increase Participation in Whole Class Discussions, What to Do When Kids Refuse to Do the Work, How to Help Students with Executive Function Issues,* and much more!

By the end of this toolbox, you'll not only have ideas to try tomorrow but also the confidence to create dynamic, student-centered learning environments that foster engagement, deeper understanding, and unforgettable classroom experiences for everyone!

Todd Finley has a rich background in education, having taught elementary and 7–12th grade English in Minneapolis. Currently, he is a tenured professor of English Education at East Carolina University. With 98 articles published with *Edutopia*, several of which have garnered over 2 million views and ranked among the top 10 most-read posts annually, Todd's work has made a significant impact on educators worldwide.

Also Available from Routledge Eye On Education
www.routledge.com/K-12

101 Answers for New Teachers and Their Mentors, Fourth Edition
Effective Teaching Tips for Daily Classroom Use
Annette Breaux

Classroom Management from the Ground Up
Todd Whitaker, Katherine Whitaker, Madeline Whitaker Good

Your First Year, Second Edition
How to Thrive and Survive as a New Teacher
Todd Whitaker, Katherine Whitaker, Madeline Whitaker Good

Prepared Classroom
Ready to Teach, Ready to Learn
Gail Boushey and Allison Behne

Real Talk for New Teachers
Tools for Building a Sustainable Career
Katy Farber and Penny Bishop

Everything New Teachers Need to Know But Are Afraid to Ask
An Honest Guide to the Nuts and Bolts of Your First Job
Amber Chandler

Classroom Cheat Codes

Effective Teaching Strategies to Power-Up Engagement

Todd Finley

NEW YORK AND LONDON

Designed cover image: Getty Images

First published 2026
by Routledge
605 Third Avenue, New York, NY 10158

and by Routledge
4 Park Square, Milton Park, Abingdon, Oxon, OX14 4RN

Routledge is an imprint of the Taylor & Francis Group, an informa business

© 2026 Todd Finley

The right of Todd Finley to be identified as author of this work has been asserted in accordance with sections 77 and 78 of the Copyright, Designs and Patents Act 1988.

All rights reserved. No part of this book may be reprinted or reproduced or utilised in any form or by any electronic, mechanical, or other means, now known or hereafter invented, including photocopying and recording, or in any information storage or retrieval system, without permission in writing from the publishers.

For Product Safety Concerns and Information please contact our EU representative GPSR@taylorandfrancis.com. Taylor & Francis Verlag GmbH, Kaufingerstraße 24, 80331 München, Germany.

Trademark notice: Product or corporate names may be trademarks or registered trademarks, and are used only for identification and explanation without intent to infringe.

ISBN: 978-1-041-04556-4 (hbk)
ISBN: 978-1-041-04555-7 (pbk)
ISBN: 978-1-003-62880-4 (ebk)

DOI: 10.4324/9781003628804

Typeset in Arial
by Apex CoVantage, LLC

Graphic elements by The Noun Project

To teachers everywhere, especially Randi, Jack, Mike, Brian, Sarah, Allen, Jennifer, Swags, and Mom.

Table of Contents

Acknowledgements	xii
Meet the Author	xiii
Preface	xiv
Introduction	xv

Chapter 1   Energize and Engage: First-Week Activities — 1

First-Week Activities	5
Ice Breakers	6
Handling a Big Class	7
Set Strong Norms	8
Rapport Builders!	9
I Wish My Education Profs Had Told Me . . .	10
Teaching, Like Writing a Persuasive Essay	11

Chapter 2   Classroom Management: Cultivating a Productive Learning Environment — 15

Reduce Classroom Commotion	19
Resistant Classes	20
Classroom Conflict	21
A Child Refuses Classwork. Now What?	22
Indicators That a Child Might Become Violent	23
Supporting a Child Who Might Become Violent	24
Tips for Dealing with Hate Speech	25

Chapter 3   The Organized Teacher: Maximizing Efficiency — 29

The Organized Teacher	33
Time Savers	34
Plan Lessons Faster	35
Tips for Managing Student Paperwork	36
Sub Tub Components	37

Chapter 4   Instructional Essentials: Core Elements of Effective Teaching — 41

Lesson Starters	45
Schema Activation Strategies	46
Metacognition	47
To Clarify Something Complex	48
The Science of Chunking	49
Engaging Text-Based Lessons	50
Alliterative Weekday Activity Themes	51
How to Engage in Deliberate Practice	52
Upgrade Presentation Handouts	53
Boost Classroom Rigor	54
Upgrade Reading Homework	55
Decrease Task Difficulty	56
Bulletin Boards Dos' and Don'ts	57
Study Tips	58
Classroom Stations	59

Year-Enders	60
Closure Activities	61
Unsung Duties	62

Chapter 5   Dynamic, Student-Centered Learning Approaches — 67

Active Learning Strategies	71
Classroom Improv Games	72
Games for Classrooms	73
Cooperative Learning	74
Gamification Tools and Strategies	75
Student-Centered Learning	76
Make Lectures Interactive	77
How to Teach Decision-Making	78
How to Reduce Cognitive Overload	79
Sticky Note Activities	80
X-Factor Teaching	81

Chapter 6   Harnessing Visual Tools — 86

Powerful PowerPoint	90
Make Thinking Visible	91
Pair Visual with Critical Thinking	92
Video Viewing Tips	93
Timeline Learning Activities	94

Chapter 7   Cultivating Effective Teacher Habits — 98

Eight Habits of Successful Teachers	102
Boost Your Teaching Confidence	103
Effective Teaching Nonverbals	104

Chapter 8   Building Literacy Skills (Reading, Writing, Listening, Speaking) — 109

How to Scaffold Texts to Unlock Meaning	113
Scaffolding English Language Arts	114
Effective Use of Text Evidence . . . Remember C.A.S.E.	115
Post-Reading Journal Alternatives	116
Book Report Alternatives	117
Vocabulary Instruction	118
How Students Conceal Reading Struggles	119
Where to Find Free Readings	120
Poem Analysis Activities	121
Techniques for Helping Kids Summarize	122
Writing Tips	123
Writing to Learn Strategies	124
Low-Stakes Writing	125
Revising and Editing Checklists	126
Listening Activities	127
Public Speaking Formats	128

Chapter 9 Supporting Diverse Learners (and Colleagues) — 133

- Inclusion — 137
- Supporting Students with Executive Function — 138
- Gender Equity Strategies for Faculty — 139
- Poverty Deficit Myths — 140
- Micro-Aggressions — 141
- I Finished Early—Now What? — 142
- Helping Introverts Participate in Discussions — 143
- Indicators of Bulimia — 144

Chapter 10 Facilitating Dynamic Classroom Discussions — 149

- How to Increase Participation in Whole Class Discussion — 153
- Make Class Discussions Constructive — 154
- Follow-Up Questions — 155
- A Discussion Goes Off-Topic. What Do You Say? — 156
- When Students Can't Answer — 157
- How to Facilitate Difficult Discussions — 158
- Talking About Race: Ground Rules — 159
- Debunk Conspiracy Theories — 160

Chapter 11 Comprehensive Testing and Assessment Techniques — 165

- Exam Prep Activities — 170
- Final Exam Alternatives — 171
- CAT (Classroom Assessment Techniques) — 172
- Test Construction Errors — 173
- Formative Assessment Tech — 174
- Creative Ways to Promote Learning When Testing — 175
- Exit Ticket Prompts — 176
- They Bombed the Test, Now What? — 177
- Advice for Kids with Test Anxiety — 178
- Teaching to the Test: The Issues — 179

Chapter 12 Streamlined Grading and Constructive Feedback — 184

- Efficient Grading Part 1 — 188
- Efficient Grading Part 2 — 189
- Ways to Solicit Student Feedback — 190

Chapter 13 EdTech Strategies — 194

- ChatGPT Time-Savers — 198
- Classroom YouTube Tips — 199
- What Can You Do with Google Docs? — 200
- Using Social Media for Education — 201
- Improve Remote Instruction — 202
- Teacher Presence During Remote Instruction — 203
- HyperDoc Templates — 204

Chapter 14 Motivating Students — 209

- How to Motivate Me — 213
- Research on Student Engagement — 214
- Teacher-Student Relationship Building — 215
- Trigger Students' Happy Brain Chemicals — 216
- Leverage Social Proof to Motivate Students — 217
- Classroom Rewards! — 218
- Ways to Say, "Good Job!" — 219
- Give Activities Engaging Names — 220
- Personality Characteristics of Most Liked Teachers — 221
- Make Students Feel Heard — 222
- Why Lessons Fail — 223

Chapter 15 Fostering Emotional Resilience — 228

- Compassion Fatigue — 232
- Withstand that Tough Tuesday — 233
- Science-Based Ways to Rest and Refocus — 234
- How to Maintain Healthy Boundaries — 235
- Stage Fright — 236
- Mindfulness Tips — 237
- Trauma-Informed Teaching — 238
- How to Help Traumatized Students — 239
- Ways to Help Stressed Teens — 240
- Helplines for Kids — 241
- Social-Emotional Learning Prompts — 242

Chapter 16 Beyond the Classroom — 247

- How to Defuse Angry Parents — 251
- Meal Prep Tips for Teachers — 252
- Interview Questions — 253
- How to Raise Teacher Pay — 254
- What Teachers Should Stand For — 255

Appendices — 259

- Appendix A: Index of Foundational Instructional Strategies — 260
- Appendix B: Index of Advanced Instructional Strategies — 263
- Appendix C: Glossary — 266
- Appendix D: Final Words — 270

Acknowledgements

I would like to thank the talented artists of The Noun Project, whose brilliant artwork helped transform ideas into accessible visuals. Deep appreciation goes to Routledge, an imprint of the Taylor & Francis Group, for their support and for believing in this project from the start.

I am also deeply grateful to the College of Education at East Carolina University for providing an academic home where educational innovation is encouraged and supported.

To teachers everywhere: your service has inspired every word.

Meet the Author

Todd Finley, PhD, is an Associate Professor and Coordinator of the English Education Program at East Carolina University. A former elementary and secondary ELA teacher, he co-founded the Tar River Writing Project and is a founding member of the Artificial Intelligence Teaching and Research Institute (AITRI). He earned his MA and PhD at the University of Minnesota.

Specializing in tech-augmented literacy and high-impact instruction, Dr. Finley is also recognized as an education generalist whose work spans curriculum, pedagogy, technology, and teacher development. He teaches, researches, and partners with schools to translate theory into practice. He has authored multiple books and over 130 articles—including many widely read pieces for *Edutopia*. His work is devoted to converting educational moon shots into teacher-friendly cheat codes that energize classrooms and elevate student learning.

He lives in North Carolina with his wife and an ever-growing pack of dogs.

Preface

There is a part of the brain called the hippocampus that transforms short-term memories into long-term ones. It helps me remember thousands of teachers that I've worked with, faces like yours who have experienced the euphoria of classroom epiphanies as well as lessons that spiraled into chaos.

Some, like me in my early years of teaching, were secretly lonely or emotionally numb, struggling with the cost of groceries. But they showed up for their students, day after day.

All of them wanted to test their hearts and minds in the classroom. They knew that real teaching demands many skills. They saw how some educators silenced a class with a frown and inspired like magicians, and observed how the prize for succeeding in the world's most significant profession is profound satisfaction.

To be a teacher means being more strategic, more moral, and more hopeful than other jobs. It means recovering immediately when you falter.

Please use your hippocampus to remember that young humans secretly wish for you to be strong, fair, creative, loving, and wise enough to make them powerful in the world. That's what *Classroom Cheat Codes: Effective Teaching Strategies to Power-Up Engagement* is for, to help you empower students.

I'll never forget how teachers like you enter this complex profession because you want the lives of your students to matter. Let's begin.

Introduction

The U.S. has never launched a large-scale, long-term, fully supported approach to schooling where teachers were given 100% autonomy to:

- explore innovative, exploratory learning methods
- involve students in co-designing the curriculum and assessment methods
- prioritize intuition and empathy over coverage
- adapt activities and materials at their full discretion to meet the needs of diverse students
- implement a multi-modal approach to evaluation over bubble sheets
- choose whatever professional development (PD) meets their needs without question

Comprehensive, holistic empowerment has never happened on a mass scale for an entire generation of teachers and learners—not all the way. But it could. If we can figure this out, it will be the biggest contribution our nation has made to humanity since the Universal Declaration of Human Rights! And we could be the ones to bring this about.

By providing actionable strategies, real-world examples, and evidence-based practices, *Cheat Codes: Effective Teaching Strategies to Power-Up Engagement* is designed to equip educators with the tools they need to reclaim their autonomy, innovate in the classroom, and truly understand and respond to the needs of their students. It's do-it-yourself PD with over 1,200 strategies. If you're ever wondering how to solve a classroom problem, look to this guide first for answers.

So, what are **Cheat Codes**? They're a form of micro-coaching, a concise collection of powerful infographics without any superfluous content. I think you'll find that it's hard to stop after reading just one.

Cheat Codes: The Origin Story

Eight years ago, I got fed up with long-winded education blogs that buried a single, often disappointing strategy at the end of the article. My big idea: Wouldn't it save teachers time if I compiled various strategies on a single page? I could use eye-catching images I found through my subscription to a graphic database called the Noun Project! *C'mon!*

This pursuit aligned with my skillset. In the doctoral program at the University of Minnesota, I developed the capacity to swiftly track down tactical instructional approaches and synthesize them into concise prose, a knack that proved handy when researching ideas for more than 100 *Edutopia* articles and over 200 *Todd's Brain* newsletters I've hammered on. Readers of those posts often compliment my ability to devise innovative solutions for classroom issues. In short, I was built for making bite-sized instructional strategies. My goal was for an educator on social media to glance at a single infographic and learn at least three creative and inspiring classroom solutions they had never encountered before.

It turns out that teachers shared my infographics widely when I posted them on X/Twitter. Within a few months, I heard from schools in the U.S. that copied the infographics and posted them in copy machine rooms and bathroom stalls (so teachers could enjoy "Poddy-PD" while doing personal business). After a while, the infographics were translated and used for PD by countries all over the world.

Over the years, dozens of teachers have asked me if they can buy the whole collection of them. The guide that you're holding answers that request.

What's New?

To update the Cheat Codes for this guide, I added more researcher input, overhauled each one into a streamlined format, and switched them from color to monochrome to make copies more legible. Workbook features, described after the next section, were developed to accompany each chapter.

I'm a professional researcher, educator, and teacher trainer, *not* a professional designer—so forgive any design crimes I've accidentally committed. Just know that this collection of Cheat Codes has been made with love. And like the best lessons, they're handmade.

Is This Guide for You?

Designed for new and veteran K-12 teachers, professors, professional development facilitators, and teacher trainers, this guide serves as a workbook and a treasure trove of classroom techniques. Ultimately, these Cheat Codes were written for me, by me, but shared with you to enrich how we teach and learn.

Chapter Format

Each chapter in *Classroom Cheat Codes: Effective Teaching Strategies to Power-Up Engagement* features a consistent set of elements designed to maximize its utility. They occur in this order.

- **Introduction**—A brief overview of key themes and objectives sets the stage for teaching problems and solutions the chapter addresses.
- **Key Chapter Strategies**—Preview some of the chapter's content with a handy outline of key ideas.
- **Memory Device**—Every chapter features one of the mnemonics from the list below to aid educators in recalling recommended strategies.
  - *Acronyms*: Forming a word from the initial letters of a series of words.
  - *Acrostics:* Creating sentences where the first letters of each word stand for another word.
  - *Chunking:* Grouping individual pieces of information into larger units.
  - *Keyword Method*: Using a familiar word or phrase to help remember new information by associating it with the keyword.
  - *Rhymes:* Using simple rhymes to remember information.

- *Visual Imagery*: Creating a mental image to remember facts or lists.
- *Narrative Mnemonic*: Crafting a story that connects information you need to remember by weaving elements into a narrative, making recall easier by following the sequence and logic of the tale.
- *Peg System*: Using a set of peg words you have memorized and creating associations between those peg words and items you need to remember.
- *Method of Loci:* Associating information with specific locations in a familiar place or along a route you know well.
- *Music/Melodic Mnemonics:* Setting information to music or a rhythm to make it easier to recall.

Cheat Codes—Central to each chapter are the infographics, edublasted with practical, tactical, evidence-based, and creative teaching methods for immediate classroom use.

Workbook: Reflecting on Chapter Topics—Thought-provoking prompts and advanced questions encourage professional learning communities (PLCs) or PD workshop participants to critically evaluate the suggested teaching methods and how they can be applied in their classrooms.

Checklist of Activities and Strategies to Try—A compilation of practical strategies included in each chapter encourages experimentation and bridges the gap between theoretical knowledge and classroom application. The Checklist also includes a dedicated section for teachers to reflect on the effectiveness of the strategies.

Readers will observe that several key concepts from each chapter are reiterated in the materials accompanying the Cheat Codes. Repetition and rephrasing serve as reinforcement of these fundamental ideas.

About the Appendices

After Chapter 16, the guide includes the Appendices.

Appendix A—Index of Foundational Instructional Strategies

Access a curated collection of Cheat Codes—proven teaching strategies tailored to address early career professionals' unique challenges and concerns. This index guides them in selecting appropriate techniques, such as classroom management, that foster instructional competence and swagger.

Appendix B—Index of Advanced Instructional Strategies

This specialized index recommends a list of Cheat Codes tailored to meet the advanced needs of experienced teachers already proficient in classroom management and teaching fundamentals. These strategies provide veteran educators with detailed methodologies, complex problem-solving approaches, and enriched content that leverages their skills and pushes the boundaries of traditional pedagogy.

Appendix C—Glossary

The glossary provides concise definitions of technical educational terms used throughout the text to ensure that all readers, regardless of their prior knowledge or experience level, can grasp the advanced concepts discussed in the book.

xviii Introduction

Appendix D—Final Words

The final page of the guide invites you to stay in touch and continue the conversation about transformational teaching. Included is a "Daily Affirmation for Teachers" written just for you.

At its core, *Cheat Codes: Effective Teaching Strategies to Power-Up Engagement* is engineered to enhance your pedagogical effectiveness so that you are well equipped with creative strategies to meet the diverse needs of your students—to make lessons unforgettable.

Chapter Overviews

Chapter 1—Energize and Engage: First-Week Activities

Jumpstart the school year! This chapter describes interactive activities for the first week, helping teachers set the semester's tone. Learn strategies like the "3000 Foot View" to preview what's coming, icebreakers to build community, and the "Awesome Wall" to motivate and inspire. It also covers managing large classes, establishing strong norms, and building rapport to foster a positive classroom environment on day one. These activities are designed to make the first week fun and foundational for the year ahead.

Chapter 2—Classroom Management: Cultivating a Productive Learning Environment

Internalize strategies that transform your lively classroom into a zone of focused learning and mutual respect. This chapter tackles everything from managing disruptive behavior to fostering cooperative and supportive student interactions. Learn about congestion avoidance, listening cues, smooth transitions, and more. Whether dealing with a noisy class or planning for your absence, these insights help create an environment where inspired learning happens.

Chapter 3—The Organized Teacher: Maximizing Efficiency

This chapter will boost your organizational skills and make life feel more like a *Slip and Slide*! From creating a welcoming classroom atmosphere to implementing savvy time-saving tips, stay on top of your game. Learn how to streamline daily tasks with tools like the 31-file-folder system for every day of the month, innovative hall passes, and strategies to avoid paper pileups. Also, delve into advanced, efficient planning techniques that ensure every lesson is impactful.

Whether you're prepping for the next day or the next month, this chapter will help you make room for the important stuff: connecting with kids.

Chapter 4—Instructional Essentials: Core Elements of Effective Teaching

From leveraging popular songs to explain complex subjects to employing narrative advance organizers for simplifying new concepts, discover innovative ways to grab and maintain your students' interest. Learn to begin lessons energetically, wield media to deepen understanding, and transform your classroom into a knowledge haven. Also, help your students acquire metacognitive skills.

Chapter 5—Dynamic, Student-Centered Learning Approaches

Shake up stale activities! This chapter introduces interactive, student-focused teaching methods that make learning come alive. From group warm-ups like role play and Reader's Theater to creative games like "Build a Story" and "String of Pearls," learn about maximum engagement. Plus, discover classroom games that integrate critical thinking and cooperation, such as "Four Corners" and "Marshmallows and Toothpicks," which challenge students to build and debate in fun, educational ways. Whether you're guiding discussions with "Circle of Voices" or setting up competitive learning scenarios with gamification tools, this chapter gives you a toolkit for fostering an active and inclusive learning environment.

Chapter 6—Harnessing Visual Tools

How do you use powerful visuals that capture eyeballs and enhance understanding? Avoid PowerPoint pitfalls, engage students through visual thinking strategies, and render complex ideas both tangible and digestible. We explore a variety of techniques, including how to energize presentations with humor and surprises, make lectures interactive with visuals, and support critical thinking with graphic organizers. Whether it's video analysis or creating impactful multimedia presentations, inform and inspire!

Chapter 7—Cultivating Effective Teacher Habits

Delve into the routines and practices that successful educators swear by, from the power of making daily lists to the art of dressing for success. Discover practical tips like turning off your phone to avoid distractions, using electronic apps to stay organized, and building resilience through friendships. Streamline prep time and enhance your classroom presence with powerful nonverbal cues. Each habit is backed by research and is designed to boost your confidence, efficiency, and overall teaching performance.

Chapter 8—Building Literacy Skills (Reading, Writing, Listening, Speaking)

Explore strategies that strengthen reading, writing, listening, and speaking skills. From facilitating structured talks with Think-Pair-Share to employing scaffolding techniques like frontloading vocabulary, each approach is crafted to deepen understanding and engagement. Experience modeling with "think-alouds" for metacognition, harness visuals to enrich reading contexts, and connect new concepts to students' prior knowledge to enhance relatability. This chapter serves as your comprehensive guide to creating a supportive literacy environment.

Chapter 9—Supporting Diverse Learners (and Colleagues)

Embrace diversity in your classroom and school with strategies like structured discussions, thoughtful scaffolding of texts, and techniques to make learning accessible for all. Enhance comprehension with pre-reading activities and empower students through tailored writing tasks. This chapter also presents practical ways to manage public speaking anxiety and tailor instruction to suit diverse learning styles, ensuring that every student feels valued and supported.

Chapter 10—Facilitating Dynamic Classroom Discussions

Rev up your classroom discussions! Learn an array of strategies to elevate participation and engagement in your class dialogues. Learn methods like the Hatful of Quotes for an immersive quote analysis or shift the dynamic with various discussion formats such as Socratic Seminars and Fishbowl discussions. This chapter also introduces practical tools to manage and direct discussions constructively, ensuring every student's voice is heard and valued. Whether it's using writing as a precursor to discussion or handling off-topic diversions with grace, these techniques are designed to make your classroom discussions more inclusive, thoughtful, and impactful.

Chapter 11—Comprehensive Testing and Assessment Techniques

This chapter unpacks a range of testing and assessment techniques tailored to diverse learning environments. From interactive activities like Peer Profs and Mock Press Conferences to appealing exam alternatives such as YouTube Exams and E-portfolios, this chapter is one-stop shopping for creating exams that measure knowledge but also enhance learning and retention.

Chapter 12—Streamlined Grading and Constructive Feedback

This chapter is a grading game-changer! Packed with effective strategies for efficient grading and delivering impactful feedback, this section also shows how to use rubrics and grading apps to cut down on time while increasing precision.

Learn feedback techniques that motivate and guide students, enhancing their learning journey. Whether you're looking to refine your grading practices or explore new methods like peer review and self-assessment, this chapter equips you with the tools to make grading less of a chore and more of an opportunity to foster student growth and achievement.

Chapter 13—EdTech Strategies

Discover how technologies like ChatGPT can revolutionize your teaching practices by generating discussion prompts, custom quizzes, and personalized learning goals. Explore the integration of Google Docs for collaborative projects and real-time feedback, and YouTube to bring diverse, engaging content into your classroom. Learn about using tech to save time and enhance learning.

Chapter 14—Motivating Students

Packed with strategies to keep your students engaged and eager to participate in class, explore game-based techniques, like Jeopardy-style reviews, that make education both fun and competitive. Learn the science behind motivation with insights from leading researchers to understand how factors like environment, personal attention, and class culture impact student engagement. Get ready to inspire your students to new heights of achievement.

Chapter 15—Fostering Emotional Resilience

Both students and teachers need tools and strategies to recognize and manage symptoms of emotional strain such as anxiety, exhaustion, and disconnection.

Assess vulnerability, reframe negative mindsets, and cultivate a supportive teaching environment that prioritizes mental health and well-being. Learn the significance of setting boundaries, practicing sleep hygiene, and incorporating humor into the classroom to maintain a balanced emotional state. These strategies will enhance your resilience, making it an essential read for educators aiming to thrive in challenging educational landscapes.

Chapter 16—Beyond the Classroom

This chapter explores essential strategies for engaging beyond the traditional teaching environment, offering insights into defusing tense situations with parents, practical meal prep tips for busy teachers, and critical interview techniques for advancing your career. By balancing your personal and professional life, you can enhance your well-being and deliver unparalleled learning experiences for your students.

From motivation to management, innovation to inspiration, each chapter is loaded with dozens of strategies. You're sure to find several that match your teaching style. *Evolve, energize, enrich, enlighten,* and *elevate* your classes to the next level!

Chapter 1

Energize and Engage: First-Week Activities

Energize and Engage: First-Week Activities

It's the first week of school, and you're facing a sea of new students' faces. Here is your opportunity to set the tone for the rest of the year. What's your game plan? How do you turn these strangers into a cohesive, motivated class ready to take on the challenges ahead?

Welcome to Chapter 1, where we explore how to create an electric atmosphere from day one.

This chapter is brimming with creative, engaging strategies designed to break the ice, gather crucial insights about your students, and establish clear, effective norms that will keep your classroom running smoothly throughout the academic year. From the "3000 Foot View" that helps map out the semester to engaging icebreakers and "The Awesome Wall" that builds community and motivation, you'll discover how to energize your students in the following pages.

Key Chapter 1 Strategies

1. Introduce yourself to your students in a way that sets a positive and welcoming tone.
2. Help students get to know each other in a fun and interactive way.
3. Learn about students' backgrounds, interests, and learning challenges.
4. Establish clear procedures, rules, and behaviors expected in the classroom.
5. Provide an overview of the semester's curriculum, key activities, and learning objectives.
6. Inspire and motivate students by showcasing past students' achievements.
7. Introduce students to the exciting activities and learning experiences of the upcoming year.

Memory Device for this Chapter
Mnemonic Phrase

> **"Every Student's Awesome Start"**
>
> **E**stablish a Welcoming Environment
>
> **S**urvey and Understand Students
>
> **A**wesome Wall and Inspiration
>
> **S**et and Reinforce Norms
>
> **S**tart with a Semester Overview

FIRST-WEEK ACTIVITIES

Effective first-week activities help to establish a positive classroom environment, foster a sense of community, and build rapport between students and teachers.

1. PROVIDE A 3000 FOOT VIEW

Talk about what is going to occur in each month by displaying a calendar. What work did previous classes enjoy most? Discuss the effort that will be required at different points in the semester.

2. SURVEY THE CLASS

How well do they understand key concepts? How do they pronounce their names? What is their contact information? What learning challenges worry them?

3. AWESOME WALL

Post cartoon versions of previous students to the "Awesome Wall." Those who were wildly successful and overcame challenges, kids that inspired you, and those that contributed to the class culture. Use cartoon versions of the faces so that kids can project themselves onto those identities. Finally, share your hope that one of the current students will earn a spot on that wall.

4. ANSWER QUESTIONS

Take time to answer questions that learners might have about the class.

5. SIZZLE REEL

Show a video to introduce new students to what activities await. This can also be shown to parents during open house.

6. SPECIFY KEY BEHAVIORS

Discuss procedures, rules, and out-of-bounds behaviors. What happens when students are late? When do they pack up before class ends? Note: Norms are best formed two weeks into the school year.

ICE BREAKERS

Icebreakers reduce anxiety, build a sense of community, and foster positive relationships, which enhance classroom dynamics and learning engagement.

1. BINGO SCAVENGER HUNT

Design bingo cards that include fun and relatable prompts. For example: has read a book this month, knows how to whistle, can name five superheroes, can do a flip, can happily eat pizza every day for a year, or has a reptile as a pet.

2. GROUP FLOWER

Direct students to write something important about themselves on paper petals and affix them to a bulletin board flower. Things that everyone has in common go in the middle.

3. BEACH BALL INTRODUCTIONS

Bring a beach ball to class with different questions. Whenever a student catches the ball, they'll introduce themselves with their name and age, and answer whatever question on the ball their pointer finger landed on (Guide, Inc., 2018).

4. THREE OF A KIND

Students find three other students they share something in common with, but not physical features. Repeat (Top Hat, 2022).

5. SNOWBALL FIGHT

Write five truths about yourself. Then "snowball fight" until the balls of paper have been scattered. Ask kids to pick up a snowball and read the list aloud. Classmates guess whose snowball they have (The Colorado Education Initiative, n.d.).

6. BLOBS AND LINES

Classmates gather in "blobs" based on commonalities like the way they came to school and lines when they need to be in a particular order. Example: alphabetical or by birthday.

HANDLING A BIG CLASS

Big classes are difficult to handle due to the challenge of providing individualized attention, managing diverse needs, and maintaining classroom order, which can hinder effective learning.

1. COMMENT BOX
Invite students to insert questions about the content or give feedback on your instruction.

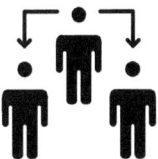
2. DELEGATE RESPONSIBILITIES
Ask students to help distribute and collect homework or lead groups. You'll often find eager volunteers who want to help.

3. TRY ATTENTION-GETTING STRATEGIES
The teacher says, "I get knocked down—" The students respond with "—but I get up again, you're never going to keep me down."

4. USE CLICKERS
Clickers help assess every learner instantly. Try SMS polling with Swift or try Plickers, a free alternative to clickers.

5. GO ELECTRIC
Try a portable voice amplifier and speaker to eliminate voice strain. These tools are commonly built into smart podiums.

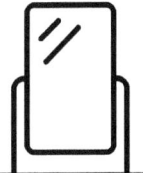
6. REFLECTION QUESTIONS
Pause in the middle of class and direct learners to write down two Qs. Then discuss the Qs with students around you (UNSW, 2022).

7. USE ADVANCED ORGANIZERS
Provide a handout with incomplete info about the day's material to be filled in by the learner.

SET STRONG NORMS

Classroom norms are the shared expectations and rules established by teachers and students that guide behavior, promote respect, and create a positive and productive learning environment.

1. INTRODUCE THREE TYPES OF NORMS
SAFETY and HEALTH (no shoving), MORAL NORMS (help peers), DISCRETIONARY NORMS (raise hands).

2. DON'T START NORMING FOR 2 WEEKS
The sequence of group formation involves, 1st, forming (members behave cautiously), and then, 2nd, storming (dominant members emerge amidst some confrontations) before norming begins.

3. SET NORMS FOR COMMON ISSUES
What are common norms for communication, when tasks are finished early, use of smartphones, student property, sub days?

4. MODEL BEHAVIOR
Teachers should model the norms they expect from students.

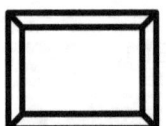

5. VISUAL REMINDERS
Post norms around the classroom as visual reminders.

6. STUDENT INVOLVEMENT
Involve students in creating norms to increase buy-in and accountability.

7. CONSISTENT ENFORCEMENT
Once the rules are in place, be consistent in their enforcement.

RAPPORT BUILDERS!

Teacher-student rapport is the positive, respectful, and trusting relationship between teachers and students, characterized by mutual understanding, and effective communication.

1. LOWER THREAT
Smile, find ways to show your palms, and keep your chin low.

2. ASK STUDENTS THEIR OPINIONS
. . . but don't judge their answers. Just stay curious and ask, "How did you come up with that?"

3. TALK MORE SLOWLY
Identify how fast your target is speaking and then speak slightly slower and slightly lower.

4. LEARN STUDENTS' NAMES QUICKLY
Use name tags, seating charts, or fun name games to help remember students' names and make them feel valued.

5. USE POSITIVE BODY LANGUAGE
Maintain open posture, eye contact, and nodding. Positive body language encourages a friendly and open atmosphere.

6. SHARE SOMETHING ABOUT YOURSELF
Offer a personal anecdote or two to humanize yourself. This can help students see you as approachable and relatable.

7. BE GENUINE
Show genuine interest in students' lives by learning about their interests, hobbies, and goals, which fosters trust and connection.

I WISH MY EDUCATION PROFS HAD TOLD ME . . .

Sometimes, the best teaching lessons come from experience, as real classroom challenges and successes provide invaluable insights that theory alone can't offer.

1. TO STOP THINKING IN BINARIES

I used to frame a completed lesson as having been categorically great or horrible. But we can often make a little addition to help the lesson succeed. Sometimes success is an inch away.

2. HAPPINESS ENGAGES KIDS

Find ways to delight in what students are doing. Contrast this with the instructor who is braced for the class to get out of hand.

3. ADOPT A S.F.S.R. ATTITUDE

Super Focused and Super Relaxed—the ideal state for any performance.

4. DON'T ALWAYS RESCUE KIDS

Productive struggle is inherent in deep learning.

5. GO TO THE LIBRARY

Go to the library every two weeks and read before bed. Build that brain.

6. AVOID ASSIGN-CORRECT PARADIGM

Seize brief moments in every class to

- identify and explain cognitive steps
- model processes
- challenge kids to achieve excellence
- take time for genre analysis
- predict problems and scaffold.

TEACHING, LIKE WRITING A PERSUASIVE ESSAY

Effective teaching involves persuasion by engaging students, inspiring curiosity, and motivating them to embrace learning through compelling and relatable methods.

1. KNOW YOUR AUDIENCE
Connect with their values, experiences, and interests. Explain how the core ideas will benefit them.

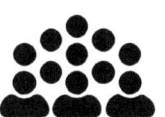

2. KEEP THEIR INTEREST
Engage and entertain. Integrate surprises. Don't spend too long on one thing.

3. IDENTIFY SIGNIFICANCE
Explain why they should care using ethos, logos, and pathos.

4. USE AN INTUITIVE STRUCTURE
State what will be covered and how the experience will be organized. Don't forget clear transitions. Disorganization leads to cognitive overload.

5. USE DELIBERATE LANGUAGE
Use language that is simple but entertaining in your distinctive voice. Take a stand. Show passion.

6. USE THE PRIMACY AND RECENCY EFFECT
Emphasize key ideas during the opening and conclusion.

7. PREDICT OBJECTIONS
What ideas will be resisted? How might those objections be overcome?

Workbook: Reflecting on Chapter 1 Topics

1. What are the key activities to include in the first week to establish a welcoming classroom environment?
2. How can we effectively gather information about students' backgrounds, interests, and learning challenges?
3. What strategies can be employed to set and reinforce class norms and expectations?
4. How can we introduce students to the course content and expectations for the semester?
5. How can the "Awesome Wall" concept be employed to inspire and motivate current students?
6. What is an alternative to thinking in binaries about your instructional practices?

Going Deeper—Advanced Questions

1. What are the multiple environmental systems that influence students' learning and behavior during the first week of class?
2. How can you design first-week activities that support students' intrinsic motivation by addressing their needs for autonomy, competence, and relatedness?
3. Evaluate the potential benefits and drawbacks of using AI-powered tools to personalize each student's first-week activities, considering data privacy issues.
4. How can school policies be designed to support teachers in implementing the first-week activities effectively, especially in under-resourced schools?

Checklist of Activities and Strategies to Try (Pick 2)

- ❑ Implement an icebreaker activity.
- ❑ Create a student survey.
- ❑ Create a class norms discussion guide with key points for discussion and a procedure for establishing norms with students involved in the process.
- ❑ Design a visual aid to show students important dates and deadlines.
- ❑ Create an "Awesome Wall" in your classroom.
- ❑ Other: _____

Describe Your Progress

1. What activities were most successful?

2. What challenges did you face?

3. How can you improve for next time?

 **References for Chapter 1**

Guide, Inc. (2018, April 7). Icebreaker: Beach Ball Toss. GUIDE, Inc. https://guideinc.org/2018/04/07/icebreaker-beach-ball-toss/

The Colorado Education Initiative. (n.d.). Student Mentoring Program: Week 1 Activities. The Colorado Education Initiative. https://www.coloradoedinitiative.org/wp-content/uploads/2014/04/SMS-Week-1.pdf

Top Hat. (2022). 25 Classroom Icebreakers For College Professors. Top Hat. https://tophat.com/blog/classroom-icebreakers/

University of New South Wales (UNSW). (2022). Active Learning Activities. UNSW Teaching. https://www.learningenvironments.unsw.edu.au/resources/active-learning

Chapter 2

Classroom Management: Cultivating a Productive Learning Environment

Classroom Management: Cultivating a Peaceful and Productive Learning Environment

Your classroom is buzzing with the energy of talking and laughing students, but amidst the chaotic playfulness, there's a need for order and structure. How do you transform this lively environment into a harmonious space where every student can thrive? If this subject gives you a Tylenol headache, you're not alone.

Classroom management invariably arises in conversations between new and veteran teachers alike. It was a big concern for me, too.

The year I started teaching 7th- to 12th-grade English in Minneapolis, I never felt more alone. Many of my students were gang members; others came to school under the influence of alcohol and stronger drugs. That year afforded me the unrelenting "opportunity" to be assaulted with a stone, two chairs, a Rambo knife, a seventh-grade girl's weak jab, and dozens of creative swear words. Fortunately, classroom order improved when I learned that successful classroom management depends on conscientiously executing a few big strategies and a lot of little ones, many of which are included in Chapter 2. Through proactive planning, clear communication, and the strategic use of positive reinforcement, you can create a classroom atmosphere where both you and your students can work productively and still have fun.

The next few pages are packed with practical strategies to ensure your classroom becomes a place of focused learning and mutual respect.

Key Chapter 2 Strategies

1. Avoid classroom congestion by strategically placing items to reduce bottlenecks and implement exit routines.
2. Provide listening cues to establish clear communication expectations.
3. Model procedures for everyday classroom activities to create consistency.
4. Plan for your absence to ensure smooth class operation.
5. Rehearse transitions to minimize disruptions.
6. Teach kids to express negative feelings.
7. Encourage students to become problem solvers.
8. Create a welcoming atmosphere.

Memory Device for this Chapter
Mnemonic Acronym

For Classroom Management, Remember C.L.A.S.S.

Congestion Avoidance

Listening Cues

Absence Planning

Smooth Transitions

Specific Exit Routines

REDUCE CLASSROOM COMMOTION

Implementing a combination of preventive, student-driven, and evidence-based strategies can significantly reduce classroom disruptions and enhance the learning environment.

1. AVOID CONGESTION
To reduce classroom bottlenecks, locate textbooks away from the pencil sharpener.

2. PROVIDE CUES TO LISTEN
Institute a signal for listening. Check out "30 Techniques to Quiet a Noisy Class": http://bit.ly/TB_Noise (Finley, 2015).

3. REHEARSE TRANSITIONS
When transitioning, kids should know which direction they should move, how fast, whether they are trading seats or moving their own chairs, and what to do once they reach their destination.

4. I.D. AN EXIT ROUTINE
For young ones, place subtle marks on the floor indicating where to stand when lining up. This decreases the chance of bumps leading to fisticuffs.

5. MODEL PROCEDURES
Model the protocols for using the restroom, passing in homework, completing work early, taking water breaks, working in centers, etc.

6. PLAN FOR YOUR ABSENCE
In your sub tub, store class photos, the schedule, office passes, rules and protocols, behavior referrals, identify the class assistant, and include a bar of chocolate.

RESISTANT CLASSES

Students who resist learning or refuse to follow the teacher's directions create a lot of fear for teachers. We've all been there. Fortunately, there are strategies that can help.

1. CELEBRATE!
Call out kids who have their effort and attitude dialed in.

2. MAKE KIDS PROBLEM SOLVERS
Say, "If you have ideas to make this class better, please share them with me."

3. LOCK IN CLASSROOM MANAGEMENT
Kids don't respect waffling or inconsistency.

4. CARE
Ask their opinion and listen without judgment. Pick up dropped pencils. Say, "I've thought of a way to make this next part less stressful."

5. SMILE
When you smile at students, they tend to smile back (Linsin, 2011).

6. ADD VALUE
Make class time count with significant, inspiring content. Help students perceive the topic or process as valuable.

7. ANGELA WATSON'S 2 X 10 STRATEGY
Spend 2 minutes for 10 days in a row speaking to a challenging student about non-school subjects.

8. X-FACTOR IT!
Do something unexpected. Bring the cheerleaders Smart Water. Turn the lights off and let students watch the snow fall while playing Beethoven's Moonlight Sonata. Bring waffles!

CLASSROOM CONFLICT

How do you talk through conflict in the classroom? Emphasize "problem-solving strategies over avoidance and punishment" (Mahvar et al., 2018). The strategies below should help.

1. WRITE FIRST
Ask learners to write about the topic in advance of the discussion so they are less emotionally reactive.

2. MAKE GROUND RULES
Before the discussion, ask students to list responses to the following prompts: *What are the qualities or characteristics of good discussions? What ground rules or guidelines should we follow in discussions?* (Carleton College, n.d.).

3. IT'S NOT A DEBATE—CONVERSATE!
"I tell them the goal of a discussion is to understand rather than win, so the tactics are different" (Krulder, 2019).

4. CONVEYING NEGATIVE EMOTIONS
"You make me feel . . ." needs to be replaced with "When you (state the behavior), I feel (one word describing emotions)" (Myers, 2010).

5. AVOID AGENDA QUESTIONS
An agenda question gives advice or challenges: "Why don't you consider . . .?" A curiosity question offers genuine inquiry: "I'm confused about . . .?" (Vogelsang & McGee, 2015).

6. DEBRIEF
At the end of the conversation, ask:

- What did you learn today?
- Who raised a good point you hadn't thought of before?
- How was our communication?
- How will this shape your thinking going forward?

A CHILD REFUSES CLASSWORK. NOW WHAT?

"Teachers should employ strategies that focus on managing behavior without using coercive threats, thus promoting self-control and autonomy in students" (Bergin & Bergin, 1999). That's the emphasis of these strategies.

1. LEARN WHAT THEY LOVE!
The first step of relationship-building is learning who the child is (without judgment).

2. CHUNK TASKS
Breaking big tasks into smaller parts makes work less intimidating.

3. SHOW CARE
Say "Do you know why I'm giving you a bit of a hard time about getting to work?"
Kids will usually say, "Because you care . . ."(Wellen Park, 2021).

4. BE CONSISTENT
Classroom routines help kids in chaos.

5. DIAGNOSE READING PROBLEMS
A reading issue is likely involved: 1) comprehension, 2) decoding, or 3) both.

6. OFFER CHOICES
Choice increases motivation. Do they want to move to a different part of the room? Do part A or part B?

7. BUILD A SUPPORT SYSTEM
Pair students with a peer buddy or mentor who can offer guidance and support. Collaborative work can ease the burden.

INDICATORS THAT A CHILD MIGHT BECOME VIOLENT

"Extremely violent behavior can appear suddenly at any time and is not accompanied by guilt. It is caused by early psychological and repeated traumas, whose importance is usually underestimated . . ." (Berger & Bonneville, 2009). When a child acts out, understanding the underlying trauma can lead to more intuitive and impactful responses.

1. THREATS OF VIOLENCE
Detailed plans in the form of letters, social media posts, drawings, or via conversations.

2. WEAK SOCIAL TIES
Socially rejected and isolated children.

3. DRUGS AND CRIMINAL ACTS
Drug use and burglaries before the age of 12.

4. VICTIM OF BULLYING
Students are picked on or victimized.

5. ANTI-SOCIAL ATTITUDES
Students who exhibit anger at the police, dishonesty, and favor rule-breaking.

6. RECENT BREAKUP
Has a significant relationship ended?

7. INSENSITIVE
The child has difficulty "acknowledging the feelings and rights of others." Lack of empathy.

SUPPORTING A CHILD WHO MIGHT BECOME VIOLENT

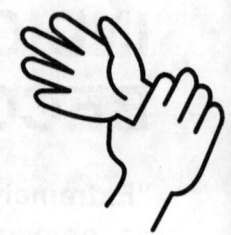

A violent child engages in behavior intended to cause physical, psychological, or financial harm to others. Addressing these behaviors requires a comprehensive understanding of the underlying causes and appropriate interventions.

1. PROTECTIVE FACTORS
- Positive social orientation
- High IQ
- Being female
- Commitment to school
- Intolerance of violence
- Attention of a loving adult (U.S. Department of Health and Human Services, 2001).

2. MENTAL HEALTH SUPPORT
Ensure access to counseling and mental health resources. Early intervention can prevent escalation.

3. CONFLICT RESOLUTION TRAINING
Teach students skills for managing conflicts peacefully. This can reduce violent tendencies.

4. PARENTAL INVOLVEMENT
Engage parents in the process. Open communication between home and school can address issues before they become severe.

5. POSITIVE PEER INFLUENCE
Encourage friendships with peers who exhibit positive behavior. A supportive social network can mitigate negative influences.

TIPS FOR DEALING WITH HATE SPEECH

"Hate speech is a term normally used to cover forms of expression aimed at persecuting people by vilifying their racial, ethnic, or other identities" (George, 2015). Such expressions often perpetuate prejudice and discrimination.

1. SHUT IT DOWN
Say with conviction, "This is not up for discussion. That kind of talk is never acceptable here."

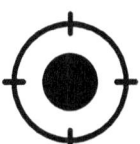

2. FOCUS ON WHAT WAS SAID
Emphasize the speech, not who said it.

3. DISCUSS THE COSTS
What does hate speech . . .

. . . do to you?
. . . do to others?
. . . do to our classroom community?

4. CLARIFY
Make sure you heard it right.

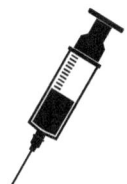

5. INOCULATE YOUR CLASSES
Dr. Richard Curwin says to have students discuss the following in small groups:

"Who decides what is hate speech: the speaker or the recipient?"
"Does the intention of the speaker matter?"
"Define teasing, sarcasm, insulting, and hate speech?"

6. IF THEY SAY, "JUST KIDDING"
Explain the difference between bonding teasing, annoying teasing (insensitive), and malicious teasing (repeated, designed to humiliate) (Wiseman, 2015).

Workbook: Reflecting on Chapter 2 Topics

1. What are the benefits of avoiding congestion in the classroom?
2. How can listening cues improve classroom management?
3. Why is it important to model procedures for students?
4. What should you include in your absence plan for a substitute teacher?
5. Why might a student refuse to do schoolwork?
6. In what ways can big tasks be broken into smaller parts?
7. What transitions should be rehearsed?
8. How can you respond if you hear hate speech in your classroom?
9. Describe a specific exit routine that can minimize end-of-class commotion.
10. How does encouraging students to become problem solvers benefit the class?
11. What impact can a teacher's smile have on the classroom environment?
12. How can we create a classroom environment where everyone feels safe and respected?

Going Deeper—Advanced Questions

1. How can modeling procedures be adapted for different age groups?
2. How can positive reinforcement be balanced with discipline in celebrating student efforts?
3. What methods would cultivate a problem-solving mindset among students?

Checklist of Activities and Strategies to Try (Pick 2)

❑ Rehearse transitions and model procedures.
❑ Spend 2 minutes for 10 days in a row speaking to a challenging student about non-school subjects.
❑ Teach students how to appropriately convey negative emotions.
❑ Pair students with a peer buddy or mentor who can offer guidance and support.
❑ Teach students skills for managing and expressing emotions.
❑ Introduce students to conflict resolution strategies.
❑ Hold a "Storytelling Session" where students share experiences of kindness and respect.
❑ Define and discuss hate speech with your students.
❑ List go-to positive reinforcement techniques.
❑ Other: _____

Describe Your Progress

1. What activities were most successful?

2. What challenges did you face?

3. How can you improve for next time?

References for Chapter 2

Bergin, C., & Bergin, D. (1999). Classroom discipline that promotes self-control. *Journal of Applied Developmental Psychology*, 20(2), 189–206.

Berger, M., & Bonneville, F. (2009). The extremely violent child. *Archives de Pédiatrie*, 16(12), 1625–31.

Carleton College. (n.d.). Potential activities to set classroom discussion environment. Carleton Academics. https://www.carleton.edu/provost/ai-seminars/climate/activities/

Curwin, R. (2017, May 1). How to respond when students use hate speech. Edutopia. https://www.edutopia.org/blog/how-respond-when-students-use-hate-speech-richard-curwin

Finley, T. (2014, October 21). 30 techniques to quiet a noisy class. Edutopia. https://www.edutopia.org/blog/30-techniques-quiet-noisy-class-todd-finley

George, C. (2015). Hate speech law and policy. In *The International Encyclopedia of Digital Communication and Society* (pp. 1–10). Wiley-VCH Verlag. https://doi.org/10.1002/9781118767771.wbiedcs139

Krulder, M. (2019, October 2). Conversations, not debates. It's not always about winning . . . Medium. https://smiz.medium.com/conversations-not-debates-1d7b29267be3

Linsin, M. (2011, July 30). Why you should smile on the first day of school. Smart Classroom Management. https://smartclassroommanagement.com/2011/07/30/smile-on-the-first-day-of-school/

Mahvar, T., Khoshknab, M. F., Pazargadi, M., & Maddah, S. S. B. (2018). Conflict management strategies in coping with students' disruptive behaviors in the classroom: A systematized review. *Journal of Advances in Medical Education & Professionalism*, 6(3), 102–14. https://pmc.ncbi.nlm.nih.gov/articles/PMC6039817/

Myers, D. G. (2010). *Social psychology* (10th ed.). McGraw-Hill.

U.S. Department of Health and Human Services. (2001). *Youth violence: A report of the Surgeon General*. https://2008election.procon.org/sourcefiles/surgeongeneralreport.pdf

Vogelsang, J., & McGee, S. (2015). Planning for difficult dialogues. Georgia Southern University. https://ww2.georgiasouthern.edu/academics/faculty-center/files/Planning-and-Managing-Difficult-Dialogues_Resource-Handout.pdf

Watson, A. (2014, October 19). The 2x10 strategy: A miraculous solution for behavior issues? The Cornerstone for Teachers. https://thecornerstoneforteachers.com/truth-for-teachers-podcast/the-2x10-strategy/

Wellen Park. (2021, August 10). *In Wellen Park, State College of Florida Collegiate School-Venice sets high education standards*. https://wellenpark.com/news/in-wellen-park-state-college-of-florida-collegiate-school-venice-sets-high-education-standards/

Wiseman, R. (2015, April 1). Just joking—helping students understand when teasing hurts. Association for Middle Level Education. https://www.amle.org/just-joking-helping-students-understand-when-teasing-hurts/

Chapter 3

The Organized Teacher: Maximizing Efficiency

The Organized Teacher: Maximizing Efficiency

Imagine learners entering a space where everything has a designated place, from color-coded file folders to neatly arranged supplies. The organized teacher, fully prepared and rested, greets each student warmly, ready to tackle the day's agenda with clarity and enthusiasm. The instructor's clutter-free desk symbolizes a mind ready to engage.

Lessons flow seamlessly, transitions are smooth, and learners thrive in an environment with clear expectations and support.

In stark contrast, picture a chaotic classroom where a disorganized teacher struggles with daily demands. *Where did I put that handout?* Papers are strewn across the desk, supplies are scattered, and the hunt for misplaced items disrupts learning. Assignments are never graded on time. The overwhelmed teacher doesn't notice that kids sense the disarray, their focus wavering. Instructions are unclear, transitions are chaotic, and the class operates like it's filled with invisible molasses.

Chapter 3 offers strategies to turn disarray into order, providing solutions to streamline routines, manage time, and create a structured, supportive environment. By embracing key principles, you can reduce stress and cultivate a classroom where learners flourish.

Key Chapter 3 Strategies

1. Introduce yourself to your students in a way that sets a positive and welcoming tone.
2. Help students get to know each other in a fun and interactive way.
3. Learn about students' backgrounds, interests, and learning challenges.
4. Establish clear procedures, rules, and behaviors expected in the classroom.
5. Provide an overview of the semester's curriculum, key activities, and learning objectives.
6. Inspire and motivate students by showcasing past students' achievements.
7. Introduce students to the exciting activities and learning experiences of the upcoming year.

Memory Device for this Chapter
Alphabetic Peg Overview

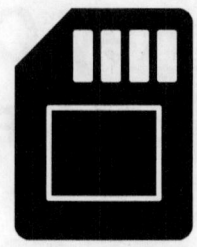

- **A**: Assign gradebook numbers
- **B**: Brainstorm with paper
- **C**: Create 31 file folders
- **D**: Digital submission organization
- **E**: Establish a welcoming environment
- **F**: Flex days scheduling
- **G**: Grading spot
- **H**: Home for everything
- **I**: Inspiration wall
- **J**: Jot down lesson changes
- **K**: Keep a short-cut utility
- **L**: Lanyard hall passes
- **M**: Meal plan
- **N**: Name tents for subs
- **O**: Over-plan for subs
- **P**: Phonetic spelling of names
- **Q**: Quick sorting with gradebook numbers
- **R**: Remind.com for communication
- **S**: Survey and understand students
- **T**: Turn-in tips
- **U**: Use a custom rubber stamp
- **V**: Visual post of due dates
- **W**: Welcome note for students
- **X**: X out missing assignments with a memo
- **Y**: Yearly sticky note improvements
- **Z**: Zero in on work time

THE ORGANIZED TEACHER

Educators who are well-organized find teaching more satisfying and feel more empowered, which reduces stress (Lee et al., 1991). Additionally, effective organization allows teachers to focus more on student engagement and less on administrative tasks.

1. THIRTY-ONE FILE FOLDERS
Create 31 file folders for each day of the month. All worksheets, tests, plans, and materials for each day are stored and ready to go (Hemphill, n.d.).

2. REMIND PARENTS
Send project due dates to parents and kids with the Remind.com App.

3. SPACE PROJECT DATES
Don't get slammed by different class projects turned in on the same day.

4. SCHEDULE FLEX DAYS
This can be a chance to re-teach, review, or get students caught up.

5. CREATE LANYARD HALL PASSES
Laminate library, office, bathroom, and hall passes with the teacher's name and room #. Attach them to a lanyard (Hegwood, 2022).

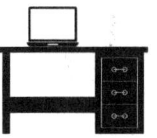
6. GRADING SPOT
Keep an area clear that you can use for grading. This is better than trying to grade on a messy desk.

7. NO MORE "BUT I TURNED THAT IN"
Have elementary and middle school kids line up in alphabetical order. Collect papers. If a child doesn't have a paper, they must write their name and "missing" and hand it in. If a kid is absent, have the child after them "in the alphabetical order write 'absent' on a paper (along with the student's name, of course) and turn it in." Staple them together (Just Add Students, 2015).

TIME SAVERS

"When teachers have more time for planning and collaborating, teachers can be more creative" (Lee & Smith, 1991). This increased creativity often leads to more engaging and dynamic lesson plans, which can improve student outcomes.

1. EVERYTHING HAS A HOME
All materials have a home. When kids try to hand you a paper, remind them where it goes.

2. USE A RUBBER STAMP
Create a custom rubber stamp (http://bit.ly/_STAMP) with your details for forms that require your name, address and phone number.

3. USE A SHORTCUT UTILITY
Create custom keyboard shortcuts to expand and replace commonly used text snippets. Try TextExpander for thank-you notes, rubrics, etc.

4. GRADEBOOK NUMBERS
Assign kids numbers that correspond with your grade book. The last child to touch submitted papers sorts them into number order and writes down the missing numbers on a cover sheet.

5. MEAL PLAN
Come home to the smell of Baked Ziti, Tater Tot Casserole, French Dip Sandwiches, Cashew Chicken, and Barley and Chickpea Risotto with "50+ Easy Slow-Cooker Recipes . . ." (http://bit.ly/_Crock-Pot; Crock Pot, n.d.).

6. PROTECT WORK TIME
Put a sign on your door during intensive work times: "Work Zone from 1:00–2:00PM. Available at 3:30 PM."

7. MINIMIZE CHOICES
Buy one brand of socks in two or three colors for quick sorting and one type of Tupperware, so lids are easy to find. Go to bed, wake up, and work out at the same time.

PLAN LESSONS FASTER

A study found that teachers plan by "1) reviewing the core competencies and basic competence from the syllabus; 2) searching for learning resources; 3) choosing learning media; 4) determining the material; 5) selecting learning method; and 6) compiling indicators and goals" (Emiliasari, 2019). That process requires a significant investment of time.

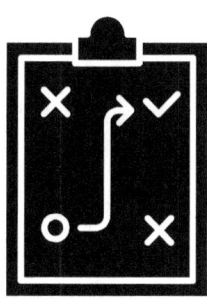

1. BRAINSTORM WITH PAPER FIRST
Spend five minutes jotting, drawing, and generating ideas. Think PLAYFULLY. Aim for ideas that will delight and clarify.

2. FOCUS
Planning is highly creative and taxing . . . When it's time to plan, do "deep work" (Newport, 2016) with intensity and focus. Find a place to work without distractions. Yup. That means no social media.

3. IF YOU GET STUCK, REACH OUT
Can't think of a good way to teach a topic? Write down what your issue is in the form of a question (which alone might prompt an epiphany). Give your question to a colleague or your online PLC. There are 3.1 million teachers in the U.S. Most like to help.

4. SAVE TIME NEXT YEAR
At the end of the lesson, when it's still fresh, take out a sticky note and write down one thing you'd change to the lesson next time to make it better. You'll thank yourself next time you're planning the next iteration.

5. SCHEDULE REGULAR PLANNING TIME
Set aside specific times each week for lesson planning. Treat it like an important meeting to ensure it gets done without last-minute stress.

6. USE GENERATIVE A.I.
ChatGPT will create a lesson plan in less than 25 seconds.

TIPS FOR MANAGING STUDENT PAPERWORK

The burden of paperwork has increased for both general education classes and special education because of budget cuts and increased class sizes (Imhoff, 2012).

1. TURN-IN TIPS
a. Make sure all papers are facing up and are headed correctly. b. Each paper includes a learner I.D. # and is sorted to match the grade book. c. Attach a recycled cover sheet with the assignment. name, period, due date, and all student names. Circle the names of kids who haven't turned in their work.

2. MAKE FIVE KEY PAPERWORK ZONES
Every paper has a home.

1. Submitted work
2. Makeup work pickup
3. Late submitted work
4. Grading in process
5. Graded work to return

3. ROGUE FILE
Some teachers also keep a rogue paper file for papers without names.

4. LATE WORK MEMO
Each paper that arrives should be accompanied by a late work memo that explains why the assignment was late and whether more help is needed.

5. POST DATES
Hang a whiteboard behind the makeup work pickup zone. Every time a graded assignment is announced, post the name and due date in chronological order for the entire semester. Check off assignments that have been graded and returned.

6. ORGANIZE DIGITAL SUBMISSIONS
Set up a clear, consistent naming convention for digital submissions. Ensure all students name their files with their name, class, and assignment title (e.g., John_Doe_English101_Essay1). This helps in quickly identifying and organizing the files.

SUB TUB COMPONENTS

Substitutes face "uncertainty and stress" that can be mitigated by detailed lesson plans, class lists, and appropriate materials (Stoddart & Cameron, 2021). Providing clear expectations and resources ensures continuity in student learning.

1. WELCOME NOTE
Leave a warm note with your appreciation. Attach a Blow Pop, because everybody loves a bubble gum center wrapped in a fruit-flavored candy shell.

2. ON-STANDBY
Assign a student helper and ask a colleague to be available for backup. Write down where/how to contact that colleague.

3. CONTENT OUTLINE
Whether using a sub tub or binder, include a table of contents so contents are easy to locate.

4. OVER-PLAN
It's better to have more activities than not enough. Create "sponge" activities just in case Plan A runs short.

5. PHONETIC SPELLING OF NAMES
Where it seems helpful, include phonetic spelling on the seating chart and class list (differentiatedteaching.com, 2024).

6. NAME TENTS
Name tents will enhance the substitute's ability to build relationships with your students.

7. WHAT IF'S
Provide a "what if" sheet that answers: What if there is a fire drill? If the tech goes south? If the art special is canceled? Who to contact for information or help.

Workbook: Reflecting on Chapter 3 Topics

1. Discuss the potential benefits and challenges of using apps like Remind.com to communicate project due dates to both students and parents.
2. Reflect on the impact of having a dedicated grading spot on your efficiency and stress levels. How could you implement this strategy in your own workspace?
3. How does scheduling flex days for re-teaching, reviewing, or catching up help maintain a balanced and effective teaching schedule?
4. How can using a custom rubber stamp and keyboard shortcuts for commonly used text snippets save time and reduce repetitive tasks?
5. Reflect on the importance of minimizing choices in your daily routine. How can this strategy be applied to your professional and personal life to increase efficiency?
6. Discuss the benefits of setting specific planning times each week for lesson planning. How can treating this time as an important meeting help in reducing last-minute stress?
7. Share an example of a successful lesson plan brainstorming session you have had.
8. What strategies can you use to protect your work time from interruptions?
9. Reflect on the importance of having a clear and consistent naming convention for digital submissions. How does this help in managing and organizing student work?
10. How can providing a detailed sub tub ensure continuity in students' learning?

Going Deeper—Advanced Questions

1. What are the psychological benefits for teachers who implement structured organizational practices in their classrooms?
2. What organizational strategies influence the overall effectiveness of instructional delivery?
3. How does the integration of technology (e.g., Remind.com, digital submissions) reshape traditional organizational practices in education?

Checklist of Activities and Strategies to Try (Pick 2)

- ❏ Create 31 file folders for daily materials.
- ❏ Use the Remind.com app to send due dates to parents and students.
- ❏ Space out project due dates across different classes.
- ❏ Schedule flex days for re-teaching and review.
- ❏ Designate a specific grading spot in your classroom.
- ❏ Assign grade book numbers to students for easier sorting.
- ❏ Implement a meal plan to streamline evening routines.
- ❏ Brainstorm lesson ideas on paper before planning.
- ❏ Schedule regular planning times each week.
- ❏ Prepare a comprehensive sub tub with detailed instructions and phonetic spellings on seating charts for substitutes.
- ❏ Keep a rogue file for unnamed papers.
- ❏ Other: _____

Describe Your Progress

1. What activities were most successful?

2. What challenges did you face?

3. How can you improve for next time?

 **References for Chapter 3**

50+ Easy Slow-Cooker Recipes. (n.d.). 50+ easy slow-cooker recipes. http://bit.ly/_Crock-Pot differentiatedteaching.com. (2024). Phonetic spelling of names. http://www.differentiatedteaching.com/phonetic-spelling-names

Emiliasari, A. (2019). Teacher planning: A study of reviewing competencies, selecting resources, and setting instructional goals. *International Journal of Teaching Methods*, 12(1), 45–60.

Hegwood, V. (2022, August 9). 28 classroom organization ideas to make your year easier. Prodigy Game Blog. https://www.prodigygame.com/main-en/blog/classroom-organization

Hemphill, S. (n.d.). Thirty-one file folders. Teaching Every After. http://www.example.com/teaching-every-after/thirty-one-file-folders

Imhoff, R. (2012). The rising paperwork burden in education: Causes and consequences. *Educational Administration Quarterly*, 48(2), 123–39.

Just Add Students. (2015, August 9). 7 organizational tips for teachers. https://justaddstudents.com/7-organizational-tips-for-teachers/

Lee, J., & Smith, K. (1991). Teachers' planning and creativity: The effects of time for collaboration on instructional innovation. *Journal of Educational Psychology*, 83(3), 500–10.

Lee, J., Smith, K., & Brown, L. (1991). The effects of organizational practices on teacher empowerment and stress. *Journal of Educational Administration*, 29(4), 230–45.

Newport, C. (2016). *Deep work: Rules for focused success in a distracted world*. Grand Central Publishing.

Stoddart, A., & Cameron, B. (2021). Reducing substitute teacher stress: The impact of detailed lesson plans and resource materials. *Journal of School Leadership*, 31(4), 345–62.

Chapter 4

Instructional Essentials: Core Elements of Effective Teaching

Instructional Essentials: Core Elements of Effective Teaching

The essence of teaching lies not only in delivering information but in inspiring and engaging students, helping them to make meaningful connections and develop critical thinking skills. In other words, what's essential is marrying great structure with inspiration. These are the new instructional essentials.

When you step into Ms. Johnson's classroom, you notice that the biology objective is written on her whiteboard in big letters. She tells a story about a young explorer navigating a magical forest, an analogy for cellular biology. Students know that she is brilliant at making abstract concepts relatable. To reinforce content knowledge, Ms. Johnson uses hands-on activities, like modeling plant cells with clay. Animations are cued up to engage diverse learning preferences.

The teacher's lessons are structured with thematic weekday activities and advance organizers. By incorporating these core elements—storytelling, interactive activities, multimedia, and structured planning—Ms. Johnson creates unforgettable experiences and inspires a lifelong love of learning.

Because the teacher's care for students is conveyed through her meticulous planning and ability to make tough concepts easily digestible, Ms. Johnson gets the ultimate reward: every day, epiphanies occur right in front of her.

Key Chapter 4 Strategies

1. Start your lesson with a compelling story or analogy to capture students' attention.
2. Incorporate diagrams, videos, and graphic organizers to help students visualize complex concepts.
3. Use a blackboard purge or vocabulary scavenger hunt to connect new information with what students already know.
4. Incorporate media to enhance understanding and engagement.
5. Have students create hierarchical concept maps to organize and connect critical concepts.
6. Allow students to choose from a variety of prompts or tasks to increase engagement.
7. Implement weekday themes to create anticipation and reduce cognitive load.
8. Connect abstract concepts to real-world scenarios to make learning relatable.
9. Simplify complex tasks into manageable steps to build confidence.
10. Wrap up lessons with a clear summary to consolidate learning and address questions.
11. Use group activities and discussions to foster collaborative learning and deeper understanding.
12. Use formative assessments on the regular to monitor progress and adjust instruction.

Memory Device for this Chapter
Narrative Mnemonic

On Alex's first day as a schoolteacher, the principal introduced them to an experienced mentor named Jamie. Jamie was known for their exceptional teaching skills and agreed to guide Alex on their journey.

Storytelling and Analogies

Jamie began by explaining the power of storytelling in the classroom. "They make abstract concepts relatable and memorable." Jamie demonstrated by weaving a story about a historical event, capturing students' attention immediately. "And don't forget analogies," Jamie added. "They help students understand complex ideas by relating them to something familiar."

Interactive Activities and Music

Next, Jamie showed Alex how to use a song about the periodic table to help students remember the elements. Jamie also introduced interactive activities like role-playing and simulations. In one science class, students pretended to be different parts of a cell, moving and interacting according to their functions.

Tell Students Why the Lesson Matters

Jamie emphasized the importance of purposeful planning. "Every lesson should have a clear objective," Jamie advised. "Students need to know what they're learning and why it matters." Later, Alex made sure their students knew the purpose of each activity.

Student Engagement Techniques

Finally, Jamie talked about various techniques to maintain student engagement. "Ask open-ended questions, encourage group discussions, and always relate the material to the students' lives," Jamie suggested. They demonstrated by leading a lively debate on a current event, prompting students to think critically and express their opinions.

Putting It All Together

With Jamie's guidance, Alex combined storytelling and analogies, used music and interactive activities, planned purposefully, and employed various engagement techniques. One day, Alex asked Jamie, "How do I ensure I'm not just entertaining the students but also helping them develop essential skills?" Jamie replied, "If students are solving a problem, creating something, or making a decision related to the content, they are developing essential skills."

With this advice, Alex was inspired to try out the tactics shared by his mentor.

LESSON STARTERS

It's worth it to burn calories coming up with a strong lesson opener. Establishing an engaging start to a lesson sets a positive tone for the rest of the class and fosters active participation.

1. PLAY A SONG
Loads of songs are written about school subjects: "We Didn't Start the Fire" (history), "Mother Nature's Son" (the environment), "I Can Add" (math) . . .

2. START WITH VOCABULARY
Post several words and let kids guess the topic.

3. BLACKBOARD PURGE
Have the class write everything they know about the topic until the blackboard is full. Ask for elaboration and correct misconceptions.

4. STORY, ANALOGY, OR POEM
Read or tell a story related to the topic. Bonus points if it's a cliffhanger that you wait until the end of class to finish. Analogies and poems can also be powerful.

5. INCOMPLETE DIAGRAM
Provide a diagram with labels removed. Have kids try to guess as many parts as they can before turning the sheet over and viewing the answers.

6. HOOK COMPONENTS
A) CAPTURE interest. B) Explain WHAT will be learned and C) WHY it matters. D) RELATE it to previous knowledge and E) TELL how the lesson will unfold.

7. START WITH MEDIA
Show YouTube clips related to the topic: author interviews, trailers, and explainers.

SCHEMA ACTIVATION STRATEGIES

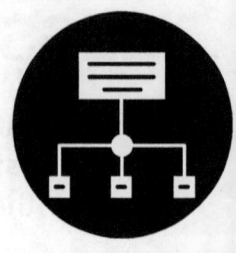

A schema is like a mental blueprint that helps us make sense of the world. It shapes how we store and organize knowledge, allowing us to link new ideas to what we already know, believe, or have encountered. This interconnected structure allows us to retrieve and apply knowledge more efficiently when faced with new learning or problem-solving scenarios.

1. MYSTERY BOX
Insert items into a box for students to pull out. Tell students that their job is to try to determine what they have in common.

2. NARRATIVE ADVANCE ORGANIZER
This kind of advance organizer introduces new material through storytelling. The teacher conveys key concepts by embedding them within a narrative, making the lesson more engaging and easier to grasp. This approach helps students connect ideas in a meaningful and memorable way.

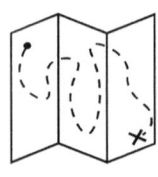

3. VOCABULARY SCAVENGER HUNT
Give each group a set of vocabulary words and challenge them to track down real-world representations of as many terms as possible over the course of a week.

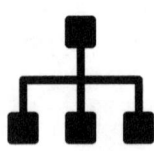

4. HIERARCHICAL CONCEPT MAPS
Students work in groups to brainstorm key ideas related to a topic and arrange them in order from broadest to most specific. This activity helps them build a structured concept map, which they can create using sticky notes or a digital tool.

5. FACT OR FIB? + JUSTIFY
Offer four to six concise "fact or fib" statements about the lesson topic. Students guess accuracy on a chart and briefly note their reasoning. Discuss answers together to clear up misconceptions. This sparks curiosity and readies them for new content.

METACOGNITION

"Metacognition refers to one's knowledge concerning one's own cognitive processes and products or anything related to them . . ." (Flavell, 1979). This awareness allows individuals to regulate their thinking and improve their problem-solving and decision-making skills.

1. MAP A STUDY PLAN
Ask kids to identify where and when they will study. What resources will be used? Why are those resources important?

2. CONCEPT MAP
Fill out a blank concept map to test knowledge (The Learning Center, n.d.).

3. RUNNING LIST
Kids keep a running list of things that confuse them—things that the class can help the teacher answer at the next class.

4. ALLOW METACOGNITIVE REFLECTION
How are you evaluating your current progress? Which strategies or techniques are you applying? What is your plan for improving your learning? How do you identify key ideas in what you read? How do you gauge your understanding and adjust as needed?

5. SAY IT ALOUD
Engaging in a Think Aloud—verbalizing your thoughts as you learn—helps clarify the material and promotes deeper understanding. This process also brings to light any areas of confusion or misunderstanding.

6. TEACHER MODELING
Aloud, teachers should walk through their cognitive process.

7. MUDDIEST POINT
At the end of class, kids write the answer to this question: "What was most confusing to me about the material being explored in class today?" (Angelo & Cross, 1993).

TO CLARIFY SOMETHING COMPLEX

"Modeling in complex texts requires that teachers analyze the text for factors of qualitative complexity and then design lessons that introduce students to that complexity" (Fisher & Frey, 2015). By carefully scaffolding these lessons, teachers can help students build the necessary skills to independently navigate and understand challenging texts.

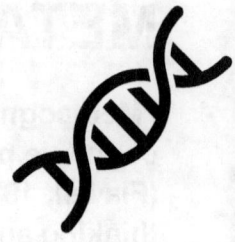

1. USE VISUALS
Photos, YouTube examples, graphic organizers, etc.

2. USE SIMILES and METAPHORS
"It's just like . . ."; "Similarly . . ."

3. EMPLOY MNEMONIC DEVICES
Stages of the writing process: "Pretty Dolls Rarely Ever Punch Criminals" (Pre-writing, Drafting, Revising, Editing, Publishing, Celebrate).

4. ANALOGIES
Use analogies to make complex ideas more relatable.

5. BREAK DOWN STEPS
Break complex tasks into smaller, more manageable steps.

6. REAL-WORLD EXAMPLES
Use real-world examples to illustrate abstract concepts.

7. STUDENT EXAMPLES
Encourage students to produce their own examples to demonstrate understanding.

THE SCIENCE OF CHUNKING

Segmenting information, or chunking, is vital for mastering both skills and knowledge. It organizes data related to problem-solving methods, thus enhancing practice performance and boosting verbal learning. By dividing information into digestible units, chunking eases cognitive load and helps learners store and retrieve complex material more effectively.

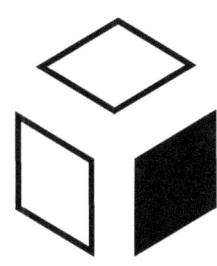

1. THE MAGIC CHUNKING NUMBER
Working memory effectively holds only four bits of information at a time- not seven (Cowan, 2001).

2. APPLY THE "GENERATION EFFECT"
We remember material better when we've generated it ourselves. Direct students to explain info in their own words.

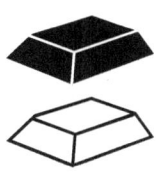
3. SHORTEN CHUNKS FOR ONLINE INFO
By breaking down information into smaller, more manageable pieces (i.e. chunks), we reduce cognitive load. This reduction helps users quickly scan, understand, and retain content—an essential factor in online environments where attention spans are often brief.

4. DOODLE CHUNKS
Direct kids to doodle an image that makes a personal connection to each chunk of information.

5. SEGMENT CLASSTIME
Chunk class time into different experiences, such as reading, stations, whole class discussions, etc.

6. LEARN CHUNKS SLOWLY
"Learning slowly so you can perform quickly seems strange, yet it's exactly how many world-class performers learn" (Coyle, 2010).

ENGAGING TEXT-BASED LESSONS

In a thriving reading classroom, students learn to become active readers. Engagement means that the reader is deeply connected to the text, investing both cognitively and emotionally. When students are deeply engaged, they are more likely to connect personally with the material, fostering a lifelong love of reading.

1. USE VISUAL THINKING

Show students a real-world photo that represents the topic. Then ask them to search for details using the following Visual Thinking Strategy (VTS): What do you notice? What do you see that makes you say that? What more can we find?

2. GIVE 3-PART HOMEWORK

Sheila Valencia, a prof. at the University of WA., recommends that all homework assignments describe three parts: 1) The purpose; 2) Directions on how readers are supposed to go about it; and 3) What readers are supposed to learn.

3. HAVE KIDS MAKE A REPORT CARD

Have students work in small groups to create an evaluation form for a literary character, historical figure, or event. Instruct them to select relevant assessment criteria and write detailed feedback to justify each score.

4. VARY YOUR PROMPTS

Go beyond typical prompts. For example, ask students to find the text's hidden assumptions, draw parallels between the themes in the text, create a set of research questions that emerge from the text.

5. RELATE HOMEWORK TO NEXT CLASS

Sheila Valencia sets up textbook homework that prepares kids for an activity in the next class. For example: "Tonight when you read Chapter 12, I want you to think about the causes of the American Revolution. As you're reading, draw a T-chart to keep track of the British perspective & the American one. When we come to class tomorrow, we're going to divide into two teams and debate" (Finley, 2014).

ALLITERATIVE WEEKDAY ACTIVITY THEMES

Implementing themed days during the week can infuse the classroom with both structure and excitement that captivates students. This consistent yet vibrant method not only simplifies lesson planning for teachers but also maintains a high level of student motivation and inquisitiveness.

1. MONDAY

- Motivation Monday (Goal setting)
- Mighty Maker Monday (Time to create)
- Method Monday (Learn a strategy)
- Mahalo Monday (What are you thankful for?)

2. TUESDAY

- Tune Tuesday (Work with background music)
- Practice-Test Tuesday (No-stakes or low-stakes quizzes)
- Talking Tuesday (Class discussion)
- Tech Tuesday (Working with tech)

3. WEDNESDAY

- Wordplay Wednesday (Vocabulary work)
- Wildcard Wednesday (Surprise!—teacher's choice)
- Worksheet Wednesday (Yup, I said the W-word)
- Watch-It Wednesday (Watch a YouTube video)

4. THURSDAY

- Think-a-Thon Thursday (Team problem-solving)
- Thankful Thursday (What are you grateful for?)
- Thorough Thursday (Revising/editing work)
- Thespian Thursday (Role-playing)

5. FRIDAY

- Fab Friday (Students' choice)
- Five-Station Friday (Station work)
- Foodie Friday (Snacks!)
- Free-Time Friday (Scheduled breather for part of the class)

HOW TO ENGAGE IN DELIBERATE PRACTICE

"Deliberate practice is a highly structured activity, the explicit goal of which is to improve performance" (Ericsson et al., 1993). It involves focused effort, immediate feedback, and repeated refinement to master specific skills.

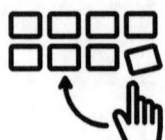

1. BE SYSTEMATIC

"Deliberate practice always follows the same pattern: break the overall process down into parts, identify your weaknesses, test new strategies for each section, and then integrate your learning into the overall process" (Clear, 2020).

2. STUDY EXPERTS

How do they think? What strategies do they use? Models are critical.

3. GET A COACH

A coach should have expertise in the skill you are trying to learn and know how much someone can be pushed before they reach independence. Coaches reinforce accountability.

4. AVOID COMFORT

Focus on tasks that are beyond your current ability. This can be frustrating, but that's the price for expertise.

5. SELF-MOTIVATE

To sustain effort, rally energy for the pursuit of excellence. It helps to "write down 10 amazing things that will happen" if you accomplish your goal (Austin, 2015).

6. ASSESS OFTEN

Know exactly how close you are to making a benchmark performance. Feedback can be quantitative or made qualitatively by a coach.

7. SIMULATE REAL CONDITIONS

Simulations are useful for practicing in more authentic conditions and analyzing progress.

UPGRADE PRESENTATION HANDOUTS

Handouts can add extra details, vivid examples, and targeted exercises that reinforce the day's lesson in surprising ways. These resources empower students to explore and digest challenging concepts at their own pace, deepening their understanding long after the lesson ends.

1. DON'T OVER-DO IT
Keep it brief. Only include the most important information.

2. INCLUDE FAQS
Curb common points of confusion.

3. INCORPORATE VISUALS
Avoid decoration, but still incorporate charts, graphic organizers, and photos that aid understanding.

4. INCLUDE DO'S AND DON'TS
If there is a skill involved, like researching, specify do's and don'ts.

5. SHARE RESOURCES
Tell kids where to find more information on the topic.

6. PROVIDE DEFINITIONS
Succinctly define critical vocabulary.

7. AID RETENTION
Make the titles memorable. Example: "Fair is Foul, and Foul is Fair"; Sound Devices in Shakespeare's "Macbeth."

8. PROMOTE SELF-ASSESSMENT
Include comprehension questions.

BOOST CLASSROOM RIGOR

"Rigor is creating an environment in which each student is expected to learn at high levels, each student is supported so he or she can learn at high levels, and each student demonstrates learning at high levels" (Blackburn, 2008). This balance of high expectations and robust support ensures that students are challenged while having the tools they need to succeed.

1. START WITH REFLECTION
Start class with a five-minute exercise where kids write answers to questions they struggled with on the last assessment.

2. SHOW YOUR WORK
Ask kids to show their work and identify content area strengths and weakness.

3. USE TOOLS
With Grooveshark, learners can create a character playlist with explanations for their song choices or make their own A.I. song with Suno.

4. CITE EVIDENCE
Have kids support conclusions with evidence.

5. ROLE PLAY
Dramatizations allow students to try on different identities.

6. INTRODUCE MESSY INQUIRY
Life isn't as unambiguous as a bubble sheet. Have kids generate questions and answer them.

7. ENCOURAGE HIGHER ORDER THINKING
Plan tasks that require higher-order thinking.

8. MAKE TASKS AUTHENTIC
Engage kids in real-world problem-solving & decision-making. Let kids learn from mistakes and successes.

UPGRADE READING HOMEWORK

"Reading homework is crucial because it reinforces what students learn in the classroom, provides an opportunity for independent practice, and helps develop a lifelong habit of reading" (Schmoker, 2006). Consistent reading assignments also foster critical thinking and comprehension skills, which are essential for academic and future success.

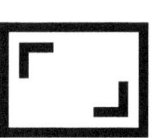

1. USE THE 52:17 RATIO
"The most productive people work for 52 mins., then break for 17 mins." The key, though, is for kids to ID how to use their energy resources best (Gifford & Gifford, 2024).

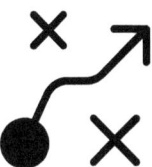

2. PLAN HOMEWORK
Learners are more likely to study if they commit to when and where they will do their readings. Provide organization time at the end of class.

3. PROVIDE A SELF-CHECK
It's not enough to sit and read; students should be encouraged to actively comprehend the assignment. A self-check or low-stakes assessment can help.

4. IDENTIFY HOW LONG IT WILL TAKE
Make a prediction about how long you anticipate the readings will take to be completed.

5. APPLY THE READINGS
"The next class, kids 'should be engaged in homework application, where they are asked to use what they have read (as in a debate).' Teachers should not cover the reading material in a lecture" (Valencia, 2014).

6. ENLIST GUARDIANS' SUPPORT
It's not enough to sit and read; students should be encouraged to actively comprehend the assignment. A self-check or low-stakes assessment can help.

DECREASE TASK DIFFICULTY

"Decreasing task difficulty to ensure success and build confidence can be essential, but it should be balanced with tasks that challenge and stretch students' abilities to foster growth and development" (Hattie, 2012). This balance encourages a gradual progression of skills, helping students develop resilience and a growth mindset.

1. ADJUST LENGTH
Lengthen how long you cover instructions, the amount of practice, and the time allotted to complete the task. Shorten the number of problems to complete.

2. STUDENT TEAMS
Make learning social to increase enjoyment and scaffold learning.

3. OFFER CHOICE
For example, students can choose whether to consume the text by reading independently, reading with another student, or by listening to a recording.

4. CREATE GUIDED NOTES
Use when presenting new content, or as study guides. Strategically replace key words in your document with blanks.

5. FISHBOWL ACTIVITY
"A small group in the center is circled by the rest of the class; the group in the middle, or fishbowl, engages in an activity, modeling how it's done for the larger group" (Alber, 2014).

6. POST DIRECTIONS
Remembering directions can interfere with performance. Writing directions reduces cognitive load.

7. CHUNK TASKS
"Show the student how to take any assignment and break it into small, manageable chunks" (Gonzalez, n.d.).

BULLETIN BOARDS DO'S AND DON'TS

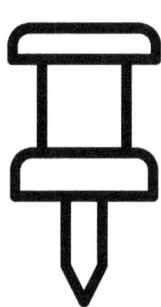

Bulletin boards can powerfully support the curriculum. When thoughtfully designed, they can reinforce key concepts, display student work, and create an engaging environment that supports active learning.

1. DO . . .
- Ensure the bulletin board has a clear purpose.
- Feature kids' work.
- Make it invite curiosity.
- Keep the bulletin board uncluttered.
- Make the height age-appropriate.
- Launch new bulletin board designs with new units.
- Use "plasticized paper" to avoid fading.
- Use sticky Velcro for heavier materials.
- Ask questions that can be answered by considering different artifacts displayed.

2. DO NOT . . .
- Post images that trivialize kids.
- Display stereotyped activities.
- Make your board too busy.
- Use spray mount (triggers asthma).
- Privilege a specific religious holiday.
- Allow misspellings or inaccurate info.
- Use purple or blue (they fade quickly).
- Forget to make a rough sketch before creating your bulletin board.
- Slap up a commercialized bulletin board.

3. OTHER TIPS
- **Student Contributions**: Allow students to contribute to the bulletin board by adding their own drawings, writings, or photos.
- **Highlight Achievements**: Dedicate a section to celebrating student achievements, both academic and extracurricular.
- **Incorporate Interactive Elements**: Add elements that students can touch, move, or interact with, such as flaps to lift or pieces to rearrange.

STUDY TIPS

Effective study strategies also help students build confidence, improve time management, and retain knowledge more effectively over the long term. By fostering active engagement with the material, these techniques transform passive reading into meaningful learning, making complex concepts more accessible and easier to recall when needed.

1. NAP
Even napping for 10 minutes boosts concentration and reduces fatigue (Zhao et al., 2010).

2. SPACE OUT YOUR STUDY SESSIONS
Students review material over a long period of time. This gives their minds time to form connections between the ideas and concepts (Sara, 2024).

3. PARAPHRASE INFORMATION
Converting information into your own language helps you internalize it more deeply.

4. LEARN, THEN SLEEP
To help reinforce memories, get your eight hours of sleep every night.

5. DON'T CRAM FOR TESTS
At the end of the semester, ask students to provide positive blurbs about your class along with their photos. And post 'em.

6. CAFFEINATE AFTER STUDYING
Two cups of coffee after studying strengthens memories for 24 hours (Borota et al., 2014).

7. STUDY AT THE SAME TIME
A routine will help to make studying second nature—equipping you mentally and emotionally to get started without delay.

CLASSROOM STATIONS

Designated learning stations serve as distinct zones where students tackle a variety of tasks at the same time, facilitating customized instruction and boosting engagement. This energetic setup transforms the classroom into an interactive hub where learners actively explore and solve problems using diverse methods.

1. INCLUDE VARIETY
Online, offline, listening, group work, floor work, visual representations, individual work, practice, problem-solving, etc.

2. GET THEM MOVING
Cue energetic tunes to prompt students to groove their way to the next station. Have them complete assignments while standing at a whiteboard, fostering movement and interaction.

3. PLAN FOR REFLECTION
After students complete a station, require them to summarize in writing or orally what they learned. This will help them internalize what they learned.

4. USE TASK CARDS
Write numbered directions at each station. Include the learning target as well as how the station should look when kids finish up.

5. MODEL NON-EXAMPLES
Model for students what they shouldn't be doing. Kids find this amusing.

6. CREATE INTUITIVE TRANSITIONS
Number stations. Use a timer. Show students which way they rotate.

7. INSTRUCTOR LEADS ONE STATION
This allows teachers the opportunity to engage directly with students with targeted, interactive instruction and assessment.

YEAR-ENDERS

The final class of the year is a time to honor each student's unique journey and progress. It's a moment to reflect on accomplishments, reminisce about shared experiences, and motivate learners to take their enthusiasm for knowledge into the next chapter. Before the final bell rings, it's also an opportunity to remind students they have the power to shape their own story.

1. GRAPH MY SEMESTER
A teacher named Meghan Mathis has kids graph and illustrate personal highs and lows of the year.

2. THE WORD
Assign each student a unique word—such as "altruistic," "dependable," or any other positive attribute—and encourage them to delve into its meaning.

3. GUESTS
Invite a former student to discuss joining the army, majoring in computer science, etc.

4. "LAST LECTURE"
Imagine you have 10–15 minutes to say the last words you will ever speak to students. Discuss what you've learned about life, about learning, about your content . . .

5. SURVEY
Have kids complete a Likert survey on texts, activities, and content they experienced over the semester.

6. VIDEO TO FUTURE CLASS
Videotape kids' answers to "What should future students know about how to get an 'A' in this class?"

7. PEER LETTERS
Kids write to one or more peers they learned the most from (best friend in class doesn't count).

CLOSURE ACTIVITIES

"Closure is that part of a lesson in which the teacher wraps things up. Closure helps students form a coherent picture, consolidate, eliminate confusion, and reinforce what they have learned" (Hunter, 1982). Closure is the final act of clarity that—at the sublime level—leaves students with both confidence and curiosity.

1. PARENT HOTLINE
Give students an interesting question about the lesson without further discussion. Email their guardians the answer so that the topic can be discussed over dinner.

2. SNOWSTORM
Students write down what they learned on a piece of scratch paper and wad it up. Given a signal, they throw their paper snowballs in the air. Then each learner picks up a nearby response and reads it aloud.

3. I WONDER
Near the end of class, ask students to write a question they still wonder about on a card. Everyone places cards into a basket. Individuals take cards. In groups, they try to address all the questions. If a group can't answer the question, ask the instructor.

4. HIDDEN EXIT SLIPS
Place sticky notes under the desks of the students before they enter class. At the end of class, have an Oprah moment and direct students to answer an exit ticket question.

5. WHY DOES IT MATTER?
Have students answer this prompt: What takeaways from the lesson will be important to know three years from now?

6. PICK A CARD
Students write a question about the day's lesson on an index card. Shuffle and then redistribute them. Each student reads their question and chooses another learner to answer.

UNSUNG DUTIES

"Teachers are often asked to do too much with too little. They are expected to be experts in their subjects, counselors for their students, and managers of ever-increasing administrative tasks, all while creating engaging and meaningful learning experiences" (Palmer, 1998). Amid the complexities of modern education, the demands placed on teachers can often feel insurmountable.

1. LEARNING NEW TECH
To enhance learning, educators stay abreast of new educational technologies.

2. NEGOTIATING BUREAUCRACY
To advocate for kids' needs, teachers often have to work their way through complex school systems and rules.

3. MENTAL PREP
Educators often spend time at home mentally preparing for the day ahead, reflecting on their practices, and strategizing ways to support their students.

4. CREATING MATERIALS
Teachers use personal time to create or modify worksheets, tests, and interactive activities.

5. COMMUNICATION
Teachers regularly communicate with parents to discuss their child's progress and any potential issues.

6. VOLUNTEERING TIME
Teachers often volunteer for school events and community service projects.

7. PD
As lifelong learners, teachers pursue professional development to keep up to date on diversity, equity, and inclusion, tech integration, social-emotional learning, data-driven instruction, classroom management, project-based learning, etc.

Workbook: Reflecting on Chapter 4 Topics

1. What strategies did you find most effective for capturing student interest?
2. How can storytelling enhance the learning experience?
3. How does activating prior knowledge help students connect with new information?
4. In what ways can concept maps aid in organizing critical concepts?
5. How can thematic weekday activities create excitement in the classroom?
6. What are the advantages of using real-world examples in teaching?
7. What are some effective mnemonic devices you could use in your teaching?
8. How can breaking down tasks into smaller steps benefit students?
9. Why is it important to include closure in your lesson plans?
10. How does peer interaction enhance learning?
11. What methods can you use to assess student understanding during lessons?

Going Deeper—Advanced Questions

1. How does the implementation of metacognitive strategies in the classroom impact students' self-regulated learning and academic performance?
2. How can thematic weekday activities be structured to address diverse learning needs and promote inclusivity?

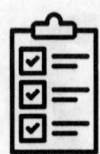

Checklist of Activities and Strategies to Try (Pick 2)

- ❑ Implement a blackboard purge to activate prior knowledge.
- ❑ To engage students, read or tell a related story, analogy, or poem.
- ❑ Show YouTube clips or multimedia content related to the lesson.
- ❑ Use a mystery bag to introduce new concepts.
- ❑ Employ narrative advance organizers to present new information.
- ❑ Create anticipation guides with thought-provoking statements.
- ❑ Plan group pre-quizzes to review and connect prior knowledge.
- ❑ Encourage students to map out their study plans.
- ❑ Use think-aloud strategies to model metacognitive processes.
- ❑ Use similes, metaphors, and analogies to clarify complex ideas.
- ❑ Break down complex tasks into manageable steps.
- ❑ Use real-world examples to illustrate abstract concepts.
- ❑ Use a choice board or learning menu to give students options.
- ❑ Use direct instruction and task cards in classroom stations.
- ❑ End lessons with a variety of engaging closure activities.
- ❑ Other: _____.

Describe Your Progress

1. What activities were most successful?

2. What challenges did you face?

3. How can you improve for next time?

 **References for Chapter 4**

Alber, R. (2014, January 24). 6 scaffolding strategies to use with your students. Edutopia. https://www.edutopia.org/blog/scaffolding-lessons-six-strategies-rebecca-alber

Angelo, T. A., & Cross, K. P. (1993). *Classroom assessment techniques: A handbook for college teachers*. Jossey-Bass.

Austin, B. (2015, December 8). The 4 fundamentals of unstoppable motivation. Stop. Start. Do. [Blog post]. https://www.stopstartdo.com/blog/the-4-fundamentals-of-unstoppable-motivation-how-to-get-motivated-to-achieve-your-goals

Blackburn, B. R. (2008). Rigor is NOT a four-letter word. https://eric.ed.gov/?id=ED527934

Borota, D., Murray, E., Keceli, G., et al. (2014). Post-study caffeine administration enhances memory consolidation in humans. *Nature Neuroscience*, 17(2), 201–3. https://doi.org/10.1038/nn.3623

Clear, J. (2020, April 13). The beginner's guide to deliberate practice. https://jamesclear.com/beginners-guide-deliberate-practice

Cowan, N. (2001). The magical number 4 in short-term memory: A reconsideration of mental storage capacity. *Behavioral and Brain Sciences*, 24(1), 87–114; discussion 114–85. https://doi.org/10.1017/s0140525x01003922

Coyle, D. (2010). *The talent code*. Arrow Books.

Ericsson, K. A., Krampe, R. T., & Tesch-Römer, C. (1993). The role of deliberate practice in the acquisition of expert performance. *Psychological Review*, 100(3), 363–406. https://doi.org/10.1037/0033-295X.100.3.363

Finley, T. (2014, August 26). Boom-Bang homework assignments. Edutopia. https://www.edutopia.org/blog/boom-bang-homework-assignments-todd-finley?qt-discussion_replies=1

Fisher, D., & Frey, N. (2015). Teacher modeling using complex informational texts. *The Reading Teacher*, 69(1), 63–69. https://doi.org/10.1002/trtr.1372

Flavell, J. H. (1979). Metacognition and cognitive monitoring: A new area of cognitive-developmental inquiry. *American Psychologist*, 34(10), 906–11. https://doi.org/10.1037/0003-066X.34.10.906

Gifford, J., & Gifford, J. (2024, October 4). Does the 52-17 rule really hold up? DeskTime Blog. DeskTime Insights. https://desktime.com/blog/52-17-updated#:~:text=The%20data%20revealed%20that%20the,workday%20to%20achieve%20maximu m%20productivity

Gonzalez, J. (n.d.). A few strategies to help slow-working students. Cult of Pedagogy. https://www.cultofpedagogy.com/slow-working-students

Hattie, J. (2012). *Visible learning for teachers: Maximizing impact on learning*. Routledge/Taylor & Francis Group. https://doi.org/10.4324/9780203181522

Hunter, M. C. (1982). *Increasing instructional effectiveness in elementary, secondary schools, colleges and universities*. TIP Publications.

Palmer, P. J. (1998). *The courage to teach: Exploring the inner landscape of a teacher's life*. Jossey-Bass.

Sara. (2024, December 10). What is spaced practice (and how to use it). Oxford Learning. https://www.oxfordlearning.com/what-is-spaced-practice/

Schmoker, M. (2006). Results now: How we can achieve unprecedented improvements in teaching and learning. https://eric.ed.gov/?id=ED494304

The Learning Center. (n.d.). Using concept maps. University of North Carolina at Chapel Hill. https://learningcenter.unc.edu/tips-and-tools/using-concept-maps/019

Valencia, S. (2014, June 27). When high school students struggle with textbook reading. Edutopia. https://www.edutopia.org/blog/students-struggle-with-textbook-reading-sheila-valencia

Zhao, D., Zhang, Q., Fu, M., Tang, Y., & Zhao, Y. (2010). Effects of physical positions on sleep architectures and post-nap functions among habitual nappers. *Biological Psychology*, 83(3), 207–13. https://doi.org/10.1016/j.biopsycho.2009.12.008

Chapter 5

Dynamic, Student-Centered Learning Approaches

Dynamic, Student-Centered Learning Approaches

Throughout my teaching career, I've seen firsthand how student-centered instruction can transform a classroom into a wonderful place to learn. Whether it's through group role plays, reader's theater, or interactive games, these methods breathe life into the curriculum. And believe me, these activities do more than just entertain; they foster critical thinking, collaboration, and a deeper understanding of the material.

One of the most powerful tools I used was the "Build a Story" activity, where each student contributes to a growing narrative, incorporating vocabulary flashcards along the way. This exercise not only enhances language skills but also encourages creativity and teamwork. Another exercise: reflecting on decisions—like what might have happened if a student had said "yes" instead of "no"—helps kids understand the impact of their choices, promoting critical thinking. Creating a "machine" with noises and gestures or guessing characters in "Party Quirks" keeps students engaged and eager to participate,

Incorporating activities like "Four Corners" discussions, marshmallow and toothpick towers, and trivia competitions further enriches the learning experience. These strategies encourage students to think critically, work collaboratively, and express their ideas confidently. The "One-Minute Debate" sharpens their persuasive skills, while the "Name Game" adds a fun twist to learning about historical figures. Each of these methods has proven to be invaluable in keeping students motivated and invested in their education.

Such strategies and others like them reduce cognitive overload and ensure that students are not only learning but thriving. Through these innovative approaches, my former middle school and high school students in Minneapolis found that classrooms could inspire joy and enthusiasm; they developed a genuine love for learning and deepened their connection to classmates.

When students lean into learning activities, time evaporates.

Key Chapter 5 Strategies

1. Design lessons that cater to diverse learning styles.
2. Use storytelling to make abstract concepts relatable.
3. Incorporate hands-on activities to reinforce learning.
4. Structure lessons to maximize student engagement.
5. Create a classroom environment that fosters academic growth.
6. Integrate thematic weekday activities to keep lessons fresh.
7. Encourage metacognitive reflection in students.
8. Use group work to enhance collaborative skills.
9. Implement feedback loops to improve learning outcomes.
10. Balance technology and low-tech tools in the classroom.

Memory Device for this Chapter
Rhyme/Rhythm Mnemonics

> Roleplay, Reader's Theater, Simon Says—these warmups are a wiz!
>
> Games and fun, in learning's mix, engagement is the perfect fix.
>
> Study hard, then take a rest, clear your mind, and do your best.
>
> [Buzz Groups] Turn and talk, share your views, ideas grow, no one can lose.

ACTIVE LEARNING STRATEGIES

"Active learning involves students in doing things and thinking about the things they are doing. This engagement in active learning leads to a deeper understanding of the material and better retention" (Hake, 1998). Active learning allows ideas to be explored, challenged, and solidified.

1. REFLECT IN WRITING
Use "quick writes" and "writing to learn strategies" Writing is a thinking tool.

2. SOLVE IT
Brainstorm solutions to a problem collaboratively or individually.

3. RELATE IT
Relate the info to something you have experienced.

4. FEEL IT
Find a way to feel intensely curious about the material so that it sticks in long-term memory.

5. GENERATE QUESTIONS
Develop questions about the topic and pose them to peers.

6. TEACH IT
Being able to fully explain the idea to a peer means that you have internalized the topic.

7. DOODLE
Sketch out how the concept relates to your life.

8. COMPARE NOTES
Share your notes with a peer, discuss the differences, and make additions or revisions.

CLASSROOM IMPROV GAMES

"Improvisational theater activities involve students in creative problem-solving and spontaneous decision-making, fostering both individual creativity and collaborative skills" (Sawyer, 2004). These activities encourage trust, adaptability, teaching students to embrace uncertainty, and think on their feet.

1. WARMUPS
Try a group role play conversation where kids sit in their own chairs. Do Reader's Theater. Play Charades or Simon Says.

2. BUILD A STORY
One kid starts with a phrase: once upon a time there lived . . . The next kid picks up where the previous kid left off and so on until everyone has contributed to the story multiple times. Show learners a vocabulary flash card word when it's their turn so they can incorporate these words (Case, 2024).

3. THE MACHINE
One student makes a repeating noise and simple gesture. A second one makes a new noise and movement which connects to the original gesture. Each child joins in until all participate in creating a machine (Ben-Zion, 2021).

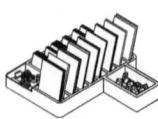

4. PARTY QUIRKS
In this guessing game, one student host leaves the room. Three other kids volunteer to play literary or historical figures and drop subtle hints about their characters when the host returns to guess who they are (Tornio, 2024).

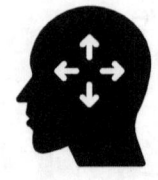

5. CHOICES
Imagine a recent experience where you said "no" to someone. Brainstorm a list of what could have happened if you'd said "yes." How would your life be different (Overcoming Obstacles, n.d.)?

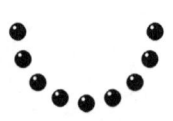

6. STRING OF PEARLS
A player steps forward and makes up the first line. Player 2 makes up a last line that has nothing to do with the first. The rest of the players each fill in a line of the story, trying to end up with a narrative that makes sense. Every time a new line is added, the players go down the string and repeat their lines first to last (Charles, 2024).

GAMES FOR CLASSROOMS

"Games are essential as they can help to reduce anxiety, increase positive feelings, and improve self-confidence because there is no fear of punishment and criticism for learners when they are practicing the target language freely" (Crocker, 2019). By incorporating games, educators empower students to embrace learning with enthusiasm.

1. FOUR CORNERS

Before the discussion, ask students to list responses to the following prompts:

- What are the qualities or characteristics of good discussions?
- What ground rules or guidelines should we follow in discussions (Carleton Academics, n.d.)?

2. MARSHMALLOWS AND TOOTHPICKS

Each team gets the same number of toothpicks and tiny marshmallows. Objective: create the tallest, most stable, and most creative tower (Mulvahill, 2023).

3. ONE-MINUTE DEBATE

Two kids have 60 seconds to persuade the class that their favorite food, hobby, sport, Netflix show, musician, soda, or animal is the best. The class votes.

4. NAME GAME

Tape names of famous people to the backs of students. Kids ask a peer one yes or no question to guess the name, then switch to another peer until they say the correct name.

5. TRIED AND TRUE GAMES

- **Vocabulary Charades**: Have students act out vocabulary words without speaking while their peers guess the word.
- **Team Trivia**: Create trivia questions related to the lesson and have teams compete to answer them.
- **Learning Stations**: Set up different stations with various activities related to the lesson for students to rotate through.
- **Story Chain**: Start a story and have each student add a sentence to continue it, promoting creativity and listening skills.

COOPERATIVE LEARNING

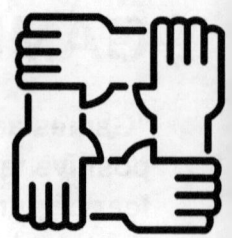

"Cooperative learning not only improves academic achievement but also promotes socialization and learning among students across different subject domains. It builds skills and knowledge through interaction between learners in groups" (Annenberg Learner, 2019).

Cooperative learning helps students develop essential interpersonal skills and prepares them for collaborative challenges beyond the classroom.

1. SHOWDOWN

Learners sit in a circle and the teacher asks a question. They must answer in secret and then when the teacher calls "showdown," all boards must be shown, Students can debate the best answer (Candler, n.d.).

2. CIRCLE OF VOICES

Give a small group a topic and allow a few minutes to organize their thoughts about it. Each student has two to three minutes of uninterrupted time to speak. Then the subgroup engages in a general discussion of the topic, without introducing new ideas. Participants should only build on what someone else has said, not on their own ideas (University of Waterloo, n.d.).

3. STUMP YOUR PARTNER

Students write a challenging question based on content up to that point (such as a chapter or lecture), then pose the question to a nearby peer. Learners hand in their questions, which can be used to create tests or exams (Academy 4 Social Civics, 2025).

4. BUZZ GROUPS

Have students turn to one to three neighbors to discuss areas of confusion, answer questions, offer examples of key concepts, or speculate on what will happen next in the class. Then have a whole class discussion.

5. WRITE-A-ROUND

"For creative writing or summarization, give a sentence starter (for example: if you give an elephant a cookie, he's going to ask for . . .). Ask all students in each team to finish that sentence. Then, they pass their paper to the right, read the one they received, and add a sentence to that one. After a few rounds, four great stories or summaries emerge. Give children time to add a conclusion and/or edit their favorite one to share with the class" (Colorín Colorado, 2018).

GAMIFICATION TOOLS AND STRATEGIES

"Gamification has the potential to increase engagement and motivation by transforming traditional lessons into an enhanced learning experience where students earn badges and achievements. This method fosters an internal drive to master the material, leading to deeper understanding and retention" (Katz & Ebben, 2022).

Moreover, gamification can inspire students to persist through challenges and collaborate effectively.

1. THREE RULES OF GAMIFICATION
Has objectives, rules, and winners.

2. TECH TOOLS
- **BuzzIn.Live**: Freemium Buzzer
- **Tic-Tac-Toe Template**: bit.ly/tic2tac (Source: Shake Up Learning)
- **Live Leaderboard Template**: bit.ly/3n94l4K
- **QR Code Treasure Hunt**: Classtools.net (H/T Zach Ramsey)
- **List Randomizer**: Make teams with Random.org
- **Badge Maker**: Accredible.com

3. GAMIFIED LEARNING PLATFORMS
- **EdPuzzle**: Editing online videos and adding interactive content to target specific learning objectives
- **Quizlet**: Flashcards
- **Kahoot**: Learning games
- **Quizizz**: Gamified quizzes, lessons, presentations, and flashcards

4. GAMING PRINCIPLES
- Beat the Clock ("Two minutes left!")
- Soften Failure (low-point quizzes)
- Booby Traps (time penalties for wrong answers)
- Easter Egg Surprises

5. LEVEL-UP SYSTEM
Implement a leveling system where kids earn points and unlock new levels or privileges.

STUDENT-CENTERED LEARNING

"[We're] changing "from directive to consultative" (McCarthy, 2015).

This shift toward a consultative approach reflects the principles of student-centered learning, where teachers act as facilitators who guide and support learners in taking ownership of their education.

1. IT'S GO TIME
Tell kids that the time to dial up concentration is when content is first presented.

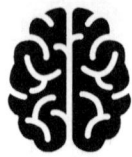
2. BRAIN BREAKS
"Concentrated study of 10–15 minutes for elementary school and 20–30 minutes for middle and high school students calls for a 3-to-5-minute break" (Wills, 2007).

3. CHECK OUT UNDERLYING CONDITIONS
Vision or hearing loss, sleep disorders, stress, diet, depression, allergy medication, and lack of exercise can degrade focus (Harvard Health Publishing, n.d.).

4. ALLOW GUM CHEWING
A study demonstrated that "participants who chewed gum had quicker reaction times and more accurate results than the participants who didn't chew gum. This was especially the case towards the end of the task" (Morgan, Johnson, & Miles, 2014).

5. PROVIDE EAR PLUGS
Let students block out audio distractions.

6. HI-LO INTEREST
Shift between highly engaging and less engaging activities (ADDitude Editors, 2023).

7. MAKE IT PERSONAL
Explain how your content is significant to students' lives. Or, have learners make that connection.

MAKE LECTURES INTERACTIVE

"An interactive lecture [is where the] the instructor breaks the lecture at least once per class to have students participate in an activity that lets them work directly with the material" (SERC, Carleton College, 2018). These activities not only reinforce understanding but also allow students to apply concepts in real time and foster a more dynamic and collaborative learning environment.

PRE-LECTURE

1. ASK A SETUP QUESTION
Pose a question about the topic that can only be answered if students listen closely to the lecture.

2. ACTIVATE SCHEMA
Ask student pairs to answer the following:
- What do you personally know about X?
- What part of the homework readings gave you the most insight about the lecture topic?

DURING LECTURE

3. SOLVE IT
Interrupt the lecture and ask student pairs to solve a problem, given info gleaned from the lecture.

4. PREDICT
Ask, "What will the rest of the presentation be about?"

POST-LECTURE

5. TALK SHOW PANEL
The teacher interviews a student panel of experts and discuss their opinions of the lecture topic.

6. WRITE A MINUTE PAPER
"What stood out as most important in today's lecture? What are you confused about?" (Stanford Teaching Commons, n.d.).

HOW TO TEACH DECISION MAKING

"Decision-making itself needs to be viewed as a skill, one that can be learned through a sequence of guided steps much as driving a car or speaking a new language can be learned" (Quist & Gregory, 2019).

Through practice, feedback, and reflection, students can develop confidence in their ability to analyze situations, weigh options, and make informed choices.

1. DECISION MAKING ANCHOR CHART

- Identify the problem/conflict to be solved.
- Gather relevant information.
- Brainstorm possible solutions.
- Identify potential consequences.
- Make a choice.
- Take action (Williamson, n.d.)!

2. LIST PROS AND CONS

Listing pros and cons is effective in all grades for helping students anticipate consequences.

3. ASK FOLLOW-UP QUESTIONS

How did you arrive at that decision? What might you do differently next time?

4. PLAY "WOULD YOU RATHER?"

Would you rather be a famous inventor or a famous writer? Would you rather start a colony on another planet or be the leader of a small country on Earth? Would you rather be able to type/text very fast or be able to read quickly? (Conversation Starters World, n.d.).

5. STUDY FAMOUSLY BAD DECISIONS

Stories of terrible decisions include the Trojan Horse, the Titanic tragedy, Hitler invading Russia, Blockbuster not buying Netflix, Chernobyl, New Coke, Russia selling Alaska to the US for only 2 cents an acre, and 12 publishing houses that rejected Harry Potter.

HOW TO REDUCE COGNITIVE OVERLOAD

"Cognitive overload occurs when a learner's working memory is overwhelmed by too much information at once, leading to a decrease in learning efficiency" (Sweller, 2020). By breaking complex tasks into smaller, manageable chunks and incorporating visuals or scaffolding techniques, teachers can reduce cognitive load, allowing students to process and retain information more effectively.

1. NO SCROLLING
Keep all content about a subject on one handout page, one slide, or one screen.

2. NO SLIDE SHOW BELLS AND WHISTLES
Students should remember the content, not the fancy transitions.

3. ELIMINATE THE REDUNDANCY EFFECT
Don't add text to a slide when the visual is self-explanatory. Don't read a text-heavy slide word-for-word (de Koning et al., 2009).

4. FRONTLOAD VOCABULARY
Provide definitions of difficult vocabulary before learners begin reading.

5. HIGHLIGHT IMPORTANT CONTENT
On handouts, use a bold font for key terms. When presenting, say, "This is the most important thing to remember."

6. DEMONSTRATE COMPLEX PROBLEMS
To help students with difficult problem procedures, show a worked example or partially worked example.

7. AVOID THE TYRANNY OF COVERAGE
Don't think of filling up class time by presenting as much info as you can. Just focus on key ideas.

STICKY NOTE ACTIVITIES

"Sticky notes can be used for a variety of classroom activities, such as providing feedback, organizing ideas, or setting personal goals. Their flexibility and ease of use make them an indispensable tool for both teachers and students" (Goodwin, 2016). Also, it's incredibly satisfying to slap stickies onto a surface like a productivity ninja.

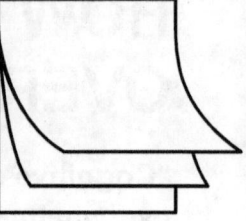

1. LOVE SWARM

When a child has surgery, a long illness, or a sad event, have the entire class cover their desk with "We Missed You!" stickies and doodles for a warm return.

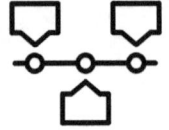

2. VISUAL TIMELINE

Have kids create a visual timeline of important moments in the chapter.

3. COLOR-CODED THINKING

As they read, learners jot down what they are thinking using color-coded strategies:

- Ask questions = orange ("Why did . . .?").
- Make predictions = green ("I think . . . will happen because . . .").
- Monitor comprehension = blue ("I'm noticing . . .").
- Make evaluations = purple ("In my opinion . . .") (Beck, n.d.).

4. MOTIVATION

Have positive sticky notes ("You've Got This, Priscilla!") waiting on each desk before a test.

5. PEER CRITIQUE

Direct kids to display essays or posters. During feedback rounds, ask learners to use green stickies for positive comments and pink for constructive criticism.

6. EXIT TICKETS

Leaving the classroom, kids identify how confident they are in their content knowledge by high and low stickies placed on a labeled piece—"High Confidence" to "Low Confidence."

X-FACTOR TEACHING

"An important aspect of the X-factor in teaching is creating an environment where students are active participants in their learning. This involves using innovative strategies that engage students and make learning more interactive and enjoyable" (Salmon, 2014). X-factor teachers make students feel like the center of the universe.

1. CURB NEGATIVE SELF-TALK
"Notice, dispute, and supplant" disruptive self-talk.

2. ENGAGE IN BRIEF, DAILY WRITING
Keep your sessions short with "ongoing awareness of what you will write the next session" (Boice, 2000, p. 85).

3. PRIORITIZE PRE-WRITING
Spend as much time and energy on pre-writing as on prose (Boice, 2000, p. 85).

4. KEEP EMOTIONS IN CHECK
Don't succumb to anxious binge-writing too close to the deadline.

5. LET GO OF EGO
Write playfully and creatively, without trying to make every sentence glorious.

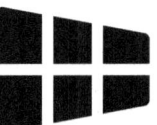
6. KEEP PERSPECTIVE
Notice whether your writing is on the correct track—solving the intended problem.

7. PROCESS OVER PRODUCT
Ask a struggling student to consult with a peer.

8. NOTICE WHEN IT'S NOT WORKING
Stop when you're fatigued or when the writing results in diminished returns.

Workbook: Reflecting on Chapter 5 Topics

1. How do role-play activities enhance student engagement and understanding of classroom material?
2. How does the "Build a Story" activity promote creativity and vocabulary development among students?
3. Reflect on a time you used a decision-making exercise in your classroom. How did it impact students' critical thinking skills?
4. How can discussing hypothetical scenarios where students make different choices help them understand the consequences of their actions?
5. What are the benefits of having students repeat the lines of the story in the "String of Pearls" activity?
6. How does the "Marshmallows and Toothpicks" activity encourage problem-solving and creativity?
7. What strategies can you use to ensure all students participate actively in "One-Minute Debates"?
8. How can "Stump Your Partner" be used as a formative assessment tool?
9. What topics or questions work best for "Buzz Groups" to stimulate meaningful discussions?
10. What are the potential challenges of using gamification in the classroom, and how can you address them?
11. What are some effective "Brain Break" activities that you can implement in your classroom?
12. What are some creative uses of sticky notes that you have found effective?

Going Deeper—Advanced Questions

1. How does the implementation of metacognitive strategies in the classroom impact students' self-regulated learning and academic performance?
2. How can thematic weekday activities be structured to address diverse learning needs and promote inclusivity?

Checklist of Activities and Strategies to Try (Pick 2)

- ❑ Conduct a group role play where students sit in their chairs and converse.
- ❑ Build a story starting with a phrase, and each student adds to the story while incorporating vocabulary flashcards.
- ❑ Reflect on a recent experience where students said "no" and brainstorm what could have happened if they said "yes."
- ❑ Set up different stations with various lesson-related activities for students to rotate through.
- ❑ Conduct a "showdown" where students sit in a circle, answer a question in secret, and reveal answers simultaneously for debate.
- ❑ Implement brain breaks with short breaks after concentrated study periods.
- ❑ Interrupt the lecture with a problem-solving activity based on the content.
- ❑ Use the game "Would You Rather?" to practice decision-making with fun hypothetical scenarios.
- ❑ Use sticky notes to create a warm return for a student after a long absence.
- ❑ Teach students to recognize when their writing is becoming counterproductive and take breaks as needed.
- ❑ Other: _____

Describe Your Progress

1. What activities were most successful?

2. What challenges did you face?

3. What can you improve for next time?

References for Chapter 5

Academy 4 Social Civics. (2025, March 19). Teaching with active learning. https://new.academy4sc.org/2025/03/19/teaching-with-active-learning/

ADDitude Editors. (2023, October 17). How to snag the attention of a distracted child. ADDitude. https://www.additudemag.com/focus-techniques-for-distracted-children/

Annenberg Learner. (2019). Teaching strategies: Cooperative learning. In *Insights into Algebra 1: Teaching for learning*. https://www.learner.org/series/insights-into-algebra-1-teaching-for-learning-2/variables-and-patterns-of-change/teaching-strategies-cooperative-learning/

Beck, A. (n.d.). Reading strategies with sticky notes. Teachers Pay Teachers. https://www.teacherspayteachers.com/Product/Reading-Strategies-with-Sticky-Notes-2053916

Ben-Zion, Y. (2021, May 4). Human machine. GIVE Guide. https://teachwithgive.org/activities/human-machine/

Boice, R. K. (2000). *Advice for new faculty members: Nihil Nimus*. Allyn & Bacon.

Candler, L. (n.d.). Show what you know! Teaching Resources by Laura Candler. https://lauracandler.com/show-what-you-know/

Carleton Academics. (n.d.). Establishing ground rules for discussions. https://serc.carleton.edu/introgeo/interactive/groundrules.html

Case, A. (2024, March 4). Weekend vocabulary storytelling. TEFLtastic. https://tefltastic.wordpress.com/worksheets/cutting-edge/ce-int/module-10/weekend-vocab-story/

Charles, D. (2024, February 5). Game library: "First line, last line." ImprovDr. https://improvdr.com/2024/02/05/game-library-first-line-last-line/

Colorín Colorado. (2018, June 22). Cooperative learning strategies ["Write-around" collaborative writing activity]. https://www.colorincolorado.org/article/cooperative-learning-strategies

Conversation Starters World. (n.d.). Would you rather questions. https://conversationstartersworld.com/would-you-rather-questions/

Crocker, M. (2019, April 3). Why games are so important in the English language classroom. ITTT TEFL Blog, International TEFL and TESOL Training. https://www.teflcourse.net/blog/why-games-are-so-important-in-the-english-language-classroom-ittt-tefl-blog/

de Koning, B. B., Tabbers, H. K., Rikers, R. M. J. P., & Paas, F. (2009). Towards a framework for attention cueing in instructional animations: Guidelines for research and design. *Educational Psychology Review*, 21(2), 113–140. https://doi.org/10.1007/s10648-009-9098-7

Goodwin, B. (2016). Tools for classroom instruction that works: Using sticky notes to enhance learning. *Educational Leadership*, 74(2), 80–1.

Hake, R. R. (1998). Interactive-engagement versus traditional methods: A six-thousand-student survey of mechanics test data for introductory physics courses. *American Journal of Physics*, 66(1), 64–74. https://doi.org/10.1119/1.18809

Harvard Health Publishing. (n.d.). Concentration & focus. Harvard Health. https://www.health.harvard.edu/topics/concentration-focus

Katz, Y. J., & Ebben, M. (2022). Gamification in education: The potential for increased engagement and motivation. *Journal of Educational Technology Development and Exchange*, 15(1), 1–15. https://doi.org/10.18785/jetde.1501.01

McCarthy, J. (2015, September 9). Student-centered learning: It starts with the teacher. Edutopia. https://www.edutopia.org/blog/student-centered-learning-starts-with-teacher-john-mccarthy

Morgan, K., Johnson, A. J., & Miles, C. (2014). Chewing gum moderates the vigilance decrement. *British Journal of Psychology*, 105(2), 214–25. https://doi.org/10.1111/bjop.12025

Mulvahill, E. (2023, August 7). 25 awesome team-building games and activities for kids (plus free Google Slides). We Are Teachers. https://www.weareteachers.com/team-building-games-and-activities/

Overcoming Obstacles. (n.d.). Lesson 3: Exploring alternatives and considering consequences. In Decision making (High school curriculum). Overcoming Obstacles. https://www.overcomingobstacles.org/portal/en/curricula/high-school/lesson-3-exploring-alternatives-and-considering-consequences

Quist, A., & Gregory, R. (2019, May 2). Teaching decision-making skills in the classroom. Arithmetic of Compassion. https://www.arithmeticofcompassion.org/blog/2019/5/1/teaching-decision-making-skills-in-the-classroom

Sawyer, R. K. (2004). Creative teaching: Collaborative discussion as disciplined improvisation. *Educational Researcher*, 33(2), 12–20. https://doi.org/10.3102/0013189X033002012

Salmon, G. (2014). *E-tivities: The key to active online learning*. Routledge.

SERC, Carleton College. (2018). Interactive lectures. https://serc.carleton.edu/introgeo/interactive/index.html

Stanford Teaching Commons. (n.d.). Formative assessment and feedback. Stanford University. https://teachingcommons.stanford.edu/teaching-guides/foundations-course-design/feedback-and-assessment/formative-assessment-and-feedback

Sweller, J. (2020). Cognitive load theory and educational technology. *Educational Technology Research and Development*, 68(1), 1–16. https://doi.org/10.1007/s11423-019-09701-3

Tornio, S. (2024, January 16). Use our FREE Guess Who template to make your own game. We Are Teachers. https://www.weareteachers.com/guess-who-template/

University of Waterloo, Centre for Teaching Excellence. (n.d.). Circle of voices. In Group work in the classroom: Types of small groups. https://uwaterloo.ca/centre-for-teaching-excellence/catalogs/tip-sheets/group-work-classroom-types-small-groups#circle_of_voices

Williamson, R. (n.d.). Decision-making process anchor chart. https://www.teacherspayteachers.com/Product/Decision-Making-Process-Anchor-Chart-1234567

Wills, J. (2007). Review of research: Brain-based teaching strategies for improving students' memory, learning, and test-taking success. *Childhood Education*, 83(5), 310–15. https://doi.org/10.1080/00094056.2007.10522940

Chapter 6

Harnessing Visual Tools

Harnessing Visual Tools

Chapter 6 is filled with practical strategies that any educator can use to bring their lessons to life and make learning a truly visual and memorable experience.

Using visuals in teaching isn't just helpful; it's essential for truly effective learning. Visual aids like diagrams, charts, and timelines can turn complex topics into easily digestible information. According to Richard Mayer's Cognitive Theory of Multimedia Learning, pairing words with relevant visuals helps students form mental models, making the material stick better (Mayer, 2009). This approach breaks down information into bite-sized chunks, which is particularly useful for learners who might struggle with just text.

Visuals also make learning more inclusive and engaging. Research shows that tools like infographics and videos can grab students' attention and keep them interested. And when kids are interested, they participate more and retain information longer. One study found that students who learned with visual aids performed better in assessments than those who got traditional text-based instruction (University of Wisconsin-Madison, 2014).

Visuals also improve critical thinking and problem-solving skills. When students create or interpret visuals like concept maps or timelines, they're analyzing and connecting ideas. The Vanderbilt University Center for Teaching suggests that these tools help students organize their knowledge and perceive patterns, which enhances their analytical abilities (Vanderbilt University Center for Teaching, 2016). By integrating more visuals into your teaching, you can ensure that children are not just memorizing but truly understanding the material.

Key Chapter 6 Strategies

1. Incorporate humor into presentations to enhance memory and learning.
2. Facilitate poster presentations to engage students in research and public speaking.
3. Apply de Bono's PMI (Plus, Minus, Interesting) method to analyze visual content (de Bono, 1985a).
4. Conduct focused interviews where students explain their thought processes.
5. Pause the instructional video and discuss key moments to reinforce understanding and engagement.
6. Implement the Visual Thinking Strategy (VTS) to foster inquiry and discussion.
7. Frontload videos with pre-teaching vocabulary and contextual information.
8. Use timelines for various subjects, from history to literature, to enhance comprehension.

Memory Device for this Chapter
Method of Loci Mnemonic

Picture yourself walking through your home and associating each room with specific strategies.

Living Room

Add humor: See a comedy show playing on the TV, representing the importance of humor to engage and enhance memory.

Kitchen

Poster presentations: See your fridge covered with research posters, symbolizing creating and presenting posters in a classroom research conference.

Bedroom

Visual Thinking Strategy (VTS): Picture art on your bedroom walls and ask questions like "What do you notice?" representing the VTS inquiry process.

Deep Analysis: See a magnifying glass on your nightstand, symbolizing deep analysis of visual content.

Garage

Double Timeline: Imagine two timelines side by side on the garage door, comparing historical events or literary movements.

POWERFUL POWERPOINT

"A more effective way to present material is with the Assertion-Evidence Method, which has been linked with better understanding and long-term retention" (Garner & Alley, 2013). This approach encourages presenters to use clear, concise assertions supported by compelling visuals or data, making complex concepts more accessible and engaging for learners.

1. BEYOND THE 5/5/5 RULE
The 5/5/5 rule (no more than 5 words per line of text, 5 lines per slide, or 5 text-heavy slides in a row) is out of date. "Edit your message until it's compelling, then support it with an equally compelling composition" (ProPoint Graphics, 2017).

2. BUILD IN SURPRISES
Wake up kids' brains with astounding stats, videos, or funny images of you. Help learners feel something with images from these sources: Morguefile, Unsplash, Compfight, Flickr, Photopin, and Image Free.

3. ADD HUMOR
Laughter wakes up the hippocampus—which is critical to memory and learning.

4. CONNECT
Make connections to previous topics, as well as kids' interests, and experiences.

5. GET THE TITLE RIGHT
It should be hooky and convey the topic's importance: "What Writing Skills will Bring You Love and Cash."

6. STATE THE CONCLUSION FIRST
While presenting, try stating the conclusion first, then chronologically describe how you arrived at that idea (Vik, 2004).

7. REPEAT YOUR MESSAGE
If the presentation is long and your message is important, repeat it.

MAKE THINKING VISIBLE

"Visible Thinking is a flexible and systematic research-based approach to integrating the development of students' thinking with content learning across subject matters . . ." (Project Zero, 2024). It empowers students to make their thought processes explicit.

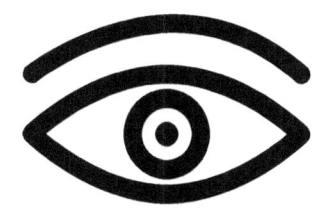

1. FOCUSED INTERVIEWS
During short teacher-student conferences, ask learners to explain their writing/thinking.

2. REMIXING
Ask students to take an assignment and remix it into a different genre, Ex: an essay could be converted into historical.

3. POSTER PRESENTATION
Direct students to create a poster on their research. Then hold a classroom "research conference" where parents, peers, teachers, and community stakeholders ask students questions about their research process and the focus of their inquiry.

4. MULTIMEDIA NARRATIVES
Kids "use music, images, timing, & graphics to convey their own complex combination of emotional & intellectual responses to some moving historical incident they were trying to portray for a public audience" (findings are a synthesis of the Visible Knowledge Project, Bass & Eynon, 2008).

5. SORT KEY VOCABULARY
Direct students to identify 10 big ideas from a unit of study & organize them from most to least important and then provide a justification.

6. DRAMATIZE
Ask students to dramatize how a historian, or scientist, or writer, or geologist, or mathematician, would think through a problem.

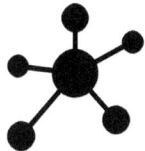
7. CONCEPT MAPPING
Concept maps represent how students organize knowledge and illustrate how detailed that knowledge is.

PAIR VISUAL WITH CRITICAL THINKING

"Thinking routines are short, easy-to-learn mini-strategies that extend and deepen students' thinking and become part of the fabric of everyday classroom life. They help reveal students' thinking to the teacher and also help students themselves to notice and name particular thinking moves, making those moves more available and useful . . ." (Project Zero, 2024). Over time, these routines cultivate a culture of curiosity and inquiry.

1. VTS
The Visual Thinking Strategy is a three-step inquiry process:
1. What do you notice?
2. What do you see that makes you say that?
3. What more can we find? Repeat . . .

2. DE BONO'S PMI
1. List all the positive aspects.
2. List all the negative effects.
3. List all the interesting aspects (adapted from de Bono, 1985b).

3. DEEP ANALYSIS
1. What does it say?
2. What does it not say?
3. What does it mean?

4. POSTER ANALYSIS
What do you notice? Who's the author? List people, things, objects, and symbols. Is there a message? Questions? Instructions? Author? Audience?

5. THE FOUR Ws
1. What do you see? What else?
2. What does it remind you of? An image? An experience?
3. What's the artist's purpose? To analyze? Persuade? Entertain?
4. So what? Why does it matter? Significance? (Adapted from Abilock, 2002)

VIDEO VIEWING TIPS

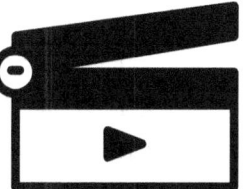

"It's important to be mindful of how often and how much we use video—it's important to have a clear purpose for using that film, documentary, or news clip" (Alber, 2019). When thoughtfully integrated, video can spark discussion, provide real-world context, and cater to diverse learners.

1. RELATE IT
Present a reading that unpacks some of the same ideas addressed in the video.

2. LESS IS MORE
An average adult's attention span is limited, and it's even shorter for children and teenagers. Keep it tight!

3. PAUSE & DISCUSS
Check out over 100 questions to ask from Teach with Movies: http://bit.ly/TeachwMovies.

4. FRONTLOAD THE VIDEO
Pre-teach vocabulary. Ask: What questions would you want to ask the filmmaker before the video begins? What do you know about the topic? Analyze the film poster and have kids generate questions about the film. Have students create a semantic web of ideas essential to the topic. Have learners rate their understanding of terms and concepts explored in the video.

5. GRAPHIC ORG. OR GUIDED NOTES
Use a graphic organizer or guided notes. See http://bit.ly/2MFNnvc.

6. PROVIDE CONTEXT
Describe the setting, the cultural impact, associated controversies, and the key reasons for showing the video.

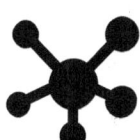
7. MAKE CONNECTIONS
Make video-to-self, video-to-other-video, and video-to-world connections.

TIMELINE LEARNING ACTIVITIES

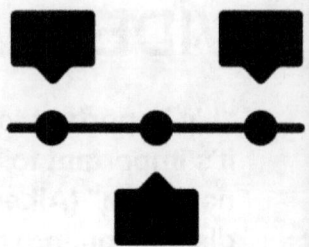

"Creating timelines allows students to identify patterns and themes among events, make comparisons across different time periods, and develop historical perspective by relating concurrent entries" (Vanderbilt University Center for Teaching, 2024). This process not only enhances critical thinking skills but also helps students visualize the interconnectedness of events.

1. COMPREHENSION
In a visual timeline, name the eight most important events in chapter four.

2. WHAT CAUSED IT?
In order, name the causes of WWI (history), the history of Earth (geography), or the ascension of Mao Zedong (political), the Big Bang Theory (astronomy), or the evolution of Impressionism (art) and Romanticism (literature).

3. AUTOBIOGRAPHIES
Create a timeline as a pre-writing strategy for memoirs or autobiographies.

4. INQUIRY PROJECT
Identify project steps and estimated completion times of different drafts.

5. SELF-ASSESSMENT
Develop a semester-long timeline that identifies learning struggles and successes.

6. DOUBLE TIMELINE
Use timelines to make side-by-side comparisons of, say, Roman Emperor inflection points.

7. TIMELINE TAPESTRY ACTIVITY
Learners work together to create a "tapestry" that visually and narratively represents the sequence of events or stages.

Workbook: Reflecting on Chapter 6 Topics

1. How can moving beyond the 5/5/5 rule make your PowerPoint presentations more engaging?
2. Why is it important to build surprises into your presentations? Give examples of how this can be done.
3. How does stating the conclusion first and then explaining the process improve understanding?
4. What strategies can you use to effectively repeat your message without sounding redundant?
5. What are the benefits of asking students to remix assignments into different genres?
6. In what ways do multimedia narratives allow students to express complex ideas?
7. How does sorting key vocabulary aid in understanding and retention of big ideas?
8. How does de Bono's PMI method encourage critical thinking?
9. What is the significance of deep analysis in understanding visual content?
10. How can the "Four Ws" method be used to analyze and understand visual artworks?

Going Deeper—Advanced Questions

1. How can the integration of humor and surprise have implications for the long-term retention of information?
2. Reflect on the impact of making thinking visible through focused interviews and poster presentations. How does this approach compare with traditional assessment methods in evaluating student understanding?
3. Analyze the benefits and challenges of using timelines in different subjects (e.g., history, literature, science). How do timelines help in identifying patterns and relationships between events or concepts?
4. How can the Visual Thinking Strategy (VTS) be adapted to subjects beyond the arts, such as mathematics or science?
5. Discuss the role of multimedia narratives in developing emotional responses to historical events. How can this approach foster a deeper connection between students and the material?

Checklist of Activities and Strategies to Try (Pick 2)

❑ Wake up kids' brains with presentations that feature astounding stats, videos, or funny images to build in surprise.

❑ Make connections to previous topics and students' interests to enhance relevance.

❑ Start a presentation with the conclusion and then explain the process to improve understanding.

❑ Use the Visual Thinking Strategy (VTS) to guide students through a three-step inquiry process.

❑ Encourage students to use de Bono's PMI method to analyze visual content.

❑ Have students create a poster presentation to share their research and field questions from peers and teachers.

❑ Ask students to remix an assignment into a different genre to deepen their understanding.

❑ Use timelines to help students visualize and understand historical events or processes.

❑ Create a graphic organizer or guided notes to help students follow along with video content.

❑ Pre-teach vocabulary and context before showing a video to enhance comprehension.

❑ Other:
_____.

Describe Your Progress

1. What activities were most successful?

2. What challenges did you face?

3. How can you improve for next time?

 **References for Chapter 6**

Abilock, D. (2002). The Four Ws: Questions for Visual Analysis. *Knowledge Quest*, 31(1), 38–40.

Alber, R. (2019, March 15). Using video content to amplify learning. Edutopia. https://www.edutopia.org/article/using-video-content-amplify-learning

Anon. (n.d.). Graphic organizers and guided notes. http://bit.ly/2MFNnvc

Bass, R., & Eynon, B. (Eds.). (2009). The difference that inquiry makes: A collaborative case study on technology and learning from the Visible Knowledge Project. Academic Commons. https://web.archive.org/web/20181216090816/https://blogs.commons.georgetown.edu/vkp/files/2009/03/bass-revised-2.pdf

de Bono, E. (1985a). *De Bono's thinking course*. British Broadcasting Corporation

de Bono, E. (1985b). *Six Thinking Hats*. Little, Brown, and Company.

Garner, J. K., & Alley, M. (2013). How the design of presentation slides affects audience comprehension: A case for the assertion-evidence approach. *International Journal of Engineering Education*, 29(6), 1564–79.

Mayer, R. E. (2009). *Multimedia learning* (2nd ed.). Cambridge University Press. https://doi.org/10.1017/CBO9780511811678

Project Zero. (2024). Visible thinking. Harvard University. https://pz.harvard.edu/

ProPoint Graphics. (2017, July 5). Debunking the presentation 6x6 rule. Forbes. https://www.forbes.com/sites/propointgraphics/2017/07/05/debunking-the-presentation-6x6-rule/

Teach with Movies. (n.d.). Discussion questions index. http://bit.ly/TeachwMovies

University of Wisconsin-Madison. (2014). Creating a poster. Undergraduate Symposium. https://www.learning.wisc.edu/ugsymposium/poster.html

Vanderbilt University Center for Teaching. (2016, April 20). Using timelines to enhance learning. https://web.archive.org/web/20160420080556/https://cft.vanderbilt.edu/guides-sub-pages/digital-timelines/

Vik, G. N. (2004). Breaking bad habits: Teaching effective PowerPoint use to working graduate students. *Business Communication Quarterly*, 67(2), 225–8.

Chapter 7

Cultivating Effective Teacher Habits

Cultivating Effective Teacher Habits

The habits teachers cultivate in our personal and professional lives can profoundly impact classroom effectiveness and spark learning. Nurturing these habits is not just another item to add to the pile of responsibilities. It's an ongoing practice that matters.

The key is consistency. Doug Lemov emphasizes in *Teach Like a Champion* that "consistent, purposeful routines not only enhance classroom management but also increase student engagement and achievement" (Lemov, 2010). This insight is particularly relevant in the classroom, where the routines we establish and the behaviors we model set the tone for our students. Effective habits like making lists, preparing for tomorrow, and reducing distractions during grading and planning are essential practices that enhance our ability to deliver high-quality instruction.

Another habit to embrace is cultivating resilience and balance. According to a study by Patricia Jennings and Mark Greenberg, "Mindfulness and emotional regulation practices help teachers reduce stress and prevent burnout, leading to more effective teaching" (Jennings & Greenberg, 2009). This resilience is bolstered by maintaining strong interpersonal relationships and engaging in hobbies and outside interests, which enrich our lives and translate into better teaching. Parker J. Palmer notes that "self-care is essential for teachers, as it directly impacts their ability to care for their students" (Palmer, 2007). *In other words, care for your students by caring for yourself!*

Incorporating these habits into our daily routines can significantly impact student outcomes. John Hattie's extensive research in *Visible Learning* found that "teacher clarity, consistent behavior, and preparedness are among the most influential factors on student achievement" (Hattie, 2009). By modeling these successful habits, we inspire our students to develop their own productive routines. Ultimately, adopting and refining key habits leads to more effective, balanced, and resilient teaching.

Key Chapter 7 Strategies

1. Use paper or electronic lists to stay organized and ensure important tasks are completed.
2. Budget 15 minutes every evening to file papers and prepare for the next day.
3. Meet with friends regularly to reduce cortisol levels, improve confidence, and boost resilience.
4. Engage in outside hobbies to enrich your life and enhance your teaching.
5. Check your email only twice a day to avoid distractions and stay focused.
6. Dress professionally to create a strong, favorable image for students.
7. Let students know the objectives of the lesson to keep students (and you) focused.
8. Stand completely still to signal students to stop, look, and listen.
9. Use animated facial expressions to become a more persuasive communicator.
10. Maintain eye contact to create a bond and engage students.
11. Use physical proximity to redirect students and increase engagement.
12. Take breaks during the day to restore physical energy and maintain effectiveness.
13. Visit the library regularly to read and expand your knowledge base.

Memory Device for this Chapter
Acronym Mnemonic

Helpful habits
Active hobbies
Balanced life
Interpersonal relationships
Time management
Simplified tasks

EIGHT HABITS OF SUCCESSFUL TEACHERS

"Because they are consistent, often unconscious patterns, [habits] constantly, daily, express our character" (Covey, 1989). By intentionally shaping our habits, we have the power to transform not just our routines but the very essence of who we are.

1. MAKE LISTS
Use paper or electronic lists with apps like Todoist.

2. PHONE HYGIENE
Mobile phone use leads to anxiety and depression (Negl & Godiyal, 2016). Turn your phone completely off after each use and place in a zippered pocket.

3. INTRODUCTION
Jerry Seinfeld hangs a calendar on his wall and for every day that he successfully writes jokes, he draws a big X and creates an XXXXX pattern. His goal is to never break the chain. There is also an app for chaining: Chains.cc.

4. PREP FOR TOMORROW
Budget 15 minutes every evening to file papers and return objects to their right location before you go home.

5. MEET WITH FRIENDS
Friendship reduces cortisol, improves confidence, and boosts resilience to trauma (Mayo Clinic Staff, 2020).

6. REDUCE DISTRACTIONS
Don't multitask. Check your email twice a day at most and avoid "response-mode" (Alton, 2018).

7. ENJOY HOBBIES
"Outside pursuits enrich lives and translate into better teaching," writes teacher Diana Senechal (2013).

BOOST YOUR TEACHING CONFIDENCE

"Children as young as 4 can distinguish between verbal markers of certainty and uncertainty ('know' versus 'think' or 'guess'). These children preferred to learn new information from a person who appeared confident and certain in their knowledge" (Smith, 2024).

Young learners are perceptive and more likely to engage with adults who demonstrate assuredness.

1. WEAR POWER CLOTHING
Leave the comfy clothes at home, Dress like money. "In a 2012 study . . . subjects who wore doctors' lab coats scored higher on attention-related tasks than did those who did not" (Styx, 2024).

2. LET KIDS KNOW THE OBJECTIVES
That means you know them too! Keep your purpose in mind.

3. DON THE CAPE
While standing in the hall, insist on classroom behaviors before kids enter class. Set expectations (Snoke, 2015).

4. BE 10% MORE ENTHUSIASTIC
There is no drawback to more passion and enthusiasm.

5. DIAL IN YOUR VOICE
Slow down, breathe, then project your voice. Practice!

6. SET UP EXPECTATIONS
Tell students up front that you don't know everything. Nobody does. If you get stumped, tell the class you'll look up the answer and tell them tomorrow.

7. PREP EARLY
Make sure you're thoroughly planned before the day starts.

EFFECTIVE TEACHING NONVERBALS

When "the nonverbal behavior of the teachers was consistent with their verbal behavior [it] significantly impacted student performance" (Chaudhry & Arif, 2012). This alignment fosters trust, clarity, and engagement in the classroom.

1. FREEZE BODY
When teachers stand completely still, their body language suggests kids should stop, look, and listen (Learners Edge, 2023).

2. ANIMATE
"Persuasive communicators exhibit more animated facial expressions . . ." (Speaking Coach, 2023).

3. EYE POWER
Eyes "are the only part of your central nervous system that make contact with the outside of your body." Eye contact activates the limbic mirror neurons. If you communicate an emotion through your eyes, your students' brain will activate similar neurons . . . Eye contact is critical for bonding (Brown et al., 2003; Marino, 2013; Perry, 2021).

4. SHOW YOUR PALMS
"Use an open-body gesture such as upturned palms and open arms (rather than crossed arms) to indicate you are open and accepting of anything your students want to share" (Williamson, n.d.).

5. DRESS UP
Teachers' formal or professional dress creates a "strong favorable image" for students (Kashem, 2019).

6. PROXIMITY
"Physical closeness to a student has been proven to redirect the student back on task. This type of strategy helps to increase student engagement [and] decrease problem behaviors" (IRIS Center, 2021).

Workbook: Reflecting on Chapter 7 Topics

1. In what ways has turning off your phone after each use impacted your anxiety levels and focus during the school day?
2. How does budgeting 15 minutes every evening for preparation affect your readiness and stress levels the following day?
3. Reflect on the benefits you've experienced from regularly meeting with friends. How has this practice influenced your resilience and confidence?
4. Describe how engaging in outside hobbies has enriched your personal life and translated into better teaching practices.
5. What changes have you noticed in student behavior and engagement when you dress professionally?
6. In what situations have you used the strategy of standing still to gain students' attention, and what were the outcomes?
7. How have animated facial expressions helped you become a more persuasive and engaging communicator?
8. Discuss the impact of maintaining eye contact on your relationship with students and their engagement in the classroom.
9. How do open-body gestures influence students' willingness to participate and share their thoughts?
10. In what ways has using physical proximity as a strategy helped to redirect off-task behavior and increase student engagement?

Going Deeper—Advanced Questions

1. Explore the relationship between teacher resilience, as cultivated through personal hobbies and social interactions, and its impact on teacher burnout rates and retention. How can educational institutions support these practices?
2. How do various forms of nonverbal cues interact with cultural differences in the classroom?
3. Investigate the effects of digital minimalism, such as limiting phone and email usage, on cognitive load and decision-making processes in teachers.

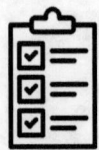

Checklist of Activities and Strategies to Try (Pick 2)

❑ Use paper or electronic lists to stay organized and ensure important tasks are completed.
❑ Budget 15 minutes every evening to file papers and prepare for the next day.
❑ Meet with friends regularly to reduce cortisol levels, improve confidence, and boost resilience.
❑ Check your email only twice a day to avoid distractions and stay focused.
❑ Dress professionally to create a strong, favorable image for students.
❑ Let students know the objectives of each lesson to keep both you and them focused.
❑ Stand completely still to signal students to stop, look, and listen.
❑ Use open body gestures to indicate you are open to student contributions.
❑ Use physical proximity to redirect students and increase engagement.
❑ Take breaks during the day to restore physical energy and maintain effectiveness.
❑ Visit the library regularly to read and expand your knowledge base.
❑ Other: _____.

Describe Your Progress

1. What activities were most successful?

2. What challenges did you face?

3. How can you improve for next time?

 **References for Chapter 7**

Alton, L. (2018, April 1). 5 signs email is ruling your life (and 7 ways to take back control). Inc. https://www.inc.com/larry-alton/5-signs-email-is-ruling-your-life-and-7-ways-to-take-back-control.html

Brown, W. E., Pageler, N. M., Menon, V., Merin, N. M., Eliez, S., & Reiss, A. L. (2003). Effect of head orientation on gaze processing in fusiform gyrus and superior temporal sulcus. *NeuroImage*, 20(1), 318–29. https://doi.org/10.1016/S1053-8119(03)00229-5

Chaudhry, A. H., & Arif, M. I. (2012). Teachers' nonverbal behavior and its impact on student achievement. *International Education Studies*, 5(4), 56–64.

Covey, S. R. (1989). *The 7 habits of highly effective people: Powerful lessons in personal change*. Free Press.

Hattie, J. (2009). *Visible learning: A synthesis of over 800 meta-analyses relating to achievement*. Routledge.

IRIS Center. (2021, September 17). Proximity control (Fundamental Skill Sheet). Vanderbilt University, Peabody College. https://iris.peabody.vanderbilt.edu/wp-content/uploads/misc_media/fss/pdfs/2018/IRIS_fundamental_skill_sheet_proximity_control.pdf

Jennings, P. A., & Greenberg, M. T. (2009). The prosocial classroom: Teacher social and emotional competence in relation to student and classroom outcomes. *Review of Educational Research*, 79(1), 491–525.

Kashem, M. (2019). Impact of teachers' attire on students' academic performance: A study on private universities in Bangladesh. *International Journal of Research in Business and Social Science*, 8(5), 1–7.

Learners Edge. (2023, January 5). Nonverbal communication in the classroom. https://www.learnersedge.com/blog/nonverbal-communication-in-the-classroom

Lemov, D. (2010). *Teach like a champion: 49 techniques that put students on the path to college*. Jossey-Bass.

Marino, A. (2013, October 10). Learn to read body language. Nonverbal communication. Alpha M. https://alpham.com/learn-to-read-body-language/

Mayo Clinic Staff. (2020, August 29). Social support: Tap this tool to beat stress. https://web.archive.org/web/20200829052723/https://www.mayoclinic.org/healthy-lifestyle/stress-management/in-depth/social-support/art-20044445

Negi, P., & Godiyal, S. (2016). Impact of mobile phone addiction among college going students: A literature review. *International Journal of Applied Research*, 2(9), 393–5.

Palmer, P. J. (2007). *The courage to teach: Exploring the inner landscape of a teacher's life* (10th-anniversary ed.). Jossey-Bass.

Perry, E. (2021, September 9). Eye contact is important (crucial really) in communication. BetterUp. https://www.betterup.com/blog/why-is-eye-contact-important

Senechal, D. (2013). *Republic of noise: The loss of solitude in schools and culture*. Rowman & Littlefield Education.

Smith, C. L. (2024). Children's sensitivity to the quality of information from others. *Child Development*, 95(1), 123–35.

Snoke, M. (2016, January 26). Classroom management: Develop clear rules and expectations. TeachHub. https://www.teachhub.com/classroom-management/2016/01/classroom-management-develop-clear-rules-and-expectations/

Speaking Coach. (2023, February 6). The power of nonverbal communication in public speaking. https://www.speaking.coach/the-power-of-nonverbal-communication-in-public-speaking/

Styx, L. (2024, May 22). Dopamine dressing: How to dress for your happiness. Verywell Mind. https://www.verywellmind.com/dopamine-dressing-how-to-dress-for-your-happiness-in-2022-5217231

Williamson, B. (n.d.). The importance of body language in teaching. EVERFI. https://everfi.com/blog/k-12/the-importance-of-body-language-in-teaching/

Chapter 8

Building Literacy Skills (Reading, Writing, Listening, Speaking)

Building Literacy Skills (Reading, Writing, Listening, Speaking)

Building literacy skills isn't just a one-time effort, but the consistent application of well-thought-out methods that enhance students' learning experiences. This chapter is one of the longest that you'll find in this guide because of the importance of literacy to all content areas; try learning any subject without reading, writing, listening, and speaking! You'll find in the next few pages dozens of inspiring strategies.

As you know, reading strategies are foundational to literacy development. Pre-reading activities, such as discussing themes and building background knowledge, significantly enhance comprehension (Shanahan & Shanahan, 2008). Moreover, integrating visuals and connecting new information to prior knowledge can make complex texts more accessible and relatable for students (Fisher, Frey, & Lapp, 2008). Remember that scaffolding texts effectively means balancing challenge and support to build students' confidence and autonomy (Tomlinson, 2014).

Writing instruction not only improves students' composing skills but also enhances their reading comprehension and learning in other subjects (Graham, MacArthur, & Fitzgerald, 2013). Therefore, embed writing tasks in content areas to improve overall academic achievement.

Listening and speaking strategies round out the literacy skills framework. Facilitating structured discussions, modeling metacognitive strategies through "think-alouds," and engaging students in Socratic seminars promote rich dialogue and reflective thinking (Zwiers & Crawford, 2011).

Finally, showing kids how to manage public speaking anxiety and present their ideas confidently prepares them for real-world scenarios, from job interviews to business resentations (Duke & Pearson, 2002). Daily implementation of literacy strategies 126 described in Chapter 8 will ensure that students are well equipped for success in school and life.

Key Chapter 8 Strategies

1. Implement "think-aloud" strategies to model metacognitive processes for students.
2. Scaffold texts by frontloading difficult vocabulary to aid comprehension.
3. Teach students about genre conventions to help them make predictions about texts.
4. Use visuals such as photos, graphic organizers, or videos to provide context before reading.
5. Connect new information to students' prior knowledge to make learning more accessible.
6. Use pre-reading activities like discussing themes and building background knowledge to enhance comprehension.
7. Use graphic organizers like Venn diagrams and story maps to visually represent key ideas.
8. Create literature circles to promote cooperative learning and in-depth discussions of texts.
9. Use the C.A.S.E. strategy (Claim, Answer, Support, Explain) to help students structure their writing with textual evidence.
10. Develop post-reading activities like journal writing, dioramas, or creative writing to reinforce comprehension.
11. Use repeated readings to help students deepen their understanding of poems or complex texts.
12. Provide book report alternatives like creating timelines or character playlists to engage students in different ways.
13. Incorporate Robert Marzano's approach to vocabulary instruction, which includes paraphrasing and using graphic organizers (Marzano, 2010).
14. Teach listening skills through activities like partner paraphrasing and reflective listening to enhance classroom engagement.
15. Design low-stakes writing activities like freewriting and cinquains to encourage creativity and reduce anxiety.

Memory Device for this Chapter
Chunking Mnemonic

Breaking Down the Chapter's Strategies into Smaller Chunks

- **Pre-Reading**: Discuss themes, build background knowledge, and state objectives.
- **During Reading**: Annotate texts, guided reading questions, and use graphic organizers.
- **Post-Reading**: Journal writing, creative activities, and text connections.

HOW TO SCAFFOLD TEXTS TO UNLOCK MEANING

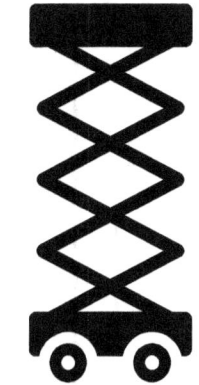

"Effective scaffolding requires a balance between challenge and support. Teachers must carefully design instructional activities that push students to extend their current capabilities while providing enough guidance to prevent frustration and disengagement" (Reiser & Tabak, 2014).

Scaffolding not only bridges the gap between what students can do independently and with help but also empowers students to embrace challenges as opportunities to learn.

1. FACILITATE STRUCTURED TALKS

Ensure these discussions are guided and purposeful, allowing students to explore various interpretations and perspectives. Implement discussion protocols such as Think-Pair-Share or Socratic Seminars to promote equitable participation and rich dialogue.

2. MODEL

Use a "think-aloud" to demonstrate metacognition.

3. REVIEW THE GENRE CONVENTIONS

Teach students about the text's genre in advance and have them make predictions about what will occur.

4. FRONTLOAD VOCABULARY

Teach the heck out of difficult vocabulary important to comprehending the text.

5. USE VISUALS

Show a photo, provide a graphic organizer, or play a video of the context before students read.

6. CONNECT TO PRIOR KNOWLEDGE

Link new information to what students already know. This can make the material more accessible and relatable.

SCAFFOLDING ENGLISH LANGUAGE ARTS

"Scaffolding in reading comprehension involves breaking down a text into manageable parts, providing context, and guiding students through each segment to build their understanding incrementally" (Walqui & van Lier, 2010). This process not only supports students in decoding complex material but also equips them with strategies to approach challenging texts independently.

1. PRE-READING ACTIVITIES
- **DISCUSSING**: Talk about the theme.
- **BUILDING BACKGROUND KNOWLEDGE**: Including historical, cultural, or social background of a text.
- **INCORPORATING MEDIA**: Play videos, podcasts, or other media.
- **I.D. PURPOSE**: Clearly state the objectives for reading.

2. ENHANCING COMPREHENSION
- **USE GRAPHIC ORG**: Venn diagrams, story maps, concept maps, etc.
- **INCORPORATE GUIDED READING Q's**: Ask about key concepts.
- **ANNOTATE THE TEXT**: Teach students to make notes on important points in the text.
- **CLOZE EXERCISES**: Students fill in the missing words in sentences or paragraphs to demonstrate comprehension.

3. COOPERATIVE LEARNING
- **LITERATURE CIRCLES**: Small group discussions with specific roles for each student.
- **FISHBOWL DISCUSSION**: Small group discusses a topic while others observe, followed by a class-wide discussion.
- **SOCRATIC SEMINAR**: Student-led discussions for exploring and analyzing texts.

4. VOCABULARY BUILDING
- **WORD WALLS**: Classroom display of key vocabulary and concepts.
- **WORD SORTS**: Sorting vocabulary words into categories.
- **VOCAB PRE-TEACHING**: Introduce key vocabulary before reading.

EFFECTIVELY USE TEXT EVIDENCE ... REMEMBER C.A.S.E.

The C.A.S.E. strategy, which stands for Claim, Answer, Support, and Explain, provides a structured approach to writing that helps students articulate their thoughts clearly and back them up with textual evidence. Using this method, students improve their analytical skills and gain confidence in constructing well-reasoned arguments.

1. C: COMPLETE
Is the evidence complete? Did you support each claim with multiple examples from different parts of the text?

2. A: ACCURATE
Is your evidence accurate—used in a way that reflects its meaning in the text? Did you choose the best evidence to support each claim?

3. S: SPECIFIC
Is your evidence specific to particular incidents or information and detailed to make a point?

4. E: EXPLAINED
Engage parents in the process. Open communication between home and school can address issues before they become severe.

5. ADDITIONAL TEXTS
- **CONNECT TO MAIN IDEAS:** Ensure each piece of evidence ties back to the main idea or argument. This strengthens your analysis.
- **USE A VARIETY OF SOURCES:** Draw evidence from a variety of sources within the text. This shows comprehensive understanding.
- **REVISE AND REFINE:** Always revise your evidence and explanations. Refining your work can uncover stronger connections and clearer arguments.

POST-READING JOURNAL ALTERNATIVES

"Post-reading activities play a crucial role in reading lessons as they help students summarize and retell the main ideas or key events from the reading, which reinforces comprehension and encourages students to identify the most important information" (Reading and Writing Haven, 2020). Activities like creative story mapping or debating engage students in synthesizing information while making connections to broader themes or personal experiences.

1. CREATE YOUR OWN EXAM
Develop five higher-level questions related to the text. Also, provide an answer key.

2. PLAY "CNN SCHOLAR"
You're the guest scholar on CNN. The first question is, "Why do you like/dislike this text?" The second question: "What was the author's purpose in writing it?" The third question: "Was the text convincing? Why or why not?"

3. APPLY IT!
Identify important information from the assigned text. Take one idea and use it to give insight into or solve a real-life problem.

4. DIORAMA
Create a diorama that depicts a key scene from the text.

5. CHARACTER DIARY
Write a diary entry from the perspective of a character in the text.

6. TEXT CONNECTIONS
Connect the text to other books, movies, or personal experiences.

7. CREATIVE WRITING
Write an alternate ending to the text or a sequel.

BOOK REPORT ALTERNATIVES

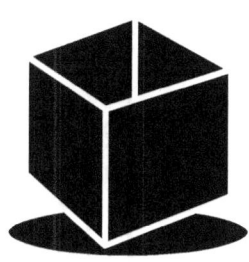

"Book reports tend to focus on summary rather than analysis, which limits students' opportunities to engage critically with the text and develop higher-order thinking skills" (Purdue OWL, 2023). Replacing traditional book reports with projects like thematic essays or multimedia presentations allows students to explore deeper interpretations and make meaningful connections to real-world contexts.

1. MAPS
To illustrate settings and key events, students can create maps using Scribblemaps.com or Animaps.com.

2. CHARACTER PLAYLISTS
With Grooveshark learners create a character playlist with explanations for their song choices.

3. QUIZZES
Kids use Socrative or Quizlet to create a quiz (with answers) on the book.

4. TIMELINES
Tell the story by sequencing significant events using TimeToast.com.

5. BILLBOARDS
Have kids create a billboard ad with Bighugelabs.com.

6. BOOK JACKETS
Design an original book cover, with a new title and blurb using Canva's Book Cover Maker: http://bit.ly/TB_Book.

7. TEN Qs
The class asks the reader Qs to assess if the book was comprehended. If answerer is successful, he or she can skip writing a book report (Purdue OWL, 2023).

VOCABULARY INSTRUCTION

"[V]ocabulary instruction should not only focus on dictionary definitions but also present words in various contexts, providing multiple exposures . . ." (Beck, McKeown, & Kucan, 2013). Integrating activities like word mapping, context-based games, and collaborative discussions can make vocabulary learning engaging and memorable.

1. VENN IT
Ask students to identify similarities and differences between words.

2. PARAPHRASE
Direct kids to define words in their own everyday vernacular.

3. DON'T INTRODUCE TOO MANY WORDS
Teachers should not overwhelm high school students with too many vocabulary test words a week. The optimal # is 5–10 words (Stahl, 1988).

4. HEIGHTEN KIDS WRITTEN VOCAB
Teach kids to use PowerThesaurus.org when writing.

5. ENCOURAGE INDEPENDENT READING
The only chance kids with poor vocab have of catching up is "extraordinary amounts of independent reading (Baker, Simmons, & Kameenui, 1998).

6. USE ROBERT MARZANO'S APPROACH
1. Teacher gives a description. 2. Kids paraphrase. 3. Students draw. 4. Kids expand word knowledge with notes and a graphic organizer. 5. Kids discuss vocab words with each other. 6. Vocab games.

7. CHOOSE APPROPRIATE WORDS
- 358 Words HS Students Should know for standardized tests (Vocab.com).
- 300 Most Difficult SAT Words (Vocab.com).
- 100 Words Every HS Grad Should Know (Quizlet).

8. PLAY VOCAB GAMES
Games like Jeopardy, Word Bingo, Skits, and Pyramid affect recall.

HOW STUDENTS CONCEAL READING STRUGGLES

"Many students with reading difficulties conceal their struggles" (Oxford Learning, 2019). A stigma-free classroom environment, where mistakes are viewed as opportunities for growth, can encourage these students to seek assistance and build their confidence as learners.

1. LISTENING SKILLS
Some readers that struggle become exceptional listeners, grasping concepts and details from lectures and class discussions.

2. MEMORIZING TEXTS
Younger children memorize shorter texts so they can "read" them when called upon.

3. VAGUE ANSWERS
When asked about a reading assignment, some kids provide generic or vague answers, relying on the teacher or classmate to fill in details.

4. EXCUSES
Watching the movie adaptation, a YouTube summary, or asking ChatGPT to outline the book can allow kids to participate in discussions.

5. OVERCOMPENSATING
Excelling in math or art diverts attention from their reading issues.

6. ASKING FOR HELP
They ask friends and family to explain assignments, framing it as not under-standing rather than being unable to read them.

7. CHEATING
Learners guess what sentences mean based on pictures.

WHERE TO FIND FREE READINGS

"Providing free readings can support student engagement and motivation by allowing teachers to select texts that are relevant and interesting . . ." (Harvard University Academic Resource Center, 2023). This approach also promotes equity, ensuring that all students have access to meaningful materials regardless of their economic background.

1. AUDIO
- Open Culture's Free Audiobooks: 900 free mp3 popular audiobooks.
- Lit2Go: Mp3 stories and poems, some with related reading strategies.
- LibriVox: Powered by volunteers, the site releases audio files of books in the public domain.

2. BOOKS
- The Reading Resource Project: Free 100-book sets for Pre-K through second grade (but you pay for shipping).
- First Book: Provides free books, but you pay for the shipping.

3. MULTIMEDIA
Listen and Read: Scholastic's site for early learners features 15 nonfiction read-along books that include images and sounds.

4. SPECIAL MENTION
Project Gutenberg: E-Books to read online or display on any device.

5. LOCAL LIBRARIES
Many local libraries offer free access to a wide range of eBooks and audio-books. Check their online resources.

6. AUTHOR WEBSITES
Many authors offer free excerpts or full texts of their works on their personal websites or blogs.

POEM ANALYSIS ACTIVITIES

"The layered nature of poetry, where each word and line can hold multiple meanings, makes it challenging for students to pin down a single interpretation" (Texas A&M University Writing Center, 2023). This complexity encourages learners to uncover its nuanced meanings.

1. CONFUSION TO SIGNIFICANCE

Based on Burke (2013), students first circle confusing lines, then mark personal connections, and finally flag the most important idea.

2. ANNOTATE IT

1. Read the poem twice without doing anything.
2. Retell the poem in writing.
3. Ask questions.
4. Think about the larger significance.
5. Find words or phrases that you find interesting.
6. Identify literary devices or the rhyme scheme and analyze how they're used (Rickert, n.d.).

3. PERSONAL AND SOCIAL APPROACH

1. Read the poem quickly and write down first impressions.
2. Re-read to confirm and develop impressions.
3. Share impressions in small groups.
4. Consider important details; negotiate a consensus interpretation.
5. Collaboratively describe evolving interpretation of the poem in writing (Edlund, 2018).

4. REPEATED READINGS

1. Read the poem aloud to students.
2. Students read again, and copy the line that is most luminous, then write for five minutes about why they chose this line, about what it makes them think or feel. They can also write questions.
3. In small groups, one kid reads the poem aloud.
4. Go around the group sharing chosen lines and reasons for choosing them.
5. Collect questions that continue to puzzle students.
6. The whole class discusses compelling ideas and asks questions. How do they view the poem now? (Adapted from Jago, 2018).

TECHNIQUES FOR HELPING KIDS SUMMARIZE

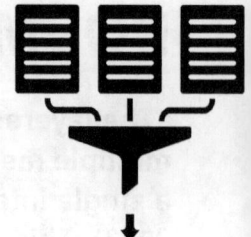

Summarizing "is a critical literacy skill that helps students understand and remember what they read, which is essential for learning across all subject areas" (Vanderbilt University Writing Studio, n.d.). By distilling key ideas, students reinforce their comprehension and learn to communicate information concisely and effectively.

1. SUMMARY BALL
Toss a ball to a student. Ask them to state a general idea about a learned topic. Then they toss the ball to another student to add more information. Repeat until the important parts of the topic are covered.

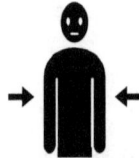

2. SLENDERIZE IT
Have students summarize a text in 35–40 words. Then have them summarize in 15–20 words. Then 10 words.

3. USE NUMBERS AND STATISTICS
Titles with numbers, like "7 Ways to Improve Your Writing," attract attention and promise clear takeaways.

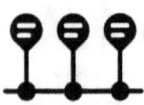

4. TIMELINES (FOR NARRATIVES)
Identify the eight important moments in a chapter. Circle the four most significant. Write a one-sentence summary.

5. ONE-SENTENCE SUMMARY
Challenge students to condense the entire lesson or reading into one comprehensive sentence. This encourages critical thinking and conciseness.

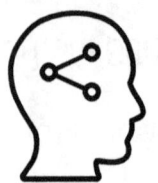

6. THINK-PAIR-SHARE
Students think about their summaries individually, pair up to discuss with a partner, and then share with the class. This collaborative approach can enhance understanding.

WRITING TIPS

"Writing instruction is crucial because it not only improves writing skills but also enhances reading comprehension and learning in subjects like science and social studies. Embedding writing tasks in content areas has been shown to boost students' overall academic achievement" (Graham & Perin, 2007). Integrating writing across the curriculum can foster deeper understanding and retention of subject-specific content.

1. CURB NEGATIVE SELF-TALK
Notice, dispute, and supplant disruptive self-talk.

2. ENGAGE IN BRIEF, DAILY WRITING
Keep your sessions short with "ongoing awareness of what you will write the next session" (Boice, 2000).

3. PRIORITIZE PRE-WRITING
Spend as much "time and energy on pre-writing as on prose" (Boice, 2000).

4. KEEP EMOTIONS IN CHECK
Don't succumb to anxious binge-writing too close to the deadline.

5. LET GO OF EGO
Write playfully and creatively, without trying to make every sentence glorious.

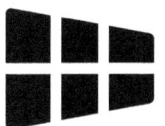
6. KEEP PERSPECTIVE
Notice whether your writing is on the correct track—solving the intended problem.

7. PROCESS OVER PRODUCT
Ask a struggling student to consult with a peer.

8. NOTICE WHEN IT'S NOT WORKING
Stop when you're fatigued or when the writing results in diminished returns.

WRITING TO LEARN STRATEGIES

"Through writing exercises, students engage in metacognition, thinking about their thinking, which helps them to identify gaps in their understanding and develop strategies for improvement" (Kramar, 2019). This process empowers them to take ownership of their learning journey across disciplines.

1. BEAT THE CLOCK
Brainstorm a list of five solutions in five minutes.

2. SPEAKER NOTES
Provide content images in PowerPoint or in Google Slides and have students fill out the speaker notes section to demonstrate understanding.

3. ROLE-STORMING
Write about the subject or question from the point of view of (pick 1): Buddha, a different gender, a conservative, a character in literature, etc. (McLeod, 2015).

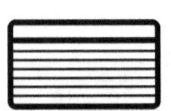

4. CRAM!
Ask students to create online flashcard questions and answers using Cram.com or Quizlet.com.

5. WHAT'S NEXT?
Direct students to predict what will happen. "What will the main character experience next?" "What will happen to the Middle East in 10 years?"

6. PASSING NOTES IN CLASS
Students write notes on scratch paper about what confuses them most about a subject. Next, they pass the notes to peers who answer the questions (adapted from East Carolina University Writing Across the Curriculum, n.d).

7. SIXTY-SECOND PAPER
In 60 seconds, learners identify the highlights of a discussion and end the "paper" with a question.

LOW-STAKES WRITING

"**Low-stakes writing assignments constitute one of the best methods you can use to solicit engagement and thinking in class. They allow students to explore course concepts without the pressure of grades, which fosters a deeper understanding and encourages participation**" (Lang, 2020). This process enables learners to articulate complex ideas that might otherwise remain unspoken.

1. STRUCTURED NOTE-TAKING
Make a T-chart. The main ideas are to the left of the line and the details are on the right. The bottom has a summary of the lecture (Fisher & Frey, 2004).

2. SENTENCE SYNTHESIS
Use three to four keywords the teacher selects to summarize the main ideas. Then share, discuss, and synthesize big concepts.

3. SKIM-SCAN-WRITE
Pairs examine text titles, headings, subheadings, captions, bold words, and visuals to create two lists: Impressions and Questions, and Quick Facts (Michigan Department of Education, 2008).

4. PROGRESSIVE CINQUAIN
Line 1: One noun that is the topic. Line 2: Two-word topic description. Line 3: Three words show the action of the topic. Line 4: Four words describe the topic and show feeling. Line 5: One synonym that restates the essence of the topic. Then pairs create a collaborative cinquain using pieces of their poems. Next form quads and repeat (Andrews, n.d.).

5. EXIT TWEET
Write a 140-word summary of a topic.

6. FREE WRITES
Allow students time to write without restrictions on a topic of their choice to encourage creativity.

REVISING AND EDITING CHECKLISTS

"Using a revising and editing checklist ensures that writers address both macro-level issues like structure and coherence, as well as micro-level concerns" (Purdue OWL, 2019). This process empowers students to develop autonomy and confidence.

1. D.A.R.E. TO REVISE
Delete Add Rearrange Exchange.

2. A.R.M.S.
- Add sentences and words.
- Remove unneeded words/sentences.
- Move sentence or word placement.
- Substitute words or sentences (Goodrich, 2016).

3. R.O.A.D. REVISING
- Replace generalities with specifics, and unclear words with clear words.
- Organize the text. Move sections, paragraphs, sentences, or words around.
- Add words or sentences for clarity and completeness. Add in content that may be necessary to strengthen the section.
- Delete unneeded words and sentences; eliminate redundancies. Remove content that doesn't fit or directly address requirements (Kayes, 2019).

4. C.H.I.M.P.S.
My work has been checked for . . .

- Capitalization
- Handwriting
- Indents
- Makes sense?
- Punctuation
- Spelling

5. C.O.P.S

- Capitalization
- Order and Organization
- Punctuation
- Spelling (The Eager Teacher, n.d.)

LISTENING ACTIVITIES

"Listening skills are closely tied to classroom engagement. When students actively listen, they are more likely to participate and engage in the learning process" (Selby, 2023). Additionally, active listening fosters a collaborative classroom culture where students feel valued and understood, ultimately enhancing their ability to build meaningful connections with peers and content.

1. PARTNER PARAPHRASE
Student A reads or tells a short story while Student B paraphrases. Then switch. (Paris, 2014)

2. LISTEN FOR WORDS
Post several words and let kids guess the topic.

3. ATTEND TO THE "INNER PERSON"
Practice listening when the speaker talks about . . .
- safety and belonging = needs.
- assertions of truth = beliefs.
- "must" and "should" = values.
- what will be achieved = goals (Straker, n.d.).

4. TURN AND TALK
Say, "I'm going to describe the process of _____. I will pause along the way and ask you to turn to a partner and explain to them what you heard" (Alber, 2013).

5. TEACH REFLECTIVE LISTENING
When listening to group members, have students jot down details, summarize points, express interest, avoid interrupting, and empathize with the feelings of the speaker, not just the facts (Stein & Hurd, 2000).

6. TELL A GROUP STORY
Each child tells one sentence of an original story. In a debrief, continuity errors are identified (Paris, 2014).

PUBLIC SPEAKING FORMATS

"By teaching students to manage their fear of public speaking and to present their ideas confidently, we prepare them for a wide range of situations, from job interviews to academic conferences. This preparation builds their self-esteem and competence" (UMN, 2020). These skills empower students to become persuasive communicators who can advocate for themselves and their ideas in personal, professional, and civic arenas.

1. STUMP SPEECH
"Together, we can . . ." Passionate prepared remarks by a student seeking to represent fellow learners.

2. INTRODUCTION
"I'm Jane Doe and I'm going to study veterinary medicine someday, so no pets ever suffer again." Introduce yourself, your goals, and why they're important.

3. PERSUASIVE SPEECH
"Let us unite in banishing fear." Motivate an audience to feel something, take action, or adopt a perspective.

4. STUART JR.'S POP-UP DEBATE
Kids "pop up" at their desks and talk. First one to speak has the floor. When multiple kids pop up, teach them to politely yield the floor. See the format here: https://davestuartjr.com/pop-up-debate.

5. POSTER PRESENTATION
"My study was designed to find out . . ." Discuss the unique features of your study, your goals, how you investigated the project, what you found out, and why it matters.

6. IGNITE TALKS
Twenty slides automatically advance every 15 seconds. See the format here: http://www.ignitetalks.io/.

Workbook: Reflecting on Chapter 8 Topics

1. In what ways can you incorporate "think-aloud" strategies to model metacognition for your students?
2. What are some effective methods for frontloading difficult vocabulary to aid in text comprehension?
3. How can teaching genre conventions help students make predictions about texts?
4. What types of visuals can you use to provide context before students begin reading a new text?
5. What are some pre-reading activities you can implement to enhance comprehension?
6. What annotation techniques can you teach your students to help them engage with and analyze texts?
7. How can graphic organizers like Venn diagrams and story maps aid in students' understanding of key ideas?
8. What are the benefits of using literature circles to promote cooperative learning and in-depth discussions of texts?
9. How can fishbowl discussions encourage student observation and participation?
10. How does the C.A.S.E. strategy (Claim, Answer, Support, Explain) help students structure their writing with textual evidence?
11. What are some post-reading activities you can use to reinforce comprehension and encourage creativity?

Going Deeper—Advanced Questions

1. What are some advanced annotation techniques that can help students delve deeper into complex texts and improve critical thinking skills?
2. How can cooperative learning strategies like literature circles and Socratic Seminars be modified to support students with different abilities?

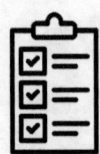

Checklist of Activities and Strategies to Try (Pick 2)

❑ Use "think-aloud" strategies to model metacognitive processes during reading.
❑ Frontload difficult vocabulary before reading complex texts.
❑ Teach genre conventions and have students make predictions about the text.
❑ Incorporate visuals such as photos, videos, or graphic organizers before reading.
❑ Conduct pre-reading activities like discussing themes and building background knowledge.
❑ Use guided reading questions to focus on key concepts during reading.
❑ Teach students to annotate texts by highlighting key points and making notes.
❑ Use graphic organizers like Venn diagrams, story maps, and concept maps.
❑ Organize literature circles for cooperative learning and in-depth text discussions.
❑ Use the C.A.S.E. strategy to help students structure their writing with textual evidence.
❑ Engage students in post-reading activities like journal writing, creative projects, and dioramas.
❑ Provide book report alternatives such as creating timelines or character playlists to engage students in different ways.
❑ Other: _____

Describe Your Progress

1. What activities were most successful?

2. What challenges did you face?

3. How can you improve for next time?

 **References for Chapter 8**

Alber, R. (2013, August 30). Say what? 5 ways to get students to listen. Edutopia. https://www.edutopia.org/blog/five-listening-strategies-rebecca-alber

Andrews, S. (n.d.). Collaborative cinquain: Pair-to-quad remix activity [Unpublished classroom handout].

Baker, S. K., Simmons, D. C., & Kameenui, E. J. (1998). Vocabulary acquisition: Research bases. In D. C. Simmons & E. J. Kameenui (Eds.), *What reading research tells us about children with diverse learning needs: Bases and basics* (pp. 183–218). Lawrence Erlbaum Associates.

Beck, I. L., McKeown, M. G., & Kucan, L. (2013). *Bringing words to life: Robust vocabulary instruction* (2nd ed.). Guilford Press.

Boice, R. (2000). *Advice for new faculty members: Nihil Nimus.* Allyn & Bacon

Burke, B. (2013). A close look at close reading: Scaffolding students with complex texts. Wisconsin Department of Public Instruction. https://nieonline.com/tbtimes/downloads/CCSS_reading.pdf

Duke, N. K., & Pearson, P. D. (2002). Effective practices for developing reading comprehension. In A. E. Farstrup & S. J. Samuels (Eds.), *What research has to say about reading instruction* (3rd ed., pp. 205–42). International Reading Association.

East Carolina University Writing Across the Curriculum. (n.d.). Writing-to-learn activities handout [Faculty resource document]. East Carolina University. https://writing.ecu.edu/wp-content/pv-uploads/sites/175/writing_to_learn_w-activities-1-1.docx

Edlund, J. R. (2018, June 29). A reader-response approach to poetry. Teaching Text Rhetorically. https://textrhet.com/2018/06/29/a-reader-response-approach-to-poetry/

Fisher, D., & Frey, N. (2004). *Improving adolescent literacy: Strategies at work*. Pearson Education.

Fisher, D., Frey, N., & Lapp, D. (2008). *In a reading state of mind: Brain research, teacher modeling, and comprehension instruction*. International Reading Association.

Goodrich, T. (2016, April 9). Revising vs. editing: ARMS and CUPS anchor chart [Image]. Pinterest. https://www.pinterest.com/pin/518125132112008904/

Graham, S., & Perin, D. (2007). *Writing next: Effective strategies to improve writing of adolescents in middle and high schools*. Carnegie Corporation of New York.

Graham, S., MacArthur, C. A., & Fitzgerald, J. (Eds.). (2013). *Best practices in writing instruction* (2nd ed.). Guilford Press.

Harvard University Academic Resource Center. (2023). Selecting engaging texts for students [Unpublished internal handout].

Jago, C. (2018, August 3). Agents of imagination: Science fiction poems in the classroom. Poetry Foundation. https://www.poetryfoundation.org/articles/147279/agents-of-imagination

Kayes, A. (2019, July 7). Revising and editing: A fun little mnemonic device to remember the difference. Proposal Reflections. https://www.proposalreflections.com/2019/07/revising-and-editing-fun-little.html

Kramar, J. (2019). Promoting student metacognition to aid the writing process [Master's capstone project, Hamline University]. https://digitalcommons.hamline.edu/cgi/viewcontent.cgi?article=1392&context=hse_cp

Lang, J. M. (2020). *Small teaching: Everyday lessons from the science of learning* (2nd ed.). Jossey-Bass.

Marzano, R. J. (2010). *Teaching basic and advanced vocabulary: A framework for direct instruction*. Association for Supervision and Curriculum Development.

McLeod, B. (2015, August 24). Become a strategic thinker with creative thinking games. Pryor Learning Solutions. https://www.pryor.com/us/blog-categories/professional-development/creative-thinking-games.html

Michigan Department of Education. (2008, May 2). Skim-Scan-Write: A reading strategy [PDF]. Michigan.gov. https://www.michigan.gov/-/media/Project/Websites/mde/Year/2008/05/02/SSWAC.pdf?rev=95d9ae8612de46e694f875c2264fc152

Oxford Learning. (2019). Why students struggle with reading. Oxford Learning. https://www.oxford-learning.com/why-students-struggle-with-reading/

Paris, C. (2014, March 11). 6 listening skills exercises to promote stronger communication. Udemy Blog. https://blog.udemy.com/listening-skills-exercises/

Purdue University Online Writing Lab. (2019). Graduate faculty guide [PDF]. Purdue OWL. https://owl.purdue.edu/writinglab/faculty/documents/20191101GradFacultyGuide.pdf

Purdue Online Writing Lab. (2023). Book reviews. https://owl.purdue.edu/owl/general_writing/common_writing_assignments/book_reviews.html

Reading and Writing Haven. (2020, December 8). Engaging post-reading activities. Reading and Writing Haven. https://web.archive.org/web/20201208120000/https://www.readingandwritinghaven.com/engaging-post-reading-activities/

Reiser, B. J., & Tabak, I. (2014). Scaffolding. In R. K. Sawyer (Ed.), *The Cambridge handbook of the learning sciences* (2nd ed., pp. 44–62). Cambridge University Press.

Rickert, D. (n.d.). Don't hate! Annotate! How to REALLY annotate a poem https://davidrickert.com/dont-hate-annotate-how-to-really-annotate-a-poem/

Selby. (2023, August 21). The importance of listening skills in school: Enhancing academic success. Everyday Speech. https://everydayspeech.com/sel-implementation/the-importance-of-listening-skills-in-school-enhancing-academic-success

Shanahan, T., & Shanahan, C. (2008). Teaching disciplinary literacy to adolescents: Rethinking content-area literacy. *Harvard Educational Review*, 78(1), 40–59.

Stahl, S. A. (1988). Five components of effective reading instruction. *Reading Teacher*, 41(8), 690–5.

Straker, D. (n.d.). Listen to the inner person. Changing Minds. https://changingminds.org/techniques/listening/listen_person.htm

Stein, R. F., & Hurd, S. N. (2000). *Using student teams in the classroom: A faculty guide*. Anker Publishing.

Texas A & M University Writing Center. (2023). Understanding poetry: Multiple meanings [Unpublished internal handout].

The Eager Teacher. (n.d.). Call the COPS: Capitalization, Organization, Punctuation, Spelling [Writing resource] [Teaching resource]. Teachers Pay Teachers. https://www.teacherspayteachers.com/Product/Call-the-COPS-Capitalization-Organization-Punctuation-Spelling-Writing-236600

Tomlinson, C. A. (2014). *The differentiated classroom: Responding to the needs of all learners* (2nd ed.). ASCD.

University of Minnesota Libraries Publishing. (2020). Stand up, speak out: The practice and ethics of public speaking (Rev. ed.). https://open.lib.umn.edu/publicspeaking/

Vanderbilt University Writing Studio. (n.d.). Effective quotes, paraphrases, and summaries [PDF handout]. Archived from https://www.vanderbilt.edu/writing/resources/handouts/effective-quotes-paraphrases-and-summaries/.

Walqui, A., & van Lier, L. (2010). *Scaffolding the academic success of adolescent English language learners: A pedagogy of promise*. WestEd.

Zwiers, J., & Crawford, M. (2011). *Academic conversations: Classroom talk that fosters critical thinking and content understandings*. Stenhouse Publishers.

Chapter 9

Supporting Diverse Learners (and Colleagues)

Supporting Diverse Learners (and Diverse Colleagues)

Renata, a junior who barely spoke English, acted like an outsider. To reach her, I started including more stories and poems from Mexico in lessons and her personality blossomed. *There you are*, I remember thinking.

If you've taught for any length of time, you've no doubt noticed a remarkable array of unique characteristics among our students and colleagues, ranging from race, ethnicity, and gender to socioeconomic status, language, religion, and learning abilities. Recognizing these differences is crucial because they shape everyone's experiences, perspectives, and learning needs.

We're all driven by emotions. Therefore, supporting diverse learners means fostering an environment where they feel emotionally and socially secure. According to Geneva Gay, "Culturally responsive teaching uses the cultural knowledge, prior experiences, frames of reference, and performance styles of ethnically diverse students to make learning encounters more relevant to and effective for them" (Gay, 2000). This involves creating an inclusive environment where every student feels seen, heard, and valued. It requires understanding that students' backgrounds influence their learning and interaction with the world.

Teachers must also demonstrate respect for their colleagues by appreciating and welcoming the diverse skills and perspectives they bring to the educational environment. This practice promotes a culture of mutual respect and collaboration, which is essential for creating a dynamic faculty and a more equitable society. As Maya Angelou powerfully stated, "In diversity, there is beauty and there is strength." Embracing this diversity isn't just beneficial, it's transformative.

Key Chapter 9 Strategies

1. Create ground rules for respectful class discussions and consistently reinforce them.
2. Identify the specific needs of each student, including those with disabilities or learning differences, students from low-income households, English language learners, students in foster care, those with caregiving responsibilities, and students from other vulnerable or underserved communities.
3. Focus class resources and time on students' cultures and employ multicultural materials.
4. Follow Universal Design for Learning (UDL) guidelines which include multiple means of engagement, representation, and action and expression.
5. Make sure students feel appreciated by allowing them to use of their home language to process information.
6. Monitor student progress using observations, formative assessments, and check-ins to make curriculum adjustments.
7. Cue important information by saying, "This is critical to remember," and then assessing comprehension.
8. Avoid shaming students by using other methods to return them to task instead of embarrassing them for not listening.
9. Implement strategies to support students with executive function challenges by creating an environment that reduces cognitive load and promotes self-regulation.
10. Redirect attribution to the original source if someone is praised for an idea that came from another person.
11. Address microaggressions by understanding and mitigating the impact of everyday verbal, nonverbal, and environmental slights that communicate hostile or negative messages to marginalized groups.
12. Begin chats with social-emotional learning activities to help students transition into academic work.

Memory Device for this Chapter
Acronym Mnemonic

Inclusion

Identify the needs of all students

Nurture diverse cultures

Create respectful discussions

Leverage UDL guidelines

Utilize formative assessments

Scaffold learning materials

Integrate multicultural resources

Organize workspace

No more one-size fits all

INCLUSION

"Inclusion is about the presence, participation, and achievement of all students, particularly those who are vulnerable to exclusionary pressures" (Ainscow, 2014). It also challenges educators to create learning environments that celebrate diversity, dismantle systemic barriers, and promote equity, ensuring every student feels valued and capable of thriving.

1. DISCUSSIONS
Create ground rules for respectful class discussions and consistently reinforce them.

2. IDENTIFY NEEDS
Knowledge of the specific needs of each student in the class is critical. "[I]t's not enough just to know which of your children have Special Educational Needs and Disabilities (SEND). You should know which, if any, of your children are on Free School Meals (FSM), which are caregivers, which are in foster care, which have English as an Additional Language (EAL) and which children are from the particularly vulnerable Roma or traveler communities" (IanBee Team, 2023).

3. YOU'RE APPRECIATED!
Work to make sure kids know they can bring their unassimilated selves to class; encourage students to use their home language to process information.

4. MONITOR PROGRESS
Use observations, formative assessment, and check-ins to make curriculum adjustments.

5. TARGET CULTURE
Focus class resources and time on students' cultures and employ multicultural materials (New America, n.d.).

6. FOLLOW UDL GUIDELINES
Universal Design for Learning forwards three principles: multiple means of engagement, multiple means of representation, and multiple means of action and expression. More information on UDL here: https://udlguidelines.cast.org/.

SUPPORTING STUDENTS WITH EXECUTIVE FUNCTION

"Supporting students with [EF] challenges requires teaching specific skills and strategies [and] an environment that reduces cognitive load and promotes self-regulation" (Dawson & Guare, 2009). Educators can empower these students to navigate complex tasks with greater independence and confidence.

1. ORGANIZED WORK AREA
Show students a photo of how the space should look when they're done working.

2. CUE IMPORTANT INFORMATION
Say, "This is critical to remember." Next, assess comprehension.

3. DON'T SHAME
"There is no need to embarrass a child by asking them for an answer when it is obvious that they are not listening, so use other methods to return them to task. Do not continually use their name to draw attention to them: 'Rebecca, look at me, please. Now!'" (Drexler, 2013).

4. TASK TREE
"A task tree is a visual strategy that will give the student step-by-step instructions on what needs to be done at the beginning of each class. Steps are shown from left to right or top to bottom and include a picture and an arrow that connects the pictures (and steps)" (Hans, n.d.).

5. CORKBOARD CHUNKING
Have students post a corkboard in their study space. One side can have pinned notecards with 15-minute tasks and the other can have tasks that take longer.

6. POST THE ACTIVITY SCHEDULE
Place this info in a spot that is visible to all learners (DiTullio, 2019).

7. PROJECT CHECKLISTS
Check out this resource: http://pblchecklist.4teachers.org/checklist.shtml (4Teachers.org, n.d.).

GENDER EQUITY STRATEGIES FOR FACULTY

"Gender equity involves understanding and addressing the power dynamics that create disparities between men and women, necessitating institutional and cultural changes to foster true equality" (Scott, 1986). Achieving this requires a commitment to dismantling biases that perpetuate inequality across all facets of society.

1. STRATEGIES

a. "Take on the emotional labor of tracking, planning, and organizing family needs, activities, and special occasions" (Smith & Johnson, 2020).
b. "Make sure you give the floor back to the speaker after asking the question" (Özler, 2020).
c. Have interviewing teams take The Harvard Implicit Bias Test.
d. If someone is praised for an idea that originally came from a woman, redirect attribution to the source.
e. Volunteer to take minutes during meetings (York University, Information and Privacy Office, n.d.).
f. "Build a supportive network of men allies who are committed to gender equity" (York University, Information and Privacy Office, n.d.).
g. Nominate women for awards and leadership positions.
h. Actively listen to women when challenged by them.
i. Learn more about avoiding gender bias in reference writing here: Avoid Gender Bias in Reference Writing (University of Arizona, n.d.).
j. Institutions must develop appropriate goals and metrics, share them with stakeholders, compare them to similar organizations, and embrace accountability for outcomes (Hirsh & Tomaskovic-Devey, 2018).
k. Learn about "The Confronting Prejudiced Responses (CPR) Model" (Ashburn-Nardo, Morris, & Goodwin, 2008).

2. GOOD NEWS ABOUT GENDER EQUITY

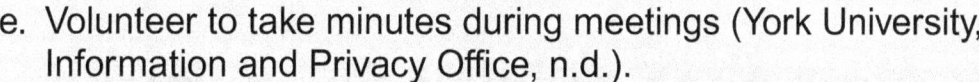

a. Beliefs can change. In 1937, 33% of Americans said they would vote for their party's nominee if she were a woman. In 2015, 92% said they would (Gallup, 2020).
b. "Gender equality helps prevent violence against women and girls and makes our communities safer and healthier" (VIC.GOV.AU).
c. "Were more women to be able to fully participate in paid work, and earn equal pay, that could add $28 trillion" to the global GDP (McKinsey Global Institute, 2015).

POVERTY DEFICIT MYTHS

"Educators must reject deficit thinking and instead adopt an equity literacy framework that emphasizes the strengths and potential of students experiencing poverty while addressing the root causes of inequity" (Gorski, 2018).

Based on multiple studies collected by Professor Paul Gorski (2008)

1. MYTH: THERE IS A "CULTURE OF POVERTY"
Poor people have wildly different clusters of behaviors and values.

2. MYTH: POOR PEOPLE ARE LAZY
Poor adults work more hours (often with one or more low-paying jobs) than rich people and possess similar levels of motivation.

3. MYTH: POOR PARENTS DON'T ATTEND SCHOOLS BECAUSE THEY DON'T VALUE EDUCATION
Low/high-income parents possess equivalent attitudes about education. But poor parents have less access to school events because of multiple jobs, no paid leave, and not enough money to pay for childcare and transportation issues.

4. MYTH: PEOPLE WHO ARE POOR WITH NON-STANDARD GRAMMAR ARE IGNORANT
All languages are equally complex, say linguists.

5. MYTH: POOR PEOPLE ABUSE DRUGS MORE THAN WEALTHY PEOPLE.
Drug use is equally distributed across all sectors of society. Abuse of alcohol, specifically, is more prevalent among wealthy people.

MICRO-AGGRESSIONS

"Microaggressions are the everyday verbal, nonverbal, and environmental slights, snubs, or insults, whether intentional or unintentional, that communicate hostile, derogatory, or negative messages to target persons based solely upon their marginalized group membership" (Sue, 2007). Recognizing and addressing these behaviors is critical for fostering inclusive environments where all individuals feel respected and valued.

1. GENDER

Whistling as a woman walks by. Message: You are a sex object. That is, women's appearance is for the enjoyment of men (Sue, 2007).

2. MICROASSAULT

"Explicit racial derogations" meant to hurt, such as calling somebody "colored" or "Oriental" (Sue et al., 2007).

3. MICRO-INVALIDATION

Negating the thoughts, feelings, or experiences of a person of color. Example: "Don't be so sensitive" (Sue et al., 2007).

4. IMITATING ACCENTS

Mimicking foreign accents reinforces stereotypes and often mocks groups for struggling with English.

5. ASCRIPTION OF INTELLIGENCE

Assigning smarts based on race or gender. "How'd you get into that school" (Aronson et al., 2002).

6. AVOID SAYING . . .

A) "Where are you from?" Message: You're not American. B) "You're so articulate." Message: Your group isn't usually as intelligent as Whites. C) "I'm not racist; I have several Black friends." Message: I'm immune to racism because I have friends of color. D) Saying to an Asian person: "Speak up more. You're so quiet." Message: Assimilate to the dominant culture. E) "You people . . ." Message: You don't belong. You are lesser (Wing et. al., 2007).

I FINISHED EARLY—NOW WHAT?

"Providing additional activities for early finishers can help maintain a high level of challenge and prevent disengagement, which is crucial for fostering a positive learning environment" (Hattie, 2009). We want to ensure that all students remain intellectually stimulated and invested in their progress.

1. BRAIN TEASERS
See Puzzle Prime or Sharp Brains for logic puzzles and visual workouts.

2. LOVE LETTERS
Provide envelopes and stationery so students can write a note of appreciation to someone they care about: parents, friends, authors, etc.

3. PRACTICE SAT WORDS
Students can download the Daily Practice for the New SAT App.

4. READ A CHOICE NOVEL
Only one-third of students read a book after high school. Let's change that.

5. ACADEMIC COMPUTER GAMES
Free learning games include Arcademics Games, Sheppard Software, Starfall, and PBS Parents Games.

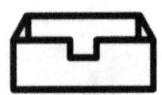
6. DESK ORGANIZATION
Marie Kondo time!

7. HOMEWORK
Do they have any unfinished homework? Is there a test they can study for?

8. INQUIRY PROJECTS
Students can spend time processing ongoing research projects.

HELPING INTROVERTS PARTICIPATE IN DISCUSSIONS

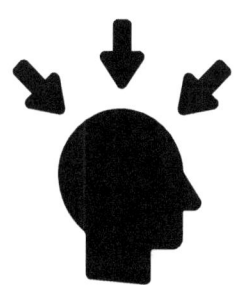

"Introverted students often feel overlooked in classroom discussions, but when teachers implement strategies that allow for thoughtful reflection and smaller group interactions, these students can thrive and contribute meaningfully" (Cain, 2012). By creating spaces for written responses, peer partnerships, and asynchronous contributions, educators can unlock the potential of introverted students.

1. PROVIDE DELIBERATION TIME
Give students a chance to write down ideas before they have to talk.

2. BEGIN CHAT WITH SEL ACTIVITY
Have students do a quick social-emotional learning exercise before the academic work starts: "Name your most often selected item of clothing. Why is it your go-to garment?"

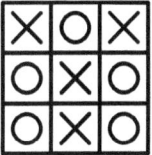

3. USE TURN-TAKING STRATEGIES
Direct learners to use concrete turn-taking strategies. Tell students you are looking for examples of generous participants inviting others into the conversation.

4. IF YOU WERE IN THE WRONG . . .
Take responsibility. State what you'll do differently. Ask, "How else can I make this right?"

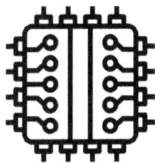

5. USE TECHNOLOGY
Incorporate tools like discussion boards or chat features in online platforms where students can contribute their thoughts without whole class speaking.

6. PAIR-SHARE
Allow students to discuss their thoughts with a partner before sharing them with the larger group. This can help build confidence and encourage participation.

INDICATORS OF BULIMIA

"Teachers should be equipped with knowledge and resources to support students with bulimia, as their daily interactions can provide the stability and encouragement these students need to pursue treatment" (Smolak, 2006). Through empathy and awareness, educators can become critical allies in breaking the cycle of shame that often accompanies eating disorders.

1. PHYSICAL INDICATORS

- "Red pinprick marks on their faces as a result of burst blood vessels" (Bulimia.com, 2022).
- Enlarged glands in the neck.
- Weight fluctuations.
- Cuts on hands from self-induced vomiting.
- Constipation.
- Eyes show broken blood vessels (Eating Disorder Hope, n.d.).
- Discolored tooth enamel.
- Breath smells like vomit.

2. BEHAVIORS

- Repeated binge eating (often more than 1–5K calories).
- Often retreat to the restroom after meals.
- Frequent dieting.

3. IMPACT ON THINKING AND FEELINGS

- Spend 70–90% of time preoccupied with food and weight (National Eating Disorders, n.d.).
- Shame and guilt.
- Irritability.
- Self-esteem issues.
- Feeling out of control.
- Problems concentrating.

4. METHODS OF PURGING

- Self-induced vomiting.
- Alternatives include diuretics, excessive exercise, laxative use, enemas, fasting, or a combination (Bulimia.com, 2022).

Workbook: Reflecting on Chapter 9 Topics

1. How do you ensure that all students feel seen and valued in your classroom?
2. What strategies do you use to identify and support the specific needs of students with disabilities or learning differences?
3. How do you incorporate multicultural materials and resources into your teaching?
4. What steps do you take to create ground rules for respectful class discussions?
5. How do you monitor and adjust your curriculum based on student progress and needs?
6. How do you organize the classroom space to support student learning and engagement?
7. What techniques do you use to highlight critical information for your students?
8. How do you manage to avoid shaming students while keeping them on task?
9. How do you implement Universal Design for Learning (UDL) principles in your classroom?
10. What methods do you use to help students develop executive function skills?
11. How do you support students from low-income backgrounds in your classroom?
12. How do you address and mitigate microaggressions in your classroom environment?
13. How do you engage students who finish their work early to maintain a high level of challenge?
14. What strategies do you use to help introverted students participate in classroom discussions?
15. How do you support students struggling with eating disorders, like bulimia, within your school?
16. How do you build a supportive network among colleagues to promote gender equity?

Going Deeper—Advanced Questions

1. In what ways do your personal biases affect your interactions with diverse learners, and how can you work to overcome them?
2. How do you critically evaluate the effectiveness of your multicultural teaching materials, and what criteria do you use to select these materials?
3. What are the potential challenges of implementing UDL principles in a diverse classroom?
4. How can you create a classroom culture that not only tolerates but celebrates diversity, and what specific actions can you take to foster this culture?
5. How do you engage with parents and communities of diverse learners?

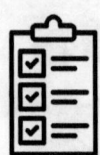
Checklist of Activities and Strategies to Try (Pick 2)

❑ Establish and consistently enforce guidelines for respectful class discussions.

❑ Prioritize and integrate multicultural materials into the curriculum, focusing resources and time on the cultural backgrounds of your students.

❑ Implement Universal Design for Learning (UDL) principles by providing multiple means of engagement, representation, and action and expression.

❑ Highlight critical information by stating, "This is critical to remember," and then checking for understanding.

❑ Encourage the use of a corkboard where students can pin notecards with 15-minute tasks on one side and longer tasks on the other.

❑ Display the activity schedule prominently in a spot that all learners can easily see.

❑ Utilize a task tree to provide step-by-step instructions with visual aids at the beginning of each class.

❑ Ensure proper credit is given by redirecting praise to the original source if someone is recognized for an idea that was not theirs.

❑ Other:
_____.

Describe Your Progress

1. What activities were most successful?

2. What challenges did you face?

3. How can you improve for next time?

 **References for Chapter 9**

4Teachers.org. (n.d.). Project based learning checklists [Web page]. http://pblchecklist.4teachers.org/checklist.shtml

Ainscow, M. (2014). From special education to effective schools for all: A review of progress so far. *European Journal of Special Needs Education*, 29(3), 309–22.

Aronson, J., Fried, C. B., & Good, C. (2002). Reducing the effects of stereotype threat on African American college students by shaping theories of intelligence. Journal of Experimental Social Psychology, 38(2), 113–25. https://doi.org/10.1006/jesp.2001.1491

Ashburn-Nardo, L., Morris, K. A., & Goodwin, S. A. (2008). The confronting prejudiced responses (CPR) model: Applying CPR in organizations. *Academy of Management Learning & Education*, 7(3), 332–42.

Bulimia.com (2022, July 8). Do I have bulimia? Signs and symptoms of eating disorders. The Bulimia Project. https://bulimia.com/bulimia-symptoms/

Cain, S. (2012). *Quiet: The power of introverts in a world that can't stop talking*. Crown Publishers.

CAST. (2018). Universal Design for Learning guidelines version 2.2. https://udlguidelines.cast.org/

Dawson, P., & Guare, R. (2009). *Smart but scattered: The revolutionary "executive skills" approach to helping kids reach their potential*. The Guilford Press.

DiTullio, G. (2018, November 9). Helping students develop executive function skills. Edutopia. https://www.edutopia.org/article/helping-students-develop-executive-function-skills

Drexler, P. (2013, April 29). Don't shame children in pursuit of discipline. *Psychology Today*. https://www.psychologytoday.com/us/blog/our-gender-ourselves/201304/dont-shame-children-in-pursuit-discipline

Eating Disorder Hope. (n.d.). Signs I have bulimia? Eating Disorder Hope. https://www.eatingdisorderhope.com/blog/signs-i-have-bulimia

Gallup. (2020, February 11). Socialism and atheism still U.S. political liabilities. Gallup. https://news.gallup.com/poll/285563/socialism-atheism-political-liabilities.aspx

Gay, G. (2000). *Culturally responsive teaching: Theory, research, and practice*. Teachers College Press.

Gorski, P. C. (2008). Peddling poverty for profit: Elements of oppression in Ruby Payne's framework. *Equity & Excellence in Education*, 41(1), 130–48.

Gorski, P. C. (2018). *Reaching and teaching students in poverty: Strategies for erasing the opportunity gap*. Teachers College Press.

Hans, J. (n.d.). Visual strategies for students with autism. n2y Blog https://www.n2y.com/blog/visual-strategies-autism/

Hattie, J. (2009). *Visible learning: A synthesis of over 800 meta-analyses relating to achievement*. Routledge.

Hirsh, E., & Tomaskovic-Devey, D. (2018). Metrics, accountability, and transparency: A recipe for institutional change? *Sociological Perspectives*, 61(1), 5–27.

IanBee Team. (2023, February 2). How to create an inclusive classroom: 12 tips for teachers. PlanBee. https://planbee.com/blogs/news/how-to-create-an-inclusive-classroom-12-tips-for-teachers

McKinsey Global Institute. (2015). The power of parity: How advancing women's equality can add $12 trillion to global growth. https://www.mckinsey.com/featured-insights/employment-and-growth/how-advancing-womens-equality-can-add-12-trillion-to-global-growth

National Eating Disorders Association. (n.d.). Warning signs and symptoms. https://www.nationaleatingdisorders.org/warning-signs-and- symptoms/

New America. (n.d.). Understanding culturally responsive teaching. https://www.newamerica.org/education-policy/reports/culturally-responsive-teaching/understanding-culturally-responsive-teaching/

Özler, B. (2020, January 13). Better conduct at seminars. World Bank Blogs—Development Impact. https://blogs.worldbank.org/en/impactevaluations/better-conduct-seminars

Scott, J. W. (1986). Gender: A useful category of historical analysis. *The American Historical Review*, 91(5), 1053–75.

Smith, J., & Johnson, A. (2020). The invisible load: Understanding the emotional labor of family life. *Journal of Family Studies*, 26(3), 345–62.

Smolak, L. (2006). Body image development in children. In T. F. Cash & T. Pruzinsky (Eds.), *Body image: A handbook of theory, research, and clinical practice* (pp. 65–73). Guilford Press.

Sue, D. W. (2007). Racial microaggressions in everyday life: Implications for clinical practice. *American Psychologist*, 62(4), 271–86.

Sue, D. W., Capodilupo, C. M., Torino, G. C., Bucceri, J. M., Holder, A. M. B., Nadal, K. L., & Esquilin, M. (2007). Racial microaggressions in everyday life: Implications for clinical practice. *American Psychologist*, 62(4), 271–86. https://doi.org/10.1037/0003-066X.62.4.271

University of Arizona, Center for the Study of Women. (n.d.). Avoiding gender bias in letter of reference writing [PDF]. https://csw.arizona.edu/sites/default/files/avoiding_gender_bias_in_letter_of_reference_writing.pdf

Wing, S., Capodilupo, C. M., Torino, G. C., Bucceri, J. M., Holder, A. M. B., Nadal, K. L., & Esquilin, M. (2007). Racial microaggressions in everyday life. *American Psychologist*, 62(4), 271–86.

York University, Information and Privacy Office. (n.d.). Tip Sheet 12—Minute-taking tips and techniques. https://ipo.info.yorku.ca/tool-and-tips/tip-sheet-12-minute-taking-tips-and-techniques/

Chapter 10

Facilitating Dynamic Classroom Discussions

DOI: 10.4324/9781003628804-10

Facilitating Dynamic Classroom Discussions

One of the most exhilarating parts of teaching is diving into a lively classroom discussion. I feel Disney-level enchantment while watching students' passion arise as they share personal stories, make connections to the real world, contribute insights, and challenge ideas. These discussions aren't just fluff, they're a game-changer for fostering critical thinking and deep learning. Even better, when students engage in purposeful discussions with clear expectations, their intellectual experience elevates.

Being adept at facilitating discussions transforms passive learners into active participants, helping them develop superpowers like articulating thoughts clearly, listening to diverse perspectives, and engaging in respectful debate. These are not just academic skills; they are life skills.

I remember observing an accomplished teacher across the hall who was a discussion- facilitating artist. Mr. Rose had an uncanny ability to ask just the right questions to provoke deep thinking and steer the conversation. Although his body was poised and still, the wheels in his mind were engaged and focused on the experience of his students. It reminded me of actor Kevin Costner; you could see his empathetic, kinetic intelligence at work. As a result of his kindness and skill, his kids felt safe and encouraged to speak up, knowing their contributions were valued. That observation had a big impact on my teaching. Since then, I've experimented with different types of discussion protocols over the years, many of which are described in this chapter.

Key Chapter 10 Strategies

1. Have students choose and discuss quotations from the readings in the Hatful of Quotes activity.
2. Establish ground rules and provide a rubric for discussions, including a post-discussion debrief.
3. Utilize formats like Socratic Seminars, Harkness Tables, Fishbowl Techniques, Philosophical Chairs, and Debates to switch up discussion formats.
4. Use tools like Random Name Picker to select students for responses in a random response system.
5. Allow students to consider questions by freewriting or discussing in small groups before whole-class discussions.
6. Interrupt tense arguments by identifying areas of agreement to shift to common ground.
7. Ensure comprehension by having students rephrase the prompt.
8. Use tools like a T-chart to organize arguments for and against a topic to be ready for conflict.
9. Use follow-up questions to encourage deeper thinking.
10. Allocate specific time for off-topic discussions.
11. Allow struggling students to consult with peers.
12. Establish and review discussion guidelines before starting the discussion.
13. Encourage students to write about their thoughts and feelings after discussions, particularly when the conversation is heated.

Memory Device for this Chapter
Letter Mnemonic

LEADER

Limit off-topic discussions with the parking lot method

Establish ground rules

Assign roles in discussions

Debrief after discussions

Engage students in reflective writing before talking starts

Rephrase prompts when kids look confused by the question

HOW TO INCREASE PARTICIPATION IN WHOLE CLASS DISCUSSION

"Class discussions are crucial for developing students' critical thinking and communication skills" (Palmer, 1998). These discussions create opportunities for students to engage with diverse perspectives, refine their arguments, and build collaborative problem-solving abilities essential for academic and real-world success.

1. TRY HATFUL OF QUOTES

1. Students choose five quotations from the readings that resonate and print enough copies so that each kid receives one. 2. Place the quotes in a hat and have each learner choose one. Multiple students will receive the same quote. 3. Everyone reads their quote and writes down their thoughts about it. 4. Students share their quotes and thoughts (ACUE, 2016).

2. SWITCH UP DISCUSSION FORMATS

- Socratic Seminar (ReadWriteThink: http://bit.ly/2wS8K2n).
- Harkness Table (Wikipedia: http://bit.ly/2N06sIP).
- Fishbowl Technique (Better Evaluation: http://bit.ly/2MVVsMD).
- Philosophical Chairs (AVID: http://bit.ly/2wSHO2J).
- Debates (Humber: http://bit.ly/2oPzg8c).

3. USE RANDOM RESPONSE SYSTEM

Paste names into the Random Name Picker and spin the wheel (see the following: http://bit.ly/2MURGTr).

4. SET EXPECTATIONS

Describe the ground rules and provide a rubric. Let introverts know what the topic of discussion will be the next day. Facilitate a post-discussion debrief.

5. PROVIDE THINK TIME

Let students consider questions by freewriting a response to a prompt. Or have them talk about the question in small groups before transitioning to a whole class discussion.

MAKE CLASS DISCUSSIONS CONSTRUCTIVE

"Constructive discussions help develop students' communication skills, making them more confident and articulate speakers" (Light, 2001). These skills are invaluable in academic settings and beyond.

1. SHIFT TO COMMON GROUND
Interrupt tense arguments by asking kids to identify areas of agreement.

2. TWEAK THE FISHBOWL FORMAT
Place introverted kids in the center first, so they have a chance and responsibility to talk.

3. REDUCE SOCIAL THREAT OF FAILURE
Ask a question that has no wrong answers. For example: "What's your reaction to this?" Kids brainstorm with others before talking in front of the entire group.

4. LEAD WITH WRITING
Pose a question and ask kids to write down possible answers before discussing.

5. ASK KIDS TO REPHRASE THE PROMPT
Paraphrasing a question shows that students comprehend what the thinking task is. You can also ask kids to brainstorm an approach to considering the question. What elements should they reflect upon? In what order?

6. BE READY FOR CONFLICT
Create a T-chart labeled "for" and "against." Give the conversation a time limit and write down each point. Then the class can vote anonymously for the "winning" argument.

7. CLARIFY THE PROBLEM
Pose an issue in class, and then ask, "What do we know about this issue?" and "How do we know if we have found an adequate solution?" Then use the criteria to assess if the conversation has come to a successful close.

FOLLOW-UP QUESTIONS

"Effective questioning, including follow-ups, enables teachers to scaffold student learning, guiding them to higher levels of cognitive processing" (Marzano, 2001). This approach helps students connect new ideas to prior knowledge, uncover underlying assumptions, and articulate more nuanced responses.

1. PROMPTS THAT FOSTER ELABORATION

- Tell me more.
- What did you observe about X?
- Clarify the last part of your answer.

2. APPLICATION QUESTIONS

- What would be the result if X?
- What would happen if X?
- What is a real-world situation like X?

3. HIGHER-ORDER THINKING QUESTIONS

- What analogy would work in this situation?
- What would happen if X?

4. WHEN STUDENTS DRAW A BLANK

A) Encourage educated guesses: "What's your best guess?" B) Reword your question: "Let me ask that a different way . . ."

5. ANALYSIS QUESTIONS

- Why do you think that?
- What do you mean by that?
- How did you come up with that answer?
- What are your assumptions based on?
- What are the pros and cons of X?
- Would X agree with your answer?
- Can you compare/contrast your answer with X's answer?
- What's another possible answer?
- What makes you think your answer is right?

A DISCUSSION GOES OFF-TOPIC. WHAT DO YOU SAY?

"Off-topic remarks in discussions can occur when students are not adequately engaged or when the material does not resonate with their interests and experiences. Connecting content to students' lives can keep discussions relevant and focused" (Tomlinson, 2014). By incorporating real-world examples or inviting students to share personal insights, teachers can create a sense of relevance that naturally steers conversations back to the subject matter.

1. ASK FOR A JUSTIFICATION
"Talk about how your response relates to our topic, Jose."

2. AFFIRM AND SHIFT
"Interesting point . . . It reminds me that rough drafts of the Constitution were written on papers made of hemp."

3. RAIN CHECK IT
"I'm really curious to learn more about your kitchen fire, but we're going to switch back to. Promise me you won't forget to tell me the rest of that story."

4. SUMMARIZE AND REDIRECT
"Let's summarize what we've covered so far and see how it connects to our main topic."

5. PARKING LOT
Create a "parking lot" space on the board for off-topic ideas and questions. Revisit them later if there's time.

6. TIME BOXING
Allocate a specific amount of time for the off-topic discussion, then gently steer back to the main topic once the time is up.

WHEN STUDENTS CAN'T ANSWER

"Students may struggle to answer questions if they do not understand the question itself. Clear and precise questioning techniques are necessary to ensure that all students comprehend what is being asked" (Brookhart, 2008). Using language that aligns with students' developmental level and providing contextual examples can bridge gaps in understanding and invite thoughtful, accurate responses.

1. REPHRASE THE QUESTION
Maybe the problem is the question, not content knowledge.

2. OFFER CANDOR
Students need honesty when their answer is incorrect (Cox, 2025).

3. DON'T MAKE IT A BIG DEAL
Don't overdo sympathy. You don't want to model emotionality. Stay chill.

4. LOOK DOWN
Making eye contact and talking taxes kids' cognitive resources (Nield, 2018).

5. REPHRASE THE PROMPT
Ask the student a lower-level question or a related question (CITL, n.d.).

6. LOWER THE SOCIAL COST
Say, "Because you're a big thinker, I gave you a tough one." "A good question is both answerable and challenging. It will inspire analysis, synthesis, interpretation, and critical thinking" (Center for Teaching and Learning, 2018).

7. HAVE THEM PHONE A FRIEND
Ask a struggling student to consult with a peer.

HOW TO FACILITATE DIFFICULT DISCUSSIONS

"Teachers must be prepared to address emotional responses and conflicts that arise during difficult discussions. Active listening and empathy are essential skills for navigating these moments" (hooks, 2003). Language that aligns with students' developmental level and provides contextual examples can bridge gaps in understanding and invite thoughtful, accurate responses.

1. WRITE FIRST
Writing about the topic in advance can make kids less emotionally reactive.

2. MAKE GROUND RULES
Before the discussion, ask students to list responses to the following prompts:
- What are the qualities or characteristics of good discussions?
- What ground rules or guidelines should we follow in discussions? (Sheridan Center for Teaching and Learning, n.d.).

3. IT'S A CONVERSATION, NOT A DEBATE
"I tell them the goal of a discussion is to understand rather than win, so the tactics are different" (Krulder, 2025).

4. HOW TO CONVEY NEGATIVE EMOTIONS
"You make me feel . . ." needs to be replaced with "When you (state the behavior), I feel (one word describing emotions)" (Myers, 2010).

5. PRAISE POSITIVE DISCUSSION MOVES
Acknowledge kids who invite others into the conversation, who show they have listened carefully to peers, and invited quiet students to participate.

6. DEBRIEF
At the end of the conversation, ask the following:
- What did you learn today?
- Who raised a good point you hadn't thought of before?
- How was our communication? What went well or could have been better?
- How will this shape your thinking going forward?

TALKING ABOUT RACE: GROUND RULES

"Facilitating discussions about race involves providing historical context and addressing systemic inequalities. This helps students understand the broader societal implications of racial issues" (Ladson-Billings, 1994). Creating a safe environment for these conversations encourages students to critically analyze their own biases and consider actionable steps toward promoting equity and justice.

1. TALK FROM EXPERIENCE
Say, "I have found . . ." rather than "People say . . ." (Bobo et al., 2004).

2. DON'T BE COLOR BLIND
Colorblindness camouflages racism—a privilege available only to dominant groups (Ullucci & Battey, 2011).

3. TEST YOUR BIAS
Try Project Implicit's free racial bias quiz.

4. SET NORMS
Don't attack people. Focus on ideas being discussed.

5. ASK FOLLOW-UP QUESTIONS
Example: "This is what I heard you say . . . Is it what you meant?" and "How do you know that?" (Flanagan & Hindley, 2017).

6. FACILITATE REFLECTIVE WRITING
Ask students to write reflections on their thoughts and feelings after discussions on race.

7. "CONE OF SILENCE"
Make a rule: What's said here, stays here.

DEBUNK CONSPIRACY THEORIES

"Educators have a responsibility to challenge conspiracy theories by teaching students how to evaluate sources and evidence critically. This is a fundamental skill for participating in a democratic society" (Konda, 2019). Moreover, equipping students with the tools to identify misinformation fosters a culture of informed citizenship, empowering them to engage thoughtfully in public discourse and resist manipulation.

1. RELATE
Say, "We're all feeling anxious about [the reliability of news, job security, the security of our families, being manipulated by politicians, etc.]." Don't call people wrong. That will backfire.

2. OFFER ALTERNATIVE EXPLANATION.
A study by Johnson and Seifert (1994) showed that "if you must mention a myth, you should mention this second, and only after clearly warning people that you're about to discuss something that isn't true." Talking about the myth first concretizes it in conspiracy theorists' minds.

3. EMPATHIZE AND LISTEN
Show empathy and actively listen to their concerns. Understanding their perspective can help in finding common ground and correcting misinformation.

4. FIGHT WITH "STICKIER IDEAS"
Example: "Since 1998, our planet has been building up heat at a rate of 4 Hiroshima A-bombs per second" (Cook, 2014).

5. GAME OUT THE IF/THEN SCENARIO
Create cognitive dissonance between reality and the conspiracy. Writes conspiracy theory expert Colin Dickey: "I try to show how these conspiracies play out. I say, 'I don't know if you're right or wrong, but if you were right, I would expect the following to happen . . .'" (Kreizman, 2020).

Workbook: Reflecting on Chapter 10 Topics

1. What are the benefits of setting clear expectations and providing a discussion rubric?
2. How can switching up discussion formats (Socratic Seminar, Harkness Table, etc.) enhance student participation?
3. Why is it important to sometimes use a random response system in classroom discussions?
4. How does providing think time before a whole class discussion benefit students?
5. How can tweaking the Fishbowl format help introverted students participate more?
6. What are the advantages of asking questions with no wrong answers?
7. How can leading with writing improve the quality of classroom discussions?
8. What is the impact of asking students to justify their responses during discussions?
9. Why is creating a "parking lot" for off-topic ideas effective?
10. In what situations should students be encouraged to "phone a friend" during discussions?
11. How do establishing and reviewing ground rules enhance the quality of classroom discussions?
12. What role does debriefing play in helping students process classroom discussions?

Going Deeper—Advanced Questions

1. How can teachers balance the need for structured discussion formats with the flexibility required to address spontaneous student contributions?
2. How can a teacher's approach to handling off-topic discussions influence the classroom's learning environment?
3. Evaluate the impact of consistent use of a random response system on student participation and equity in classroom discussions.
4. How can educators assess the long-term effects of discussion-based learning on students' critical thinking and communication skills?

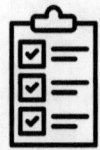

Checklist of Activities and Strategies to Try (Pick 2)

- ❑ Have students choose quotations from the readings, place them in a hat, and draw them to discuss their thoughts in the Hatful of Quotes activity.
- ❑ Describe the ground rules for discussions and provide a rubric. Include a post-discussion debrief to set expectations.
- ❑ Use various formats like Socratic Seminars, Harkness Tables, Fishbowl Techniques, Philosophical Chairs, and Debates to switch up discussion formats.
- ❑ Interrupt tense arguments by asking students to identify areas of agreement to shift to common ground.
- ❑ Direct students to draw a T-chart labeled "for" and "against" to organize arguments.
- ❑ Ask questions with no wrong answers to reduce the social threat of failure.
- ❑ Pose a question and then ask students to write down possible answers before the discussion begins.
- ❑ Use follow-up questions like "Tell me more" or "What did you observe about X?" to deepen the discussion and promote elaboration with questions.
- ❑ Create a parking lot for off-topic ideas and questions to revisit later if time allows.
- ❑ Encourage students to write reflections on their thoughts and feelings after discussions.
- ❑ Other: _____.

Describe Your Progress

1. What activities were most successful?

2. What challenges did you face?

3. How can you improve for next time?

 **References for Chapter 10**

Association of College and University Educators. (2016). Hatful of quotes [Implementation guide]. https://learn.acue.org/wp-content/uploads/2025/02/ETP_AL6_Hatful_IG.pdf

AVID. (n.d.). Student learning: Student-centered teaching, learning activities & instruction. https://www.avid.org/student-learning

BetterEvaluation. (n.d.). Fishbowl technique. https://www.betterevaluation.org/methods-approaches/methods/fishbowl-technique

Bobo, L. D., Hudley, C., & Michel, C. (Eds.). (2004). *The Black studies reader*. Routledge.

Brookhart, S. M. (2008). *How to give effective feedback to your students*. Association for Supervision and Curriculum Development.

Center for Innovative Teaching and Learning at Indiana University Bloomington. (n.d.). Discussions: Teaching strategies. https://citl.indiana.edu/teaching-resources/teaching-strategies/discussions/index.html

Center for Teaching and Learning. (2018). Asking questions to improve learning [PDF]. Washington University in St. Louis. https://ctl.wustl.edu/wp-content/uploads/2018/08/Asking-questions-to-improve-learning.pdf

Classtools.net. (n.d.). Random name picker. https://www.classtools.net/random-name-picker/

Cook, J. (2014). The 97% consensus on global warming. *Bulletin of the Atomic Scientists*, 70(5), 66–78.

Cox, J. (2025, April 4). The right way to give student feedback. TeachHub. https://www.teachhub.com/professional-development/2025/04/the-right-way-to-give-student-feedback/

Flanagan, J. C., & Hindley, A. (2017). *Effective questioning strategies in the classroom*. Bloomsbury Academic.

hooks, b. (2003). *Teaching community: A pedagogy of hope*. Routledge.

Humber College Institute of Technology & Advanced Learning. (n.d.). Teaching strategies and frameworks. https://humber.ca/innovativelearning/teaching-strategies-and-frameworks/

Johnson, H. M., & Seifert, C. M. (1994). Sources of the continued influence effect: When misinformation in memory affects later inferences. *Journal of Experimental Psychology: Learning, Memory, and Cognition*, 20(6), 1420–36.

Konda, T. M. (2019). *Conspiracies of conspiracies: How delusions have overrun America*. University of Chicago Press.

Kreizman, M. (Host). (2020, September 24). Colin Dickey on why Americans are so keen to believe conspiracies [Audio podcast episode]. The Maris Review. Lit Hub Radio. https://lithub.com/colin-dickey-on-why-americans-are-so-keen-to-believe-conspiracies/

Krulder, J. (2025, August 4). "I tell them the goal of a discussion is to understand rather than win, so the tactics are different." Personal communication.

Ladson-Billings, G. (1994). *The dreamkeepers: Successful teachers of African American children*. Jossey-Bass.

Light, G. (2001). *Learning and teaching in higher education: The reflective professional*. Paul Chapman Publishing.

Marzano, R. J. (2001). *Classroom instruction that works: Research-based strategies for increasing student achievement*. Association for Supervision and Curriculum Development.

Myers, D. G. (2010). *Social psychology* (10th ed.). McGraw-Hill.

Nield, D. (2018, April 22). This is why it's so hard to maintain eye contact while having a conversation. ScienceAlert. https://www.sciencealert.com/why-hard-keep-eye-contact-conversation-science-overload

Palmer, P. J. (1998). *The courage to teach: Exploring the inner landscape of a teacher's life.* Jossey-Bass.

ReadWriteThink. (n.d.). Socratic seminars. http://www.readwritethink.org/professional-development/strategy-guides/socratic-seminars-30600.html

Sheridan Center for Teaching and Learning. (n.d.). Sample guidelines for classroom discussion agreements. Brown University. https://sheridan.brown.edu/resources/classroom-practices/discussions-seminars/sample-guidelines-classroom-discussion

Tomlinson, C. A. (2014). *The differentiated classroom: Responding to the needs of all learners* (2nd ed.). Association for Supervision and Curriculum Development.

Ullucci, K., & Battey, D. (2011). Exposing color blindness/grounding color consciousness. *Urban Education*, 46(6), 1195–225.

Wikipedia contributors. (n.d.). Harkness table. In Wikipedia, The Free Encyclopedia. https://en.wikipedia.org/wiki/Harkness_table

Chapter 11

Comprehensive Testing and Assessment Techniques

Comprehensive Testing and Assessment Techniques

Effective testing and assessment, when wielded with precision and thoughtfulness, can transform a learning environment into a thriving ecosystem of inquiry and intellectual development. "Assessment is not about you as a teacher; it's about your students" (Brookhart, 2017). This assertion underscores the shift from teacher-centered to student-centered evaluation, a fundamental principle in contemporary educational theory. As the saying goes, *teaching is about what's caught, not what's taught.* And that is only determined by assessment.

Creating quality assessments demands more of teachers than relying on the questions provided by commercial textbook companies. That's because we aren't living in the 1970s when exams rewarded top scores to kids who were great at rote recall. Today, we need to assess kids on deeper learning (analysis, application, evaluation, and synthesis) and assess them in multiple ways.

Today, kids can and should learn while being tested—one of the functions of formative assessment. An ongoing process used by teachers to evaluate students' learning and understanding through regular feedback, formative assessment helps identify what instructional adjustments are needed. Moreover, the integration of formative assessments into daily teaching practices has been championed as a catalyst for continuous improvement and engagement. Dylan Wiliam (2011), wrote, "Formative assessment is the bridge between teaching and learning." By providing timely and constructive feedback, teachers can guide students toward higher levels of success.

Equally significant is the incorporation of diverse assessment techniques that cater to the varied needs of students. "Effective assessment practices are those that allow students multiple ways to demonstrate their understanding" (Tomlinson et al., 2003). This inclusive approach fosters a more equitable and supportive learning environment.

Key Chapter 11 Strategies

1. In Peer Profs, learners teach a section of the material to the class.
2. In a Mock Press Conference, students act as experts in an assigned subject, fielding questions from peers and the teacher.
3. Mind Mapping involves the class creating mind maps to visually organize concepts.
4. Flashcard Frenzy has kids collaboratively create and test each other's flashcards.
5. Quiz Circuit is a relay race where each leg involves a quiz question and physical challenge.
6. In Trashketball, kids answer review questions in teams to earn a chance to shoot a paper ball into a trash can for extra points.
7. A Group Poster Exam has learners receive a grade based on design, content, oral presentation, and response to questions.
8. In a YouTube Exam, groups pick five important topics from the year and explain them in a video.
9. The Memo strategy requires learners to write a memo with headings like background, problem, possible solutions with pros and cons, final recommendation, and possible impact.
10. Cloze has kids fill in the blanks with the correct terms in a passage from the readings or an outline.
11. Empty Outline directs students to list important terms for understanding a given topic or concept.
12. Human Tableau asks teams of students to create living scenes or model processes to demonstrate their understanding.
13. Paraphrase It involves asking learners to translate into everyday language an explanation of what was learned.

Memory Device for this Chapter
Chunking

Chunk 1: Student-Centered Activities

- **Mock Press Conference:** Students act as experts in an assigned subject, fielding questions from peers and the teacher.
- **Group Poster Exam:** Learners receive a grade based on design, content, oral presentation, and response to questions.
- **Letter to a Friend:** Write a well-supported letter about the content using informal language.

Chunk 2: Technology-Based Activities

- **Plickers:** Students use cards to answer questions that the teacher scans with their device.
- **Quiz Tech**: Use Kahoot or Quizizz to create online interactive quizzes.
- **Quiz Circuit:** A relay race where each leg involves a quiz question and physical challenge.

Chunk 3: Alternative Assessments

- **Simulation:** Students make choices based on a real-life scenario.
- **Memo**: Learners write a memo with headings like background, problem, possible solutions with pros and cons, final recommendation, and possible impact.
- **Cloze:** Kids fill in the blanks with the correct terms in a passage from the readings or an outline.

Chunk 4: Creative Ways to Promote Learning During Testing

- **Celebration of Learning**: Never use the word testing, call it a "celebration of learning" day.
- **Combination-Test:** Let the students take the quiz individually, then in a group, with a combined grade.
- **Justify Your Answers:** After students take the exam, let them view the test key and explain why they chose the wrong answers.

Chunk 5: Exit Ticket Prompts

- **3 Ticket Folders:** Students deposit their exit tickets in a folder labeled "Got It," "More Practice, Please,:" or "I Need Some Help."
- **The Big Question:** Ask what will be important to remember about today's lesson a year from now.
- **Choose a Prompt:** Write one thing learned today, what was difficult, an "aha" moment, etc.

Chunk 6: Post-Exam Reflection and Support

- **Use Exam Wrappers:** Learn from error analysis prompts on exam wrappers.
- **Offer Time to Regroup**: Debrief the test and offer help sessions.
- **Re-Teach**: Provide targeted instruction on the most missed content.

EXAM PREP ACTIVITIES

"Effective exam preparation involves not just memorization, but the development of a deep understanding of the material through active learning techniques such as self-quizzing, summarizing, and teaching others" (Dunlosky et al., 2013). Helping students to identify misinformation fosters a culture of informed citizenship, empowering them to engage thoughtfully in public discourse and resist manipulation.

1. PEER PROFS
Learners teach a section of the material to the class.

2. MOCK PRESS CONFERENCE
Students act as experts in an assigned subject, fielding questions from "reporters" (peers and the teacher).

3. FLASHCARD FRENZY
Collaboratively, kids create and test each other's flashcards.

4. MIND MAPPING
The class creates mind maps to visually organize concepts.

5. QUIZ TECH
Use Kahoot or Quizizz to create online interactive quizzes.

6. QUIZ CIRCUIT
A relay race where each leg involves a quiz question and physical challenge: cone weave, bean bag balance, hula-hoop rotation, bean bag toss, floor agility ladder, spoon and egg race, and jump roping.

7. TRASHKETBALL
Kids answer review questions in teams. Correct answers earn a chance to shoot a paper ball into a trash can for extra points.

FINAL EXAM ALTERNATIVES

"Exam alternatives can foster deeper learning and engagement by allowing students to apply their knowledge creatively and contextually" (Brookhart, 2013). Projects, presentations, or portfolios, can demonstrate students' understanding in dynamic, real-world scenarios.

1. GROUP POSTER EXAM
Learners receive a grade based on design, content, oral presentation, and response to questions.

2. LETTER TO A FRIEND
Write a well-supported letter about the content—using informal language (Motz, 2023).

3. EXPLORE IT
Kids choose a theme that interests them and explore it further. They present what they learned with a podcast, blog post, etc.

4. MEMO
Learners write a memo with these headings: "background, problem, possible solutions with pros and cons, final recommendation" and "possible impact" (Peterson, n.d.).

5. E-OPTIONS
- Adaptive Testing: The test is calibrated to the students' abilities.
- Simulation: Students make choices based on a real-life scenario.
- E-portfolio: Learner artifacts and reflections

6. YOUTUBE EXAM
Groups pick five important topics from the year and explain them in a video. Gather the videos together in a course YouTube channel (Potash, 2024).

7. CLOZE
Kids are given a passage from the readings, or an outline, or slides with content. They fill in the blanks with the correct terms. Word banks can be provided (Collier County Public Schools, n.d.).

CAT (CLASSROOM ASSESSMENT TECHNIQUES)

"Classroom Assessment Techniques (CATs) are generally simple, non-graded, anonymous, in-class activities designed to give you and your students useful feedback on the teaching-learning process as it is happening" (Vanderbilt University Center for Teaching, n.d.). By using CATs, educators can make real-time adjustments to instruction, ensuring that learning objectives align with students' evolving needs.

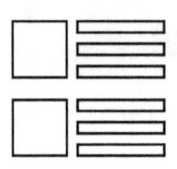

1. EMPTY OUTLINE
Direct students to list 5–10 terms that are important for understanding a given topic or concept. Aim for 2–3 minutes (Indiana University Center for Teaching and Learning, n.d.).

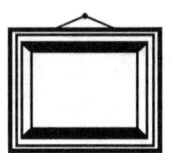

2. HUMAN TABLEAU
Ask teams of students to "create 'living" scenes or model processes" to demonstrate their understanding of something they have recently learned (Angelo & Cross, 1993).

3. PARAPHRASE IT
Ask learners to translate into everyday or simple language an explanation of what was learned. One sign that a concept is internalized is when students can offer a simple and clear explanation.

4. APPLICATION CARDS
Students describe real-world applications of "important principles, generalizations, theories, or procedures" (Johns Hopkins Bloomberg School of Public Health, n.d.).

5. WDWWWWHW
Ask learners to answer, "Who does what to whom, when, where, how and why?' (WDWWWWHW) about a given topic and then create a single informative, grammatical, and long summary sentence" (Johns Hopkins Bloomberg School of Public Health, n.d.).

TEST CONSTRUCTION ERRORS

"Test construction errors occur when items on a test do not align with the learning objectives or when they fail to measure the intended knowledge or skills" (Indiana University Center for Innovative Teaching and Learning, n.d.). These misalignments can lead to misleading results.

1. PAGE-FLIPPING!
Keep test questions on one page so kids don't have to flip papers back and forth.

2. APPROPRIATE EMPHASIS
Ask more questions about the most important info—not the content easiest to test. Match prompts with curriculum objectives.

3. TRICK QUESTIONS
How can a man go eight days without sleep? Answer: By sleeping during the nighttime). Test the content, not test savvy.

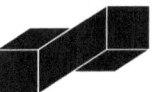

4. AMBIGUOUS QUESTIONS
There should be no more than one way to interpret a question.

5. NOT PROVIDING A WARMUP
Never start with the most challenging questions.

6. LONGEST ANSWER IS CORRECT
Choosing the longest answer is the go-to move when students are guessing on a multiple-choice question.

7. NO RUBRIC FOR THE ESSAY PORTION
You and your students should know what you're looking for and how much the response is worth.

FORMATIVE ASSESSMENT TECH

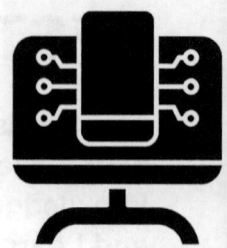

"Utilizing digital formative assessment tools can transform the educational process by enabling continuous feedback and allowing students to identify their strengths and areas for improvement" (Estrada-Araoz et al., 2023). These tools also allow teachers to adapt instruction to meet individual needs in real time.

1. PLICKERS
See the Plickers site here: https://www.plickers.com/. Students use cards to answer questions that the teacher scans with their device—a fast way to capture data.

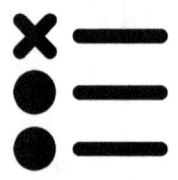

2. POLLEVERYWHERE
See PollEverwhere here: https://www.polleverywhere.com/. Ask a question during a presentation. Kids respond on the web or via text. Answers are charted in real time. The tool integrates with Google Slides, Keynote, and PowerPoint.

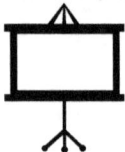

3. SLIDO
See the Slido site at https://www.sli.do/. Have kids ask questions about a text or concept, then let them vote on their favorites.

4. QUICK KEY
See the Quick Key site here: https://get.quickkeyapp.com/. This iOS and Android optical scanner quickly grades bubble sheets. The tool also integrates with Google Docs.

5. SOCRATIVE
See the Socrative site here: https://www.socrative.com/. Kids use computers or smart phones to answer quiz questions. Quizzes are scored automatically and show up in your dashboard. Also, the tool lets you download or email the report.

6. NEARPOD
See the Nearpod site here: https://nearpod.com. The tool creates interactive presentations by integrating quizzes and polls that kids respond to.

CREATIVE WAYS TO PROMOTE LEARNING WHEN TESTING

"Testing can promote long-term learning and the application of knowledge to new situations, especially when creative methods are used to engage students in meaningful ways" (Carpenter, 2012). In other words, testing isn't just testing—it's also effective instruction.

1. CELEBRATION OF LEARNING
Never use the word testing. Call it "celebration of learning" day!

2. BEST TESTER INTERVIEW
Facilitate a Q&A with the best test taker. What study tips worked with them?

3. COMBINATION TEST
Let the students take the quiz individually, then in a group. Their grade can be a combination of both scores.

4. JUSTIFY YOUR ANSWERS
After students take the exam, let them view the test key, and in green pen, score their own essays and explain why they chose the wrong answer for the possibility of partial credit.

5. OFFER A REVIEW SESSION
Put students in groups to discuss what might be on the test and construct answers.

6. RETURN GRADED TESTS WITH AN "EXAM WRAPPER"

After a finished test, return the exams "wrapped" in a sheet with reflection prompts. Annie Murphy Paul (2013) writes that the following questions will improve learners' study skills: 1. What problems posed the most difficulty for me on the exam? 2. How did I study for the exam? 3. What would I do differently if I had to retake the exam? 4. For my next exam, I want to remember to . . .

EXIT TICKET PROMPTS

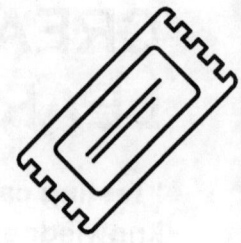

An exit ticket is a quick, informal assessment given at the end of a lesson to gauge students' understanding, gather feedback, or prompt reflection on key concepts. They also allow educators to quickly identify misconceptions and tailor upcoming lessons to student needs.

1. 3 TICKET FOLDERS
After kids write their names, what they learned, and any lingering questions, direct students "to deposit their exit tickets in a folder or bin labeled either 'Got It,' 'More Practice, Please,' or 'I Need Some Help'" (Savage & Savage, 2010).

2. THE BIG QUESTION
A year from now, what will be important for you to remember about today's lesson?

3. AFTER EXAM PROMPTS
- How much time did you spend reading? Re-reading? Reviewing? Using note cards?
- What study approach worked best for you?
- How would you categorize mistakes made on the exam?
- What do you need to do to prepare for the next exam?

4. CHOOSE A PROMPT
- Write one thing you learned today.
- What gave you the most difficulty today? Why?
- Something that really helped me learn today was . . .
- My "aha" moment or epiphany today was . . .
- Working with others today made easier or harder. Explain.
- Describe a connection you see between today's material and your life (Fisher & Frey, 2004).

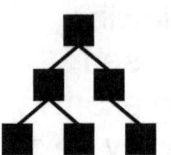

5. BLOOM'S TAXONOMY PROMPTS
Remember: Describe _____.
Understand: What would happen if _____?
Apply: How would you alter _____ to _____?
Analyze: Discuss the pros and cons of _____.
Evaluate: List criteria to judge _____.
Create: What would happen if _____?

THEY BOMBED THE TEST, NOW WHAT?

"Failing an exam can lead to significant emotional stress" (Swinburne University of Technology and Deakin University, 2020). We need to help students view failure as a stepping-stone toward improvement.

1. DON'T STRESS
Don't frame the situation as hopeless; frame this as an indicator of what still needs to be learned.

2. MODIFY ASSESSMENT PLANS
Introduce more low-stakes assessments to reveal learners' level of mastery earlier.

3. USE EXAM WRAPPERS
Have kids learn from error analysis prompts on exam wrappers. For examples, see the Eberly Center for Teaching Excellence & Educational Innovation (n.d.).

http://bit.ly/2OiSMG7.

4. OFFER TIME TO REGROUP
Debrief the test and offer a time when individuals can get help.

5. RE-TEACH
Provide targeted instruction on "most missed" content.

6. TEACH STUDY SKILLS, IF NEEDED
NEA recommends a host of study skills (NEA, n.d.).

7. REFLECT ON THE "PROBLEM"
- Was the test valid?
- Did they prepare enough?
- What content was most difficult?
- What content was handled well?
- How could the information have been taught differently or more effectively?
- Did the students have a big reason to care about the content?

ADVICE FOR KIDS WITH TEST ANXIETY

"Test anxiety can significantly impact a student's quality of life (Lohiya et al., 2021). Schools need to create a supportive test environment that prioritizes student well-being alongside academic achievement.

1. DON'T LET YOUR TESTS DEFINE YOU
You're more than a grade.

2. GET THE BIG PICTURE
Mentally allocate how much time you'll spend on each section. If there's time to recheck answers later, even better.

3. DON'T PROCRASTINATE
Study "over a longer period of time . . ." Slow absorption of the material retained better than what you memorize in a last-minute cram session (Mometrix Test Prep, n.d.).

4. USE POSITIVE SELF-TALK
"I'm a clear-eyed test assassin."

5. AVOID CAFFEINE
You might become too wired to focus effectively

6. DON'T RACE
Plan to use all of the available time, even if most students finish quickly.

7. USE GOOD SLEEP HYGEINE
Getting enough rest will help you focus on test day.

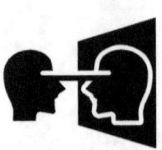
8. BOLSTER YOUR SELF-IMAGE
"Students often develop negative self-images when they experience failures on exams." Post a list of your positive qualities. Say them aloud. Remember past test successes (Mashayekh & Hashemi, 2011).

TEACHING TO THE TEST: THE ISSUES

"The need to meet specific testing standards pressures teachers to 'teach to the test' rather than providing a broad curriculum, limiting the development of higher-order thinking skills" (American University, 2023). To counter this, educators can integrate test-related content into engaging, interdisciplinary activities that foster creativity, critical thinking, and problem-solving.

1. TEST PREP DOESN'T TRANSFER
Proof: Altering the test format craters scores.

2. IT'S MALPRACTICE
Taxpayers don't pay us to "game the system" (Singer, 2016).

3. ITEM-TEACHING INVALIDATES TEST
Drilling weakens valid test results (Popham, 2001).

4. IT ALTERS THE GOAL OF LEARNING
From life-long learning to raising scores.

5. IT NARROWS THE CURRICULUM
Kids "experience far more facts and routines than conceptual understanding and problem-solving . . ." (Resnick & Zurawsky, 2005).

6. IT'S DEMORALIZING
45% of surveyed teachers think of quitting because of standardized testing (NEA, 2022).

7. IT MISPLACES PRIORITIES
Mastering exam formats is different than mastering content.

8. WE SHOULD AIM HIGHER
A state exam is a "minimum-standards test" (Johnson, 2007).

Workbook: Reflecting on Chapter 11 Topics

1. In what ways can Peer Profs and Mock Press Conferences enhance student engagement and knowledge retention?

2. How does the use of games like Trashketball align with the principles of active learning and formative assessment?

3. How can Adaptive Testing and Simulations be created to provide more personalized learning experiences?

4. In what ways can the creation of E-Portfolios and YouTube Exams help students develop digital literacy skills?

5. How does the strategy of Dig Deeper promote deeper understanding and critical thinking among students?

6. What are the advantages of using Classroom Assessment Techniques (CATs) such as Empty Outlines and Human Tableaus in assessing student understanding?

7. How can the use of Paraphrase It and WDWWWWHW improve students' ability to articulate their learning?

8. What strategies from Chapter 11 can be implemented to help students recover and learn from poor test performance?

9. How can teachers balance the need for comprehensive assessment with the potential stress and anxiety it may cause students?

Going Deeper—Advanced Questions

1. How do formative and summative assessment techniques detailed in Chapter 11 contribute to educational equity and inclusivity?

2. How can digital formative assessment tools be leveraged to create a dynamic and adaptive learning ecosystem, and what are the potential challenges and ethical considerations associated with their implementation?

3. How do the strategies for addressing test anxiety and promoting resilience in Chapter 11 align with current psychological research on stress, performance, and growth mindset?

Checklist of Activities and Strategies to Try (Pick 2)

- ❏ Have learners create posters on assigned topics and grade them based on design, content, oral presentation, and response to questions.
- ❏ Assign students to write a well-supported letter about the content using informal language.
- ❏ Have students compile an e-portfolio of their work and reflections throughout the course.
- ❏ Encourage students to choose a theme that interests them, explore it further, and present their findings through a podcast or blog post.
- ❏ Ask learners to write a memo with headings like background, problem, possible solutions with pros and cons, final recommendation, and possible impact.
- ❏ Provide passages from readings with blanks for key terms that students fill in, with or without a word bank.
- ❏ Have students describe real-world applications of important principles, generalizations, theories, or procedures.
- ❏ Use PollEverywhere or StrawPoll to ask questions during presentations, allowing students to respond via web or text, with results charted in real-time.
- ❏ After a test, return exams with a reflection sheet prompting students to think about their study habits and what they can improve for the next exam.
- ❏ Other:

_____.

Describe Your Progress

1. What activities were most successful?

2. What challenges did you face?

3. How can you improve for next time?

 **References for Chapter 11**

American University. (2020, July 2). Effects of standardized testing on students & teachers: Key benefits & challenges. American University School of Education Online. https://soeonline.american.edu/blog/effects-of-standardized-testing/

Angelo, T. A., & Cross, K. P. (1993). *Classroom assessment techniques: A handbook for college teachers* (2nd ed.). San Francisco, CA: Jossey-Bass.

Brookhart, S. M. (2017). *How to give effective feedback to your students* (2nd ed.). ASCD.

Carpenter, S. K. (2012). Testing enhances the transfer of learning. *Current Directions in Psychological Science*, 21(5), 279–83.

Collier County Public Schools. (n.d.). Cloze [Literacy-tips handout]. https://www.collierschools.com/cms/lib/FL01903251/Centricity/Domain/220/Literacy%20Tips/Cloze.pdf

Dunlosky, J., Rawson, K. A., Marsh, E. J., Nathan, M. J., & Willingham, D. T. (2013). Improving students' learning with effective learning techniques: Promising directions from cognitive and educational psychology. *Psychological Science in the Public Interest*, 14(1), 4–58.

Eberly Center for Teaching Excellence & Educational Innovation. (n.d.). Exam wrappers. Carnegie Mellon University. https://www.cmu.edu/teaching/designteach/teach/examwrappers/

Estrada-Araoz, E. G., Sayed, B. T., Niyazova, G. G., & Lami, D. (2023). Comparing the effects of computerized formative assessment versus computerized dynamic assessment on developing EFL learners' reading motivation, reading self-concept, autonomy, and self-regulation. *Language Testing in Asia*, 13(1), 39. https://doi.org/10.1186/s40468-023-00253-1

Indiana University Center for Innovative Teaching and Learning. (n.d.). Classroom assessment techniques: Assessing student learning. https://citl.indiana.edu/teaching-resources/assessing-student-learning/classroom-assessment-techniques/index.html

Johns Hopkins Bloomberg School of Public Health, Center for Teaching and Learning with Technology. (n.d.). Classroom assessment techniques [PDF handout]. https://crlt.umich.edu/sites/default/files/resource_files/ClassroomAssessmentTechniquesHopkins.pdf

Johnson, L. (2007). *Raising standards or raising barriers? Inequality and high-stakes testing in public education*. Century Foundation Press.

Lohiya, N., Kajale, N., Lohiya, N., Khadilkar, A., Khadilkar, V., Gondhalekar, K., & Agarkhedkar, S. (2021). Test anxiety among school-going children and adolescents, factors affecting and impact on quality of life: A multicenter study. *Indian Journal of Pediatrics*, 88(9), 892–8. https://doi.org/10.1007/s12098-021-03676-x

Mashayekh, M., & Hashemi, T. (2011). Recognizing, reducing and coping with test anxiety: Causes, solutions and recommendations. *Procedia—Social and Behavioral Sciences*, 30, 2149–55. https://doi.org/10.1016/j.sbspro.2011.10.417

Mometrix Test Preparation. (n.d.). Prepare for any test [Webpage]. Mometrix Academy. https://www.mometrix.com/academy/

Motz, B. A. (2023). Write a well-supported letter about the content [Class assignment handout]. Department of Psychological and Brain Sciences, Indiana University Bloomington.

National Education Association. (2022, February 1). Survey: Alarming number of educators may soon leave the profession. https://www.nea.org/nea-today/all-news-articles/survey-alarming-number-educators-may-soon-leave-profession

National Education Association. (n.d.). Helping your child do well in school. https://www.nea.org/professional-excellence/student-engagement/tools-tips/helping-your-child-do-well-school

Nearpod. (n.d.). Interactive lessons and assessments. https://nearpod.com

Paul, A. M. (2013, October 7). Smart strategies that help students learn how to learn. MindShift. KQED. https://www.kqed.org/mindshift/31942/smart-strategies-that-help-students-learn-how-to-learn

Peterson, M. J. (n.d.). Writing effective memos [Class handout]. Department of Political Science, University of Massachusetts Amherst. https://people.umass.edu/polsc356/writing-effective-memos.pdf

Plickers. (n.d.). Plickers: Simple, powerful classroom polling. https://get.plickers.com/

Poll Everywhere. (n.d.). Interactive audience participation. https://www.polleverywhere.com/

Popham, W. J. (2001). *The truth about testing: An educator's call to action*. Association for Supervision and Curriculum Development.

Potash, B. (2024, September 10). 6 creative video project ideas for ELA. Spark Creativity. https://nowsparkcreativity.com/2024/09/6-creative-video-project-ideas-for-ela.html

Quick Key. (n.d.). Quick Key: Mobile assessment made easy. https://get.quickkeyapp.com/

Resnick, L. B., & Zurawsky, C. 2005, Spring). Getting back on course: Standards-based reform and accountability. *American Educator*, 29(1), 8–46. https://www.aft.org/ae/spring2005/resnick_zurawsky

Savage, T. V., & Savage, M. K. (2010). *Successful classroom management and discipline: Teaching self-control and responsibility*. SAGE Publications.

Singer, S. M. (2016, November 3). Why teaching to the test is educational malpractice. *Gadfly on the Wall*. https://gadflyonthewallblog.com/2016/11/03/why-teaching-to-the-test-is-educational-malpractice/

Slido. (n.d.). Audience interaction made easy. https://www.sli.do/

Socrative. (n.d.). Formative assessment made easy. https://www.socrative.com/

Swinburne University of Technology and Deakin University. (2020). The impact of academic failure on student well-being. https://www.swinburne.edu.au/news/2020/08/when-students-fail-many-do-nothing-about-it-heres-how-unis-can-help-them-get-back-on-track/?utm_source=chatgpt.com

Tomlinson, C. A., Brighton, C., Hertberg, H., Callahan, C. M., Moon, T. R., Brimijoin, K., Conover, L. A., & Reynolds, T. (2003). Differentiating instruction in response to student readiness, interest, and learning profile in academically diverse classrooms. *Journal for the Education of the Gifted*, 27(2/3), 119–45. https://files.eric.ed.gov/fulltext/EJ787917.pdf

Vanderbilt University Center for Teaching. (n.d.). Classroom assessment techniques [PDF]. https://cft.vanderbilt.edu/wp-content/uploads/sites/59/CATs.pdf

Wiliam, D. (2011). Assessment: The bridge between teaching and learning [PDF]. https://www.researchgate.net/profile/Dylan-Wiliam/publication/258423377_Assessment_The_bridge_between_teaching_and_learning/links/60077c79a6fdccdcb8689787/Assessment-The-bridge-between-teaching-and-learning.pdf?origin=publication_detail

Chapter 12

Streamlined Grading and Constructive Feedback

Streamlined Grading and Constructive Feedback

Teachers often find themselves wiped out by a tsunami of grading that extends well into the weekends. The sheer volume of students' assignments, essays, and projects demands not only extensive time but also thoughtful feedback. For most of us, finding a balance between providing comprehensive feedback and maintaining a manageable workload is more aspirational than actual.

Efficient grading practices are essential for allowing teachers to dedicate more time to planning engaging lessons and interacting with students. Furthermore, speedy feedback helps students understand their strengths and weaknesses, enabling them to apply your commentary more quickly.

And do we even need to mention the need to safeguard teachers' mental health by freeing up their weekends?

The faster we grade and evaluate student work, the quicker they can use that feedback to level up their skills. Meanwhile, letting students assess their teachers demonstrates to every child in our classroom that we value a culture of improvement. Everyone benefits from feedback.

Key Chapter 12 Strategies

1. Teachers place check marks by lines with errors, and students identify and correct them.
2. Try auto-graded quizzes to quickly assess academic strengths and weaknesses.
3. Use participation points for quick writes or homework.
4. Show examples of successful work to reduce the need for extensive feedback.
5. Employ tools like spell check and Grammarly before submission, and teachers use frequently used comments.
6. Mark error patterns instead of every mistake to help students recognize issues.
7. Limit the time spent grading each paper—using a timer—to increase efficiency.
8. Collect early drafts to catch problems before the final submission.
9. Learners fill in rubrics for their own work to identify errors.
10. Hold group conferences for students with similar errors to address common issues.
11. Mark up one paragraph as a model and ask students to edit the rest based on it.
12. Invite students to mark up the syllabus, providing feedback on clarity and comprehensiveness.

Memory Device for this Chapter
Visual Mnemonic

RICH FEEDBACK

Picture a classroom where essays are marked with colorful check marks indicating grammar spots for kids to address. Students gather in small groups, animated in enthusiastic discussions about common mistakes and areas for improvement. The groups use color-coded charts and diagrams to dissect grammar rules and writing techniques, making the learning process interactive and visually stimulating. This classroom is a collaborative learning environment, where efficient feedback is appreciated by all students.

EFFICIENT GRADING PART 1

"Teachers who grade efficiently can focus more on instructional planning and student interaction . . ." (Marzano, 2018). We're in the people business, not the paperwork business.

1. CHECK MARKS
For essays, put check marks by lines that have grammar, punctuation, or spelling errors. Then learners identify what the problem is and make their own improvements.

2. GROUP WORK
Cooperative learning takes a lot of pre-planning and expectation-building but can substantially reduce the amount of work to the grade.

3. DON'T GRADE EVERYTHING
Use participation points for quick writes or homework.

4. LETTER TO THE CLASS
Read a set of papers, write a letter to the class identifying exemplars and specific problem areas, and then give students time to revise/edit as they use the letter as a resource.

5. LEVERAGE TECH
Direct kids to spell check and run Grammarly on their papers before turning them in. Cut and paste frequently used comments.

6. SHOW EXEMPLARS
If students know what success looks like, they are less likely to require substantial constructive feedback from the instructor.

7. AUTO-GRADED QUIZZES
Recycle questions year-to-year, and process grades quickly. Get a snapshot of academic strengths and weaknesses.

8. FOR TEST . . .
Let students score peers' work as you walk through an exam, but make sure the papers have codes, not names, so that the test takers are anonymous.

EFFICIENT GRADING PART 2

According to a recent survey by the National Education Association (NEA), teachers work an estimated 53 hours per week, which is seven hours more than the average working adult (National Education Association, 2023). **This workload highlights the need for systemic support, including streamlined administrative tasks and adequate planning time.**

1. NOTE ERROR PATTERNS
Tell kids that you mark error patterns, not every comma splice.

2. WALK THROUGH THE RUBRIC EARLY
Discuss the rubric before they begin the assignment to guide their work and reduce the need for extensive comments.

3. USE FORMATIVE ASSESSMENTS
Collect early drafts before the final due date to catch problems. This reduces the comments you must make later and makes feedback useful.

4. KIDS FILL IN A RUBRIC FIRST
If kids know their errors, they don't need further comments.

5. SET A TIMER
Identify the maximum time you spend grading and responding to each paper, so you don't linger. When the timer goes off, move to the next paper.

6. BYPASS ADDING
Avoid rubric math. Use checklists.

7. CONFERENCE!
When several students have similar errors, hold a group conference.

8. DON'T EDIT THE WHOLE PAPER
Mark up one paragraph of a student's essay as a model and ask the young writer to edit the rest of the essay.

WAYS TO SOLICIT STUDENT FEEDBACK

Feedback is the pulse that drives refinement and transformation. For teachers, it's a force multiplier that upgrades professional teaching and the learning experience itself. In its absence, stagnation lurks; in its presence, mastery sharpens, ideas flourish, and education ascends to new heights. Constructive feedback also empowers teachers to address specific challenges and adapt to diverse student needs.

1. ONE-POINT RAISE

Choose one focus area of your course for students to rate on a scale of 1 to 10. Then ask them to answer this prompt in writing: "What would raise that rating by one point" (Huston, n.d.).

2. ANNOTATE IT

Invite students to mark up the syllabus. Talk through their suggestions.

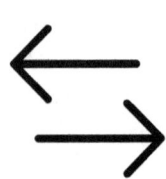

3. SWITCH-AND-REPORT

Direct learners to write their feedback on an anonymous note, fold it, and drop it into a hat. Then ask learners to pick one out of the basket. Kids are invited to paraphrase what peers wrote as you record the class comments.

4. POSSIBLE PROMPTS

- How helpful is my feedback on your assignments?
- What would you like to see more of? Less of?
- When do you learn best in this course?
- How is the pace of the class?
- How much time per week on average do you spend on homework for this class? Other classes?
- Do I encourage discussion from all participants?
- Do we talk about the readings enough? Too much?
- Are the assessments fair? How could they be improved?

Workbook: Reflecting on Chapter 12 Topics

1. How does using check marks to identify errors in student essays help students take ownership of their learning and improvement?
2. In what ways does group work reduce the grading workload for teachers while enhancing student collaboration?
3. What are the benefits and challenges of implementing peer grading in your classroom?
4. How can the strategy of not grading everything, such as using participation points for homework, impact student motivation and learning outcomes?
5. How does showing exemplars of successful work help reduce the need for extensive constructive feedback?
6. What are the advantages of marking error patterns rather than individual errors in student work?
7. Would setting a timer for grading each paper increase grading efficiency and consistency?
8. How do formative assessments, such as collecting early drafts, help catch and address issues before final submission?
9. How can using self-assessment using rubrics empower students to identify and correct their own errors before submitting their work?

Going Deeper—Advanced Questions

1. How does the integration of technology in grading and feedback processes influence the teacher-student dynamic and the perception of feedback's value?
2. Critically assess the effectiveness of group conferences in addressing common student errors. How do these conferences compare to one-on-one feedback sessions in terms of efficiency, depth of understanding, and student engagement?
3. Discuss the balance between peer support and individual accountability.

Checklist of Activities and Strategies to Try (Pick 2)

- ❑ For essays, place check marks by lines with grammar, punctuation, or spelling errors, and have students identify and correct the issues themselves.
- ❑ Implement cooperative learning projects that reduce individual grading workload.
- ❑ Use auto-graded quizzes to quickly process grades and get a snapshot of academic strengths and weaknesses.
- ❑ Allow students to score peers' anonymous work during exams for efficiency and unbiased feedback.
- ❑ Assign participation points for quick writes or homework to save grading time.
- ❑ Provide students with examples of successful work to reduce the need for extensive constructive feedback.
- ❑ Write a letter to the class after reading a set of papers, highlighting exemplars and common issues, then give students time to revise their work.
- ❑ Mark error patterns rather than every individual mistake to help students recognize recurring issues and improve their work.
- ❑ Limit the time spent grading each paper to avoid lingering and increase efficiency.
- ❑ Other: _____.

Describe Your Progress

1. What activities were most successful?

2. What challenges did you face?

3. How can you improve for next time?

 **References for Chapter 12**

Huston, T. (n.d.). What is the best way to solicit teaching feedback from students before the class? [Answer on Academia Stack Exchange]. Academia.SE. https://academia.stackexchange.com/q/37962

Marzano, R. J. (2018). *The handbook for the new art and science of teaching*. ASCD.

National Education Association. (2023, September 18). Survey: Teachers work more hours per week than other working adults. NEA Today. https://www.nea.org/nea-today/all-news-articles/survey-teachers-work-more-hours-week-other-working-adults

Chapter 13

EdTech Strategies

EdTech Strategies

Educational technology is a seismic force, shattering the constraints of traditional teaching and catapulting learning into a new dimension. When used thoughtfully, technology makes concepts morph from abstract to electrifying, passive consumption flips into active creation, and the very essence of education is rewritten. This isn't just enhancement—it's an evolution. This chapter explores the many ways technology can create dynamic, interactive, and personalized learning experiences.

These innovations not only make learning more engaging but also provide teachers with valuable data to tailor instruction and improve outcomes.

Today, kids can use tablets to collaborate on projects in real time or instantly take an online visit to a distant place where a historical event occurred. Technology also allows kids to receive instant feedback on their work, helping them to correct mistakes and deepen their understanding on the spot. This is the promise of educational technology—a promise that, when fulfilled, can make learning more accessible, inclusive, and effective.

Key Chapter 13 Strategies

1. Monitor comprehension by asking questions, visualizing, inferring, predicting, and synthesizing information from texts.
2. Use a "Have-Need-Want" graphic organizer to support comprehension before, during, and after reading.
3. Break down texts into manageable chunks and guide students through each part with questions and discussions.
4. Engage students in summarizing text sections in their own words to confirm understanding.
5. Encourage students to make connections between the text and their own experiences or prior knowledge.
6. Promote active reading by having students note important information and questions as they read.
7. Use collaborative reading strategies such as partner or group discussions to deepen comprehension.
8. Incorporate visual aids, like charts or diagrams, to help students organize and recall information.
9. Guide students in determining the importance of information to focus on key ideas.
10. Facilitate synthesis by helping students integrate ideas across texts and form conclusions.
11. Encourage prediction about upcoming content to maintain engagement and purpose.

Memory Device for this Chapter
Chunking Mnemonic

ChatGPT Capabilities Chunked into Three Categories

Planning:

Develop Lesson Plans, IEPs, and Homework

Assessment:

Create Quizzes, Assess Essays with a ChatGPT-Created Rubric, and Develop Writing Commentary

Multimedia:

Develop Slide Shows, Interactive Simulations, and Text Compacting

CHATGPT TIME-SAVERS

ChatGPT can streamline planning when you're developing unit outlines, lesson plans, slide shows, and discussion questions, significantly reducing the time spent on these tasks. Its ability to generate ideas and resources in seconds enables teachers to focus more on tailoring materials to their students' unique needs and fostering engaging, personalized instruction.

1. PASSAGE QUESTIONS
ChatGPT can create questions for any text and provide an answer key. It also can create homework writing prompts (DelSignore, n.d.).

2. DISCUSSION PROMPTS
Use ChatGPT to write engaging and open-ended prompts for whole class discussion on any topic.

3. IEP GOALS
"Input information about the student's abilities and ChatGPT will generate specific measurable goals for the student to work towards" (Erintegration, 2023).

4. QUIZZES
Align all your quiz questions on a topic or reading with the Common Core State Standards.

5. LESSON PLANS
Teachers can ask Chat GPT to write the first draft of a lesson plan. It will even create a PBL lesson.

6. SLIDE SHOWS
Chat GPT can outline a slide show for a text or topic. Then you supply the visuals.

7. DIFFERENTIATION
Chat GPT can create chapter summaries for kids that need it. It can also act as a text compactor.

CLASSROOM YOUTUBE TIPS

Using YouTube isn't just for cat videos and conspiracy theories—it's one of the best tools teachers have for making lessons more engaging, relevant, and accessible.

1. ESTABLISH A CLASSROOM VIBE
Set a calming classroom mood with seven hours of drone footage: https://www.youtube.com/watch?v=lM02vNMRRB0 (Nature Relaxation Films, 2019).

2. TEACH KIDS HOW TO STUDY
Jim Kwik's "Limitless: Upgrade Your Brain, Learn Anything Faster, and Unlock Your Exceptional Life" explains how to study and remember more (Kwik, 2023).

3. BLOW MINDS
Cue up "27 Minutes of Incredible Facts" on YouTube (https://www.youtube.com/watch?v=n1Z8lqQDywY) and guide your students on an exhilarating ride through the cosmos with Professor Brian Cox as their pilot (Science Time, 2022).

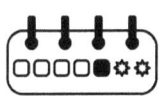
4. INSPIRATION FRIDAY
Show "Who Do You Want to Be?" (https://www.youtube.com/watch?v=R7iN71uJcG0) or "Don't Waste Time" (https://www.youtube.com/watch?v=GKf-xcnEJVo).

5. TEACH TALK SKILLS
Have students watch the YouTube video of social science expert Vanessa Van Edwards (2025) discussing "The #1 Trick to Be More Interesting in Any Conversation" (http://www.youtube.com/watch?v=DLxYiSym1c0).

6. EXPLAIN CONCEPTS AND SKILLS
Watch Khan Academy's "Adding & Subtracting Fractions" (https://www.youtube.com/watch?v=52ZlXsFJULI) "The Fabric of Space Time" by OROS (http://www.youtube.com/watch?v=v-sapLiDSnQ), and how Bob Ross paints "Island in the Wilderness" (http://www.youtube.com/watch?v=ILWEXRAnQd0). Also, check out The Education Channel (https://www.uctv.tv/education/).

WHAT CAN YOU DO WITH GOOGLE DOCS?

"Platforms like Google Docs are integral to coursework, helping students stay updated with assignments, access resources, and submit work efficiently. This fosters a more organized and productive academic environment" (Kim, 2024). The collaborative features of such platforms enable seamless peer interactions and real-time feedback, further enriching the learning experience.

1. INSTA-OPEN A BLANK NEW DOC
Type "doc.new" in the URL box and watch what happens.

2. TAG COLLABORATORS
When adding a comment, type "+" and then begin to type your collaborator's name. A popup will allow you to select the name from your Gmail contacts and will automatically notify your collaborator via email.

3. INSERT A TABLE OF CONTENTS
Just click "insert" and find "table of contents" at the bottom of the menu.

4. TYPE WITHOUT FINGERS
Find "Tools" on the Google Docs menu and select "voice typing." Then speak into the microphone and watch your words appear on the screen.

5. SHARE FOLDERS
Allow an entire class or only specific individuals to access everything in an online folder. In Google Drive, find the folder you wish to share. Right-click on it and then select "share." Control whether students can view, edit, and comment on files in the folder.

6. OFFER REAL-TIME FEEDBACK
While students are composing essay drafts in Google Docs, pop in and provide real-time feedback. Just click "insert" and then "comment."

USING SOCIAL MEDIA FOR EDUCATION

"Twitter [X] is a great way to add context to content, especially when students need to study a topic and find experts in the field to ask questions" (KQED, n.d.). By leveraging social media's real-time updates and hashtag communities, students can also track the latest trends, debates, and discoveries in their field of study.

1. TALK TO WRITERS
Follow local journalists and popular authors in children's and YA literature.

2. LIVE TWEET SPECIAL EVENTS . . .
. . . like field trips, class celebrations, awards ceremonies, and sporting events" (Finalsite, 2024).

3. PROFESSIONAL DEVELOPMENT
Connect with other educators. Follow "#" interest areas (Carpenter & Krutka, 2015).

4. ASK A PROFESSOR
Learners can directly ask experts questions.

5. SOCIAL MEDIA MOTIVATION
Check out:

- By Mari Andrew—https://www.instagram.com/bymariandrew/
- Chris Burth—https://www.instagram.com/chrisburth_/
- Daniel Pink—https://www.instagram.com/danielpink/
- Edutopia—https://www.instagram.com/edutopia
- Forged Over 40—https://www.instagram.com/forged_over_40/
- Meditation and Mindfulness—https://www.instagram.com/meditation_and_mindfulness/
- Natural Wonders—https://www.instagram.com/naturalwonders/
- Pop Sci—https://www.instagram.com/popsci/
- The Met—https://www.instagram.com/metmuseum/
- We Rate Dogs—https://www.instagram.com/weratedogs/

IMPROVE REMOTE INSTRUCTION

"[R]esearchers found that 18% of parents pointed to greater flexibility in a child's schedule [. . .] related to remote learning" (Daniela et al., 2021). This provides opportunities for extracurricular enrichment and self-paced mastery of subjects.

1. CHUNK LESSONS

Think in terms of 10-minute lesson increments. Long lectures [. . .] are even more ineffective online (Vai, n.d.).

2. ADD NOVELTY AND ENGAGEMENT

Make room for surprises. Incorporate funny visuals, short videos, timed challenges, and opportunities for kids to disclose information. Example: "Share a goofy photo of your pet on the discussion forum."

3. TRY TO AVOID . . .

- Spotty communication
- Not considering accessibility
- Inconsistent navigation
- Slow feedback

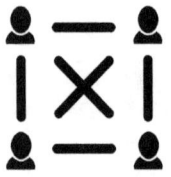

4. USE MULTIPLE CHANNELS

"Instead of simply posting info only in the announcements area, or only in the feedback area, or sending it only via email, include the information in all three of these places" (Sull, 2013).

5. INTEGRATE 3 TYPES OF INTERACTIONS

- Learner-content interaction
- Learner-instructor interaction
- Learner-learner interaction

6. BE FLEXIBLE AND ADAPTABLE

Be prepared to adjust your plans based on student feedback and any technical challenges that arise. Flexibility is key to successful remote instruction.

TEACHER PRESENCE DURING REMOTE INSTRUCTION

"[T]eacher presence is engaging students as much as the subjects" (Bouvier, 2024). This highlights the importance of relational teaching, where the teacher's enthusiasm, empathy, and ability to connect with students warms hearts.

1. SWEAT IMAGES
Use images and animated gifs from Unsplash that inspire you.

2. USE HUMOR IF . . .
. . . you're naturally funny. But sarcasm doesn't translate well online.

3. EXPLAIN WHY . . .
. . . assignments can help grow knowledge and skills.

4. PERSONALIZE CONTENT
Tell a story (using text, audio, or video) that relates to the course topics. Bonus points if the story involves previous students.

5. DON'T OZ
Let students see what your life looks like behind the professional curtain. Post a pet or family photo. Share what book is on your nightstand. Describe what you recently learned about your discipline.

6. PRESENT HIGHLIGHTS
At the end of the week, share which peer made an insightful comment on the discussion forum or asked a great question.

7. USE MULTIPLE CHANNELS
Engage students through various communication channels like emails, discussion boards, and video calls to ensure everyone stays connected.

HYPERDOC TEMPLATES

"HyperDocs streamline both the planning and delivery of lessons by consolidating all resources and activities into one document" (Powis, 2024). Beyond efficiency, they allow students to complete tasks at their own pace within a cohesive and user-friendly framework.

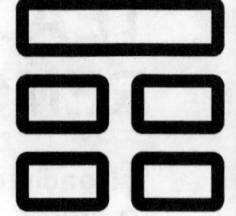

1. BASIC LESSON PLAN
This model sequences activities into cognitive steps: explore, explain, apply, share, and reflect. Link: https://bit.ly/bb_Hyper1 (The HyperDocHandbook, n.d.).

2. MENU OF ACTIVITES
This model incorporates visually engaging activities. To differentiate the activities, students choose their own adventure. Link https://bit.ly/bb_Hyper2 (Mr. Mac's Feedback Form, n.d.).

3. CLOSE READING
Kids retell the main points of a reading, provide text evidence to justify their interpretations, and share their thinking about the text. Link: https://bit.ly/bb_Hyper5 (Justus, n.d.).

4. COMPARE VIEWPOINTS
Create a re-usable Hyperdoc template that scaffolds comparison so that students investigate a topic or text from at least two different viewpoints. Link: https://bit.ly/bb_Hyper2 (Mr. Mac's Feedback Form, n.d.).

5. CHOOSE A PROJECT
Using Google Slides, kids read an essential question, then choose from three options: travel poster and guide, journal, or newspaper. Link: https://bit.ly/bb_Hyper4 (Logue, n.d.).

6. COMPREHENSION
This is more of a general guide then a HyperDoc, but can be used with assigned texts to grow readers. Steps: monitor comprehension, visualize, infer, predict, ask questions, determine importance, and synthesize. Link: http://bit.ly/bb_Hyper7 (Venezia, n.d.).

Workbook: Reflecting on Chapter 13 Topics

1. How does using check marks to identify errors in student essays help students take ownership of their learning and improvement?

2. In what ways does group work reduce the grading workload for teachers while enhancing student collaboration?

3. What are the benefits and challenges of implementing peer grading in your classroom?

4. How can the strategy of not grading everything, such as using participation points for homework, impact student motivation and learning outcomes?

5. How does showing exemplars of successful work help reduce the need for extensive constructive feedback?

6. What are the advantages of marking error patterns rather than individual errors in student work?

7. Would setting a timer for grading each paper increase grading efficiency and consistency?

8. How do formative assessments, such as collecting early drafts, help catch and address issues before final submission?

9. How can using self-assessment using rubrics empower students to identify and correct their own errors before submitting their work?

Going Deeper—Advanced Questions

1. How does the integration of technology in grading and feedback processes influence the teacher-student dynamic and the perception of feedback's value?

2. Critically assess the effectiveness of group conferences in addressing common student errors. How do these conferences compare to one-on-one feedback sessions in terms of efficiency, depth of understanding, and student engagement?

3. Discuss the balance between peer support and individual accountability.

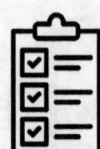

Checklist of Activities and Strategies to Try (Pick 2)

- ❑ Use ChatGPT to generate passage questions and answer keys for any text.
- ❑ Ask ChatGPT to draft a lesson plan, including project-based learning activities.
- ❑ Set a classroom vibe with ambient videos, such as drone footage or a cozy fireplace scene.
- ❑ Use YouTube to explain challenging concepts.
- ❑ Use Google Docs' voice typing tool—speak into the microphone and watch your words appear.
- ❑ Have students live-tweet special events like field trips, class celebrations, or awards ceremonies.
- ❑ Chunk online lessons into ten-minute segments for better engagement.
- ❑ Communicate important information using multiple channels—announcements, email, and feedback areas.
- ❑ Spotlight insightful student contributions at the end of each week.
- ❑ Use the "Menu of Activities" HyperDoc, where students choose their own adventure with visually engaging options.
- ❑ Other: _____.

Describe Your Progress

1. What activities were most successful?

2. What challenges did you face?

3. How can you improve for next time?

 **References for Chapter 13**

Bouvier, A. (2024). The role of teacher presence in student engagement. *Journal of Online Learning*, 18(2), 45–59.

Carpenter, J. P., & Krutka, D. G. (2015). How and why educators use Twitter: A survey of the field. *Journal of Research on Technology in Education*, 46(4), 415–38. https://www.researchgate.net/publication/264785433_How_and_Why_Educators_Use_Twitter_A_Survey_of_the_Field

Daniela, L., Rubene, Z., & Rūdolfa, A. (2021). Parents' perspectives on remote learning in the pandemic context. *Sustainability*, 13(7), 3640. https://doi.org/10.3390/su13073640

DelSignore, P. (n.d.). How to use ChatGPT to create AI art prompts. Medium. https://medium.com/@pdelsignore/how-to-use-chatgpt-to-create-ai-art-prompts-7a63e402814d

Erintegration. (2023, January 18). ChatGPT in the classroom: 10 timesaving tips for elementary teachers. https://www.erintegration.com/2023/01/18/chatgpt-in-the-classroom-10-timesaving-tips-for-elementary-teachers/

Finalsite. (2024, October 28). Creating your school's social media plan: A 10 step guide. Finalsite Blog. https://www.finalsite.com/blog/p/~board/b/post/school-social-media-plan-10-step-guide

Justus, R. (n.d.). Hyperdoc: Digital close reading https://bit.ly/bb_Hyper5

Khan Academy. (n.d.). Adding and subtracting fractions [Video]. YouTube. https://www.youtube.com/watch?v=52ZIXsFJULI

Kim, K. (2024, April 10). Getting started with Google Classroom. Azusa Pacific University, IT Support Center. https://support.apu.edu/kb/article/300-getting-started-with-google-classroom/

KQED. (n.d.). Guide to using Twitter in your teaching practice. KQED Education. https://www.kqed.org/education/how-to-use-twitter-in-your-teaching-practice

Kwik, J. (2023). *Limitless: Upgrade your brain, learn anything faster, and unlock your exceptional life* (Expanded edition). Hay House Inc.

Logue, J. (n.d.). West Africa project. https://bit.ly/bb_Hyper4

Motivation2Study. (2017, August 14). WHO DO YOU WANT TO BE? Best Motivational Video for Students & Success in Life [Video]. YouTube. http://www.youtube.com/watch?v=R7iN71uJcG0

Motiversity. (2023, August 15). DON'T WASTE YOUR TIME Powerful Motivational Speech. Grant Cardone [Video]. YouTube. http://www.youtube.com/watch?v=GKf-xcnEJVo

Mr. Mac. (n.d.). Menu activity. https://bit.ly/bb_Hyper2

Mr. Mac's Feedback Form. (n.d.). Choose your own adventure activities. https://bit.ly/bb_Hyper

Nature Relaxation Films. (2019, January 1). 7 HOUR 4K DRONE FILM: "Earth from Above" + Music by Nature Relaxation™ (Ambient AppleTV Style) [Video]. YouTube. https://www.youtube.com/watch?v=lM02vNMRRB0

OROS. (2020, August 3). The Fabric of Space Time [Video]. YouTube. http://www.youtube.com/watch?v=v-sapLiDSnQ

Powis, S. (2024). Streamlining lesson planning with HyperDocs. *Educational Technology Journal*, 12(1), 22–30.

Ross, Bob. (2016, November 28). Bob Ross—Island in the Wilderness (Season 29 Episode 1) [Video]. YouTube. http://www.youtube.com/watch?v=ILWEXRAnQd0

Science Time. (2022, April 27). 27 minutes of incredible science facts with Professor Brian Cox [Video]. YouTube. https://www.youtube.com/watch?v=n1Z8lqQDywY

Sull, E. C. (2013, October 1). Teaching online with Errol: Communicating with students in the online classroom: The joy of technology. The Teaching Professor. https://www.teachingprofessor.com/topics/online-teaching-and-learning/teaching-strategies-techniques/teaching_online_with_errol_communicating_with_students_in_the_online/

The Education Channel. (n.d.). UCTV, University of California Television. https://www.uctv.tv/education/

The HyperDoc Handbook. (n.d.). Basic lesson plan model. https://bit.ly/bb_Hyper1

Vai, M. (n.d.). Effective online strategies to improve your online teaching. Retrieved from https://www.facultyfocus.com/articles/online-education/effective-online-strategies-to-improve-your-online-teaching/

Van Edwards, Vanessa. (2025, April 15). The #1 Trick to Be More Interesting in Any Conversation [Video]. YouTube. http://www.youtube.com/watch?v=DLxYiSym1c0

Venezia, S. (n.d.). Reading comprehension strategies: How will I grow as a reader today? http://bit.ly/bb_Hyper7

Chapter 14

Motivating Students

Motivating Students

Motivation in education makes the difference between perfunctory performance and passionate pursuit of knowledge. As research demonstrates, fostering a motivated classroom environment increases engagement (Parrish, 2022) and academic success (University of Cambridge, 2024). It's about students leaning forward toward you and the curriculum.

So how do you motivate children? What resonates with kids includes praise and recognition, choice and autonomy, a relevant and authentic curriculum, and strong relationships with teachers and peers. All of these actions involve care. In a review of student engagement and dropout patterns, it was found that students often felt neglected or consciously ignored by their schools. This lack of support led many to feel that their teachers did not care about their academic struggles or personal well-being. One of the researchers noted, "The majority are lower income, not necessarily living in poverty, but come from struggling families. Many are kids of color. But the most common through line is having some kind of learning challenge that doesn't get addressed and the student feels academically abandoned" (NEA, 2024).

Techniques for motivation are often missing from research; this chapter is designed to remedy that. After all, as Beth Pandolpho (2018) writes, "Regardless of how busy we are, we cannot underestimate the importance of cultivating a classroom culture in which students feel valued and respected because if our students aren't learning, the other tasks are meaningless."

Key Chapter 14 Strategies

1. Vary activities to avoid passive information reception for too long.
2. Gamify learning with competition, scorecards, and adapting games like Jeopardy to teach content.
3. Give process instructions to challenge students to work more carefully, quickly, and deliberately.
4. Make learning authentic through Project-Based Learning (PBL) to solve real problems.
5. Make class fun by incorporating humor, which enhances motivation and retention.
6. Notice students' emotions and show you care by acknowledging their feelings.
7. Activate flashbulb memory with surprising content or humorous videos to aid retention.
8. Make life connections by explaining how lessons are useful in students' lives.
9. Identify commonalities between teachers and students to help bridge achievement gaps.
10. Avoid over-praising to prevent damaging self-esteem and disengagement.
11. Use the picture superiority effect to combine text with relevant images for better recall.
12. Engage in culturally responsive teaching by connecting curriculum to diverse experiences.
13. Create dopamine triggers through music, novelty, gratitude, and achieving goals.
14. Leverage social proof by showcasing former students' success and using data walls.
15. Build strong teacher-student relationships by listening, showing enthusiasm, and sharing good news with each class.

Memory Device for this Chapter
Chunking Mnemonic

Grouping Strategies into Categories

Engagement Techniques:
Vary Activities, Gamify Learning, Integrate Humor, and Make Class Fun

Personal Connection:
Notice Students, Acknowledge Emotions, and Foster Belonging

Academic Support:
Authentic Learning, Activate "Flashbulb" Memory, and Provide Second Chances

HOW TO MOTIVATE ME

"Constructs such as self-efficacy, self-determination, and self-regulation are central to motivated action" (Dweck, 2003). They foster resilience and adaptability in the face of challenges.

1. VARY ACTIVITIES
Don't make me passively receive information for too long.

2. GAMIFY LEARNING
Set up competition with a score card. Play beat-the-clock. Adapt old games like Jeopardy to teach content.

3. GIVE PROCESS INSTRUCTIONS
Challenge me to work more carefully, more quickly, and more deliberately.

4. CELEBRATE
Cheer me on for making progress. Recognize mastery. Timely feedback is critical (Amabile, 1988).

5. MAKE LEARNING AUTHENTIC
Use problem-based learning so I can research, solve problems, and create things I believe are significant.

6. MAKE CLASS FUN
Find ways to make me laugh. Dopamine is motivating and improves retention.

7. NOTICE ME
If I look happy or sad, say something that shows you notice me and care.

8. I CRAVE BELONGING
Don't let other kids make fun of each other. Use class rituals and slogans. Please explain why the class matters and why I matter.

RESEARCH ON STUDENT ENGAGEMENT

"Student engagement is a complex construct that involves behavioral, emotional, and cognitive dimensions" (Fredricks et al., 2021). Addressing these sustains curiosity and fosters deeper academic achievement.

1. LISTEN, BE ENTHUSIASTIC
Urban youth of color are more engaged when they perceive teachers to be authentically and enthusiastically leading their learning, and when they feel heard.

2. ACTIVATE FLASHBULB MEMORY
To activate "flashbulb memory," surprise kids before or after introducing content you want them to remember. Jokes and YouTube videos will do the trick (Go.Nature, n.d.).

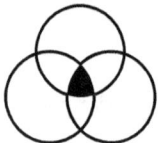

3. I.D. WHAT YOU HAVE IN COMMON
White teachers who discuss what they have in common with their Black learners helped close the achievement gap (Gehlbach et al., 2016).

4. DON'T OVER-PRAISE
"Praise-bombing struggling Black learners for mediocre essays damages their self-esteem and may speed up academic disengagement." Feedback that is specific, critical, and articulates belief in students' abilities elevates writing performance (Yeager & Dweck, 2012).

5. MAKE A LIFE CONNECTION
Motivation and academic achievement were enhanced when students wrote about why the science lesson was useful in their lives (O'Keefe & Linnenbrink-Garcia, 2014).

6. USE PICTURE SUPERIORITY EFFECT
"When we read text alone, we are likely to remember only 10% of the information three days later. If that information is presented to us as text combined with a relevant image, we are likely to remember 65% of the information 3 days later" (Medina, 2008).

TEACHER-STUDENT RELATIONSHIP BUILDING

"Positive teacher-student relationships during adolescence are linked to higher levels of school engagement" (Roorda et al., 2017). Trust and support are a learning super vitamin.

1. SAY THIS
"I'm fallible. If you feel like I'm not hearing you or misunderstanding something, please tell me."

2. SMILE
Adolescents' brains tend to read adults' neutral expressions as angry expressions (Siegel, 2013).

3. SECOND CHANCES
When kids make decisions that don't work out, debrief, then let them try again.

4. CULTURALLY RESPONSIVE TEACHING
Link curriculum to students' diverse experiences and showcase multiple cultures.

5. RED FLAG
Hand every kid a red flag to use once a semester. If it's waived, they get the floor and everyone's undivided attention (Collins, 2001).

6. ASK . . .
. . . about kids' opinions. But don't respond with your own judgment/opinion, unless asked.

7. KNOW YOUR KIDS
Know what they love and what they worry about.

8. SHARE GOOD NEWS EACH CLASS
Share the number of days until Halloween, the cool thing they'll learn this week, the fact that so many kids are making strong grades, that there's a pep assembly tomorrow, that you'll tell your favorite story at the end of class . . . etc.

TRIGGER STUDENTS' HAPPY BRAIN CHEMICALS

"Our recent research has shown that firing of dopamine neurons acts as the brain's teaching signal" (Lee et al., 2024). Dopamine helps the brain adapt and optimize decision-making based on past experiences.

1. DOPAMINE

How It Feels: Blissful, with enhanced motivation and concentration. The feeling is addictive.

How It's Triggered:
- Music
- Meditation
- Novelty
- Gratitude
- Exercise
- Sunlight
- Eating protein and probiotics
- Adequate sleep
- Achieving goals

2. ENDORPHINS

How They Feel: Like morphine. They reduce pain and stress; they can also trigger euphoria.

How They're Triggered:
- Laughter
- Exercise

3. OXYTOCIN

How It Feels: Elevated mood and fuzzy feelings of contentment. Lowered stress and anxiety. Increased trust and bonding with others.

How It's Triggered:
- Hugs
- Yoga and meditation
- Music
- Sharing appreciation
- Time with friends
- Bonding over novel experiences

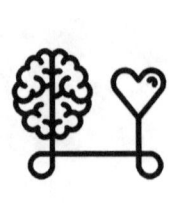

LEVERAGE SOCIAL PROOF TO MOTIVATE STUDENTS

"When we are uncertain, we are willing to place an enormous amount of trust in the collective knowledge of the crowd" (UNESCO, 2024). This reliance on collective wisdom highlights the power of social proof in decision-making, demonstrating how shared experiences and insights can alleviate doubt and guide our choices.

Social Proof is a psychological phenomenon in which the behavior of others influences people.

1. AVOID NEGATIVE SOCIAL PROOF
Never talk about the bad behavior of previous classes. That only promotes those behaviors. Also, explain what kids should do rather than giving them a list of things not to do.

2. SHOW FORMER STUDENT EXEMPLARS
Invite former students who benefited from your class or content area to visit your classroom and participate in a Q and A.

3. CREATE A CLASS SIZZLE REEL
During the first week of class, show students a fast-paced video that includes clips of student interviews, photos of previous students, student-created mind maps, and quotations about the content—all set to the theme song to *Mission Impossible*.

4. USE DATA WALLS
Display anonymized data showing class progress on certain goals or standards. Seeing collective improvement can motivate students to continue their efforts.

5. POST TESTIMONIAL POSTERS
At the end of the semester, ask students to provide positive blurbs about your class along with their photos. Post them for next year's students.

CLASSROOM REWARDS!

"There is a literature on whether classroom reward systems work. By 'work,' we mean whether they achieve the goal of better classroom or schoolwide behavior. The answer is, basically, yes" (Murphy et al., 2020). However, their effectiveness often depends on how rewards are implemented, with an emphasis on fostering intrinsic motivation.

1. VIP Chair
2. Sit at the Teacher's Desk
3. Extra Computer Time
4. Earbud Pass
5. "Awesome" Silicone Wristband
6. Gum Pass
7. Photo in the Class Newsletter
8. Phone Call Home
9. Announcements Reader
10. Hero Hoodie
11. Team Captain
12. Name Chalked on Sidewalk
13. Tell a Clean Joke
14. Class Assistant
15. Spin the Reward Wheel
16. Game Host for Review Game
17. Sit with Learning Buddy (Intervention Central, n.d.)
18. Decorate Ceiling Tile (PBIS, n.d.)
19. Uniform Pass for Casual Dress
20. Art Supplies (Clay)
21. Homework Pass
22. Admission to School Event
23. "#Hero" Screensaver
24. Student of the Week
25. Stickers
26. Fidget Toy Time
27. Assignment Extension
28. Smart Phone Pass
29. Temporary Tattoos

WAYS TO SAY, "GOOD JOB!"

"[S]pecific and sincere praise can improve classroom behavior and student engagement" (Royer & Ennis, 2024). When delivered consistently, such praise not only reinforces positive behaviors but also cultivates a sense of belonging and confidence.

- Wow!
- Oh!
- Yes!
- Cool!
- Yay!
- Yeah!
- Super!
- Oooh!
- Strong!
- Respect!
- Sweet!
- Beautiful!
- Caramba!
- Inspiring!
- Stylin'!
- Fierce!
- Bold!
- Holy!
- Aces!
- Powerful!
- Sensational!
- Dazzling!
- Amazement!
- Swaggerific!
- Crackerjack!
- Wonderment!
- Sensational!
- Stand up!
- All you!
- 100 Percent!
- Oh yeah!
- Don't stop!
- You were born for this!
- Tell me how you did that.
- That's what hard work looks like.
- Once again, you're dialed to a 103.
- From the outside, you see a placid face. On the inside, I'm jumping up and down for you!
- Raise your hand . . . Say "I did that."
- Way to sweat excellence.
- You are in it to win it!
- How does working like that make you feel?
- Your effort's on like lip balm.
- Tell your mom about today!
- On the inside, I'm jumping up and down for you!
- You are your own unfair advantage!
- I'm starting to believe in unicorns and calorie-free peanut butter.
- Did you spritz with a little extra Chuck Norris/Captain Marvel/Shuri this morning?
- I appreciate you.
- I'm never-ever forgetting that.
- For you, steak dinner and cocoa pie.
- I'll remember that one.
- Super cool.
- Up high!
- Mic drop!
- Love it!
- You're extraordinary.
- Inform NASA.

GIVE ACTIVITIES ENGAGING NAMES

"Engaged students do not just absorb content, they try to make meaning of what they study. Engaged learners care about the subject, feel motivated or excited to learn, and take ownership of their learning" (Headleand, 2024). Creating fun names signals students that you're invested in their engagement.

1. ACTIVATE THE "CURIOSITY GAP"
Pique students' curiosity by creating a gap between what students know and don't know. This Buzzfeed title generator shows how: https://perchance.org/buzzfeedtitlegenerator

2. COPY WINSTON CHURCHILL
Intermix contrasting emotional words.

3. USE NUMBERS AND STATISTICS
Titles with numbers, like "7 Ways to Improve Your Writing," attract attention and promise clear takeaways.

4. MAKE IT PERSONAL
Titles that address the reader directly, such as "How You Can Master Grammar," create a personal connection.

5. USE STRONG VERBS
Action-oriented titles with strong verbs, like "Transform Your Essays," suggest dynamic and impactful content.

6. KEEP IT SHORT AND SWEET
Concise titles are easier to read and remember. Aim for brevity without sacrificing clarity or intrigue.

PERSONALITY CHARACTERISTICS OF MOST LIKED TEACHERS

"When children like us, they will do anything to please us. They work harder, they become more readily inspired and they develop their own aspirations" (Alcott, 2017). This dynamic illustrates the profound impact of emotional connection in education.

1. EXTROVERSION
They are talkative. They are energetic.

2. AGREEABLENESS
They are merciful. They are forgiving.

3. AMICABILITY
They are lovable.

4. EMOTIONAL STABILITY
They treat students fairly. They are reliable.

5. CONSCIENTIOUSNESS
They care about their lessons and are well disciplined.

6. OPENNESS TO EXPERIENCE
They are open to new ideas and situations.

7. ADDITIONAL TRAITS
- **EMPATHY**: Understanding and sharing the feelings of students.
- **CREATIVITY**: Bringing innovative ideas and approaches to the classroom.
- **RESPECTFULNESS**: Treating all students with respect and fairness.
- **PATIENCE**: Demonstrating patience, especially when students struggle to understand concepts.

MAKE STUDENTS FEEL HEARD

"Teachers can play an important role by building intentional and meaningful connections with their students that make them feel seen, heard and safe" (Li, 2024). Educators, through these relationships, can inspire learners to be world changers!

1. GET FEEDBACK
Regularly solicit kids' feelings about your instruction and schoolwork.

2. DON'T INTERRUPT
Listen . . . Teachers say a lot by not talking.

3. NOTE THINGS YOU HAVE IN COMMON
Say, "I get upset by that too," or "That's exactly how I see it."

4. ENJOY LISTENING
Relish having a warm interaction.

5. EMPOWER THEM
Give kids a chance to work with adults to address problems in the classroom.

6. CHECK PERCEPTIONS
"Say that again, please, to ensure that I understand you."

7. RELAX YOUR BODY
"A relaxed stance communicates that you are calm and models the behavior you are wanting from the student" (Apperson Team, 2019).

8. ACKNOWLEDGE COMPETENCE
Students need to be appreciated for what they can do—including emotional and academic skills—especially when they are struggling.

WHY LESSONS FAIL

"Teachers should view failed lessons as opportunities for growth and learning. Reflecting on what didn't work provides invaluable insights that can guide future instructional strategies" (Narciss & Alemdag, 2024). Reframing setbacks as invaluable learning experiences helps students realize that every stumble is a stepping stone toward deeper understanding and creative problem-solving.

1. UNCLEAR CONTENT OR PROCEDURES
Try checking for understanding and modeling. Be ready to bail on the lesson, make adjustments, and try again tomorrow.

2. UNEXPECTED INTERRUPTIONS
Surprise assembly? Match the novelty of the occasion with a special lesson: debate, visual representation, or dramatization.

3. NOT ENGAGING
Use a hook. Tell a story. Display a real-world image, and have kids solve real-world problems.

4. PACING
Do you need to slow the lesson down?

5. TOO HARD OR TOO EASY
Too hard? Make your teaching simpler, narrow the focus, or take a break. Too easy? Challenge kids to complete the assignment faster.

6. SOME TIPS

- **Frequent Check-Ins**: Regularly check in with students to ensure they are following along and engaged.
- **Adapt to Learning Styles**: Incorporate various teaching methods to cater to different learning styles.
- **Incorporate Student Feedback**: Ask for feedback on lessons and adjust future ones accordingly.
- **Set Clear Objectives**: Clearly outline the lesson's objectives and how they will be achieved.

Workbook: Reflecting on Chapter 14 Topics

1. Provide an example of a game-based learning activity that you found particularly engaging.
2. Describe a project-based learning (PBL) activity your learners participated in. How did it help them understand the subject better?
3. How does humor in the classroom affect kids' learning and retention of information?
4. Why is it important for teachers to notice students' emotions?
5. How do class rituals and slogans contribute to a sense of belonging? Share an example of a ritual or slogan from your class that makes children feel included.
6. Can you recall a specific instance where combining images with text was effective?
7. Why is it important for teachers to acknowledge common interests and cultural backgrounds? How does this help bridge achievement gaps?
8. How does providing second chances and the opportunity to learn from mistakes affect kids' willingness to take risks and try again?

Going Deeper—Advanced Questions

1. In what ways can project-based learning (PBL) be optimized to simultaneously address content objectives, students' interests, and cognitive development?
2. How can varying pedagogical strategies be tailored to optimize neurochemical triggers for enhanced student motivation and learning outcomes?
3. How can teachers promote resilience and high academic standards without damaging self-esteem?

 ## Checklist of Activities and Strategies to Try (Pick 2)

- ☐ Introduce games such as Jeopardy or beat-the-clock to make learning competitive and fun.
- ☐ Celebrate small achievements with stickers, certificates, or a class leaderboard.
- ☐ Implement project-based learning (PBL) to solve real-world problems and make learning meaningful.
- ☐ Incorporate humor with jokes and funny videos to enhance engagement and retention.
- ☐ Notice and respond to students' emotions with simple acknowledgments.
- ☐ Foster a sense of belonging with class rituals, group activities, and inclusive language.
- ☐ Use surprising content like unexpected facts or funny videos to activate flashbulb memory.
- ☐ Combine text with relevant images to improve memory retention.
- ☐ Allow students to revise work after feedback to promote a growth mindset.
- ☐ Highlight former students' success stories to motivate current students.
- ☐ Show a video at the start of the year highlighting fun moments from past classes to build excitement.
- ☐ Other: _____.

Describe Your Progress

1. What activities were most successful?

2. What challenges did you face?

3. How can you improve for next time?

 **References for Chapter 14**

Alcott, B. (2017). Does teacher encouragement influence students' educational progress? A propensity-score matching analysis. *Research in Higher Education*, 58(7), 773–804. https://doi.org/10.1007/s11162-017-9446-2

Amabile, T. M. (1988). A model of creativity and innovation in organizations. *Research in Organizational Behavior*, 10, 123–67.

Apperson Team. (2019, November 27). Keep calm and teach on: 10 ways to calm an upset student [Blog post]. https://www.apperson.com/classroom-management/keep-calm-and-teach-on-10-ways-to-calm-an-upset-student

Collins, R. (2001). Red flags in classroom management: Strategies for student accountability. *Educational Leadership Review*, 28(1), 22–9. https://www.examplejournal.com/collins2001

Dweck, C. S. (2003). *Self-theories: Their role in motivation, personality, and development*. Psychology Press.

Fredricks, J. A., Blumenfeld, P. C., & Paris, A. H. (2021). *Student engagement: Theory, research, and practice*. Guilford Press.

Gehlbach, H., Brinkworth, M. E., King, A. M., Hsu, L. M., McIntyre, J., & Rogers, T. (2016). Creating birds of similar feathers: Leveraging similarity to improve teacher-student relationships and academic achievement. *Journal of Educational Psychology*, 108(3), 342–52. https://doi.org/10.1037/edu0000042

Go.Nature. (n.d.). Activating flashbulb memory in the classroom. https://www.go.nature.com/flashbulb-memory

Headleand, C. (2024, May 7). What is student engagement? THE Campus. https://www.timeshighereducation.com/campus/what-student-engagement

Intervention Central. (n.d.). Jackpot! Ideas for classroom rewards. https://www.interventioncentral.org/behavioral-interventions/rewards/jackpot-ideas-classroom-rewards

Lee, R. S., Sagiv, Y., Engelhard, B., Witten, I. B., & Daw, N. D. (2024). A feature-specific prediction error model explains dopaminergic heterogeneity. *Nature Neuroscience*, 27(8), 1574–86. https://doi.org/10.1038/s41593-024-01689-1

Li, Y. (2024). The impact of teacher-student relationships on students' mental health. *Lecture Notes in Educational Psychology and Public Media*, 33(1), 30–5. https://doi.org/10.54254/2753-7048/33/20231375

Medina, J. (2008). *Brain rules: 12 principles for surviving and thriving at work, home, and school*. Pear Press.

Murphy, J. M., Hawkins, R. O., & Nabors, L. A. (2020). Combining social skills instruction and the Good Behavior Game to support students with emotional and behavioral disorders. *Contemporary School Psychology*, 24(2), 228–38. https://doi.org/10.1007/s40688-019-00226-3

Narciss, S., & Alemdag, E. (2024). Learning from errors and failure in educational contexts: New insights and future directions for research and practice. *British Journal of Educational Psychology*. Advance online publication. https://doi.org/10.1111/bjep.12716

National Education Association. (2024). Teachers feel academically abandoned: Insights from the 2024 teacher survey. https://www.nea.org/nea-today/all-news-articles/what-new-survey-says-about-teachers-plans-leave-their-jobs

O'Keefe, P., & Linnenbrink-Garcia, L. (2014). The role of interest in optimizing performance and self-regulation. *Journal of Experimental Social Psychology*, 53, 70–8. https://doi.org/10.1016/j.jesp.2014.02.004

Pandolpho, B. (2018, July 12). Strategies to help your students feel heard. Edutopia. https://www.edutopia.org/article/strategies-help-your-students-feel-heard/

Parrish, A. K. (2022, November 17). To increase student engagement, focus on motivation. Edutopia. https://www.edutopia.org/article/to-increase-student-engagement-focus-on-motivation/

Perchance. (n.d.). Buzzfeed title generator. https://perchance.org/buzzfeedtitlegenerator

PBIS Rewards. (n.d.). PBIS incentives: Over 250 ideas. https://www.pbisrewards.com/pbis-incentives/

Roorda, D. L., Jak, S., Zee, M., Oort, F. J., & Koomen, H. M. Y. (2017). Affective teacher-student relationships and students' engagement and achievement: A meta-analytic update. *School Psychology Review*, 46(3), 239–61. https://doi.org/10.17105/SPR-2017-0035.V46-3

Royer, D. J., & Ennis, R. P. (2024). Student-delivered behavior-specific praise: A systematic literature review and meta-analysis. *Frontiers in Education*, 9, Article 1444394. https://doi.org/10.3389/feduc.2024.1444394

Siegel, D. J. (2013). Brainstorm: The power and purpose of the teenage brain. TarcherPerigee.

THE. (2024). Engaged learning: How students make meaning of their studies. THE Journal. https://www.thejournal.com/engaged-learning

UNESCO. (2024). Futures of education initiative: Mobilising collective intelligence for a new social contract. https://en.unesco.org/futuresofeducation/initiative

University of Cambridge. (2024). *Investigation of daily motivation regulation as a multilevel mediator of undergraduate students' intrinsic and extrinsic motivation and academic achievement.* Cambridge University Press.

Yeager, D. S., & Dweck, C. S. (2012). Mindsets that promote resilience: When students believe that personal characteristics can be developed. *Educational Psychologist*, 47(4), 302–14. https://doi.org/10.1080/00461520.2012.722805

Chapter 15

Fostering Emotional Resilience

Fostering Emotional Resilience

Teachers are afforded a unique opportunity to cultivate emotional resilience in their students—a skill that not only supports academic success but also fortifies students against sometimes intimidating challenges that arise daily—for some children more than others. According to Rajendran and Videka (2006), "[R]esilience, in the educational context, is the ability to overcome setbacks and chronic difficulties" (p. 4).

Teachers encourage this disposition by modeling resilience and providing a predictable, nurturing environment. This skill is not innate for all kids; it requires deliberate cultivation by caregivers. What does the emotional life of students have to do with school? When learners feel emotionally supported, they are more likely to engage in class, thus enhancing their overall academic experience.

Make no mistake; trauma touches the lives of many students. Let's do the math. Data from the Centers for Disease Control and Prevention (CDC) suggest that nearly 35% of children have experienced a trauma that could affect their development and behavior (2021). Given a classroom of 30 students, the following calculations can be made: 30×0.35=10.53 times 0.35 = 10.53×0.35=10.5 students. Therefore, in a class of 30 students, approximately 11 students may be experiencing trauma.

Based on the expertise of psychologists and researchers, practical tools and insights regarding how to foster emotional resilience are described in this chapter. You, as a teacher, can impact students' lifelong ability to navigate and thrive in the face of adversity. Think of yourself as an architect of resilience and a bringer of hope.

Key Chapter 15 Strategies

1. Recognize signs of compassion fatigue like anger, cynicism, and chronic exhaustion.
2. Take the Professional Quality of Life Scale Quiz to gauge your risk for compassion fatigue.
3. Instead of thinking you have nothing left to give, tell yourself, "I have the skills and patience to be helpful for the next hour."
4. Establish and maintain healthy boundaries in work and personal life to prevent burnout.
5. Track sleep, maintain a regular bedtime, and turn off electronics 30 minutes before bed.
6. Find reasons to laugh daily, as it lowers blood pressure and cortisol levels.
7. Combine brisk walking with talking to a friend to release endorphins and reduce stress.
8. Practice box-breathing by inhaling, holding, exhaling, and holding for four seconds each to reduce stress.
9. Schedule enjoyable activities for midweek to look forward to.
10. Meditation can increase happiness and decrease stress.
11. Use apps like My Fitness Pal to plan healthy meals and improve focus and productivity.
12. Engage in 30 minutes of exercise daily as recommended by Mayo Clinic.
13. Interrupt negative thinking by saying "Stop," taking a big breath, and focusing on positive experiences.
14. Listen to music that boosts confidence and happiness by triggering dopamine release.
15. Avoid interpreting blank faces as uninterested or angry during presentations.
16. Release nervous energy by jumping and laughing before a presentation.

Memory Device for this Chapter
Acrostics Mnemonics

BALANCE

Boundaries set early
Avoid negativity
Laugh
Active walking and talking
Nurture self-care
Control thoughts
Exercise regularly

THRIVE

Take deep breaths
Handle feelings mindfully
Reflect on positives
Incorporate laughter
Visualize calm scenarios
Engage in meditation

COMPASSION FATIGUE

"The lack of awareness of CF often leads to the development of more serious psychological symptomatology. Consequently, individuals may not present to treatment until symptoms have progressed to cause significant disruption in current functioning" (Barnett & Cooper, 2009). By promoting early education and proactive mental health screenings, practitioners and communities can bridge the gap between initial symptoms and effective treatment.

1. RECOGNIZE SYMPTOMS
- Anger
- Cynicism
- Avoidance
- Anxiousness
- Chronic Exhaustion
- Disconnection
- Fear
- Hopelessness
- Inability to Handle Complexity and Listen
- Guilt
- Loss of Creativity
- Poor Self-Care
- Sleeplessness

2. ASSESS YOUR VULNERABILITY
Take the free Professional Quality of Life Scale Quiz (NovoPsych, 2021).

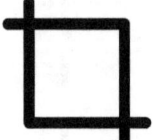

3. DON'T SUPPRESS—RE-FRAME
Don't think you have nothing left to give. Instead say, "I have the skills and patience to be helpful for the next hour."

4. AVOID NEGATIVITY ZONES
Stay away from chronic complainers.

5. SET BOUNDARIES
Learn to set and maintain healthy boundaries in your work and personal life to prevent burnout.

WITHSTAND THAT TOUGH TUESDAY

"[R]esilience is dynamic and multidimensional, and it is possible to cultivate it through the interaction of one's own resources and the resources provided by their environment" (Peixoto et al., 2020). By actively leveraging personal strengths alongside the nurturing support of their communities, individuals are empowered to transform challenges into catalysts for growth.

1. PRACTICE SLEEP HYGIENE
- Track your sleep with a sleep app (like Sleep Cycle).
- Go to bed at the same time (+/- 20 minutes).
- Turn off electronics 30 minutes before bedtime.
- Think of 10 things you are grateful for before closing your eyes.
- Follow the prescribed amount of sleep (7–9 hours).

2. LAUGH
Laughing lowers blood pressure, cortisol, and enhances immune function (Holden, 1993). Find reasons to laugh with friends or in every social encounter. Visit "The Onion," "Pictures of Walls," and "Textastrophe."

3. DON'T SUPPRESS FEELINGS
Suppressing feelings elevates anxiety.

4. TRY BOX-BREATHING
Used by teachers and Navy Seals, box breathing lowers stress and increases focus. Breathe in for four seconds through your nose. Hold for four. Breathe out for four. Hold for four. Repeat. Feel calm wash over you like a summer mist.

5. WALK AND TALK
Brisk walking releases endorphins. So does talking with a friend. Combine both.

6. PLAN A MIDWEEK TREAT
Schedule something you enjoy for Tuesday, like a favorite meal or a quick outing, to look forward to.

SCIENCE-BASED WAYS TO REST AND REFOCUS

"Rest helps teachers recharge, leading to more creativity and patience. A well-rested teacher is better equipped to handle the challenges of the upcoming school year" (Spencer, 2022). By investing in quality rest, teachers not only boost their own creativity and patience but also set a powerful example for self-care.

1. MEDITATE FOR 11 MINUTES
Eleven minutes gives 90% of the results of longer sessions. Benefits: increased happiness, decreased anxiety and stress, and increased ability to regulate emotions.

2. SLEEP HYGIENE
1) Track your sleep with Sleep Cycle; 2) Go to bed at the same time (+/− 20 minutes); 3) Turn off electronics 30 minutes before bedtime; 4) Follow the prescribed amount of sleep: 18–25 = 7–9 hrs; 26–64 = 7–9 hrs; 65+ = 7–8 hours.

3. EXERCISE
The Mayo Clinic recommends 30 minutes per day.

4. EAT MINDFULLY
My Fitness Pal (free app) helps plan healthy meals. Benefits include as much as 66% more productivity, better focus, and stress reduction.

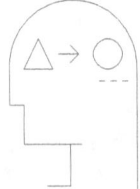
5. MAKE A STATE CHANGE
Stop thinking negatively: 1) say "Stop" and stand up; 2) take a big breath and shake your arms; 3) focus on an elated life experience; 4) praise yourself with a closed fist and say, "Yes!"

6. PRACTICE DEEP BREATHING
Take a few minutes each day to practice deep breathing exercises. This can reduce stress and improve focus.

HOW TO MAINTAIN HEALTHY BOUNDARIES

"Boundaries are the gateway to healthy relationships. Setting limits won't disrupt a healthy relationship; it prioritizes the self-care we need to look after ourselves and others" (Tawwab, 2021). We need to safeguard our well-being.

1. SET BOUNDARIES EARLY
Setting boundaries early in the classroom establishes clear expectations, fosters respect, and prevents misbehavior, creating a structured and positive learning environment.

3. WAYS TO SAY NO
I wish I could, but I've got too much on my plate. I'm sorry, but it's not a good time. I really appreciate that opportunity, but I'll have to pass this time.

4. KEEP THE RADIUS FLEXIBLE
You can set different boundaries depending on the person or situation—your comfort level doesn't have to be the same for everyone. Flexible boundaries allow you to conserve your energy and prioritize self-care.

5. USE POLITICAL DISCUSSION AIKIDO
If someone tries to draw you into a political conversation just to pick a fight, stay calm and say, "We clearly watch different news programs. We're still good with each other . . . right?"

6. SHUT DOWN BLAME
When someone falsely accuses you of something, just say, "That's not the way I see it." This usually ends the discussion.

7. READ THE CONTEXT
Some school cultures are safe for sharing personal information; others are not. It's wise to know the difference.

STAGE FRIGHT

The fear of public speaking ties back to an ancient survival instinct... When facing something frightening, the body instinctively shuts down nonessential functions... Here's a hack to override that evolutionary response while teaching: Picture the students as tiny, harmless bunnies—your prey. Teachers can harness this ancient survival instinct to transform paralyzing fear into a focused, energized state

1. PLAY YOUR PUMP-UP JAM
Research shows that music triggers a release of dopamine to the brain. It boosts confidence and happiness.

2. FOCUS ON THE "FRIENDLY EYEBALLS"
Avoid interpreting blank audience faces as uninterested or angry.

3. REINTERPRET PHYSICAL SYMPTOMS
Try to reinterpret your anxiety as excitement. You care about your performance.

4. CONTROL ADRENALINE
Count chairs or ceiling tiles. Tap your foot. Rhythmic actions keep "adrenaline in check" (NAEYC, 2015).

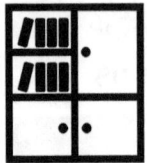
5. USE ANCILLARY MATERIALS
Posters, handouts, advance organizers, or a slide show help to organize your talk and keep the focus on the content, not on your jitters.

6. MOVE AND LAUGH
Release nervous energy by jumping up and down 15 times in the bathroom. It will make you laugh. Pro Tip: Check the stalls first.

7. LOOK FORWARD
Plant playful surprises in the presentation to look forward to: A slide featuring your dog, an energizer, a short video, or a review game.

MINDFULNESS TIPS

"Mindfulness-based training supports teachers in cultivating self- awareness, emotional regulation, unconditional presence, self-compassion, and resilience" (Ergas, 2014). Teachers can model an emotionally intelligent approach to challenges, inspiring students to cultivate these skills.

1. 5-3-1

Meditate 5 minutes a day. Write down 3 good things that happened today. Perform 1 act of kindness (Center for Healthy Minds, U. of Wisconsin-Madison, n.d.).

2. HANDLE THE MONKEY MIND

When the mind wanders during meditation, don't judge. Gently release the thought and direct attention back to your breath.

3. STANDING MEDITATION

Standing meditation builds physical stability, enhances mindfulness, and cultivates inner calm by grounding the body and focusing the mind.

4. POPULAR APP

Insight Timer is the #1 meditation app on Android and iOS stores. It offers 14K free guided meditations: https://insighttimer.com/

5. OPENING AND CALMING SESSION

Dr. Tara Brach, founder of Insight Meditation Community of Wash. D.C., offers dozens of free guided meditations: tarabrach.com. Check out her podcast.

6. BINAURAL BEATS

Check out Leiterland's anthology assignment directions for 30 literary works from 5 categories (poetry, music, movies, novels, and short stories) located here: http://t.ly/4lUY.

7. TRAFFIC LIGHT

Display a mindfulness traffic light poster in your classroom as a visual cue to *pause* and find joy, *observe* and embrace the moment with a smile, and *respond* thoughtfully by contributing your best to the situation at hand.

TRAUMA-INFORMED TEACHING

"Treating the classroom as a 'sanctuary' where students can feel safe, connected, and empowered to learn is crucial. The emotional state of the instructor plays a significant role in this environment" (Imad, 2021). Educators can leverage their positive emotional states to inspire trust and transform every lesson into an opportunity for students to flourish.

1. CONSISTENT AGENDA
Unpredictability is not the friend of traumatized kids.

2. PRIVATE PRAISE
Kids with "low self-concept and social anxiety are particularly uncomfortable with public praise . . . Instead, give a 'thumbs up' or positive note on a sticky note" (Minahan, 2019).

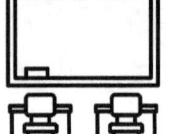

3. CLASSROOM DESIGN
Classes should be organized, not overly stimulating. Use natural light and neutral colors (Hanover Research, 2011).

4. TWO-STEP TRANSITION
Make transitions more "palatable." "Go from recess to two minutes of reading, to the spelling quiz. The intermediary step does more than compliant student behavior momentum. Kids are seated, they are quiet, with body and mind, so the transition isn't as jarring" (Martinelli, n.d.).

5. RECOGNIZE STRENGTHS
To offset negative thinking, point out areas of competence. Example: "You're good at being patient; you could be a coder in the future."

6. AVOID CONFRONTATIONS
Kids with PTSD can respond to adults with defiance when they're agitated. Be careful not to jump to assumption that a child is purposefully testing you.

7. CALM-DOWN STRATEGIES
Show students how to use deep breathing and self-talk.

HOW TO HELP TRAUMATIZED STUDENTS

"Exposure to trauma can impact learning, behavior, and social, emotional, and psychological functioning" (Kuban & Steele, 2011). Integrating trauma-informed strategies into educational settings can foster healing and resilience.

1. CONNECT

Talk to the kids, not at them. You don't have to have all the answers to connect.

2. WATCH FOR SYMPTOMS

Feelings of 1) Intense fear; 2) helplessness, 3) loss of control, and 4) threat of annihilation (Herman, 1992). The amygdala senses danger even when it's not present.

3. BREATHE

Direct kids to inhale deep green and exhale smoky gray. Kids who are angry can imagine exhaling red (Desautels, 2016).

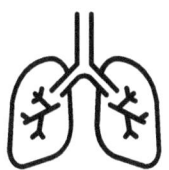

4. STICK TO A ROUTINE

Write the schedule on the board and follow it. Predictability "anchors" students (Bram, 2024).

5. REFLECT

When kids have negative thoughts, suggest self-talk or journaling about feelings. Also, planning actions to address those feelings can be helpful (Center on the Developing Child, Harvard University, 2017).

6. TYPES OF CHILDHOOD TRAUMA

- Physical abuse   Verbal abuse
- Sexual abuse   Physical neglect
- Emotional neglect. Alcoholic parent
- Home violence   Family member in jail or has a mental illness
- Family member left/disappeared

The presence of four of these traits (above) increases depression by 460% and attempted suicide by 1,220% (Washington State Department of Social and Health Services, n.d.).

WAYS TO HELP STRESSED TEENS

"Teaching your teens the tools they need to develop resilience and manage their emotions is life-changing" (Willsey, 2020). Teens need to confidently transform challenges into opportunities for growth, self-discovery, and lasting well-being.

1. TASK SKILLS
Teach students how to make lists and plan how to break big tasks into doable parts.

2. HOW MUCH SLEEP?
Teens need 8–10 hours to regulate hormones (Natural Sleep Foundation, 2023).

3. SIGNS OF EMOTIONAL CRISIS
1. Neglect of personal hygiene.
2. Dramatic change in sleep habits—sleeping more often or not sleeping well.
3. Weight gain or loss.
4. Decline in performance at work or school.
5. Significant changes in mood, such as irritability, anger, anxiety or sadness.
6. Withdrawal from routine activities and relationships (APA, 2013).

4. WHAT TO SAY TO TEENS AFTER AN ACADEMIC MISFIRE
1. This is not your whole story.
2. How you feel at this moment is not how you're going to feel forever.
3. What is your next step (J. Spencer, 2022)?

5. EXERCISE
Regular exercise is an awesome way to lower stress (E. Spencer, 2022).

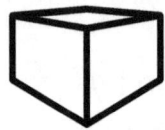

6. KEEP PERSPECTIVE
Help kids keep a proper perspective. They shouldn't inflate the danger, nor underestimate it.

HELPLINES FOR KIDS

"Kids Helpline provides crucial 24/7 support through telephone, webchat, and email, offering children and young people a vital outlet for counseling and information, particularly during challenging times" (Batchelor et al., 2021). Kids Helplines cultivates a foundation of ongoing support and resilience, ensuring that every young person feels valued, understood, and empowered to overcome life's challenges.

1. THURSDAY'S CHILD

Alcoholism, Anorexia, Bulimia, Child Abduction, Child Abuse, Child Exploitation, Cutting, Date Rape, Depression, Drug Abuse, Grief, Runaways, Pregnancy, STDs, Underage Prostitution. Call 1-800-USA-KIDS.

2. RAPE, ABUSE, AND INCEST

24/7 Call 800-656-HOPE (4673). Also, check out http://www.rainn.org.

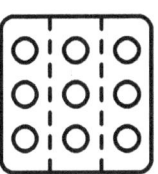

3. PLANNED PARENTHOOD

This organization provides high-quality, affordable health care for women, men, and young people, plus sex education: 24/7 800-230-PLAN (7526).

4. LGBTQIA YOUTH CRISIS HOTLINE

Trevor Lifeline is a 24/7 suicide prevention for LGBTQ youth. Call 1-866-4-U-Trevor.

5. SUICIDE PREVENTION LIFELINE

This line provides free and confidential support for you or your loved ones 24 hours a day, seven days a week. Call 1-800-273-8255.

6. ALATEEN

For kids, 13–18, who have been affected by someone else's drinking. Chat Meetings: http://bit.ly/TB_help.

SOCIAL-EMOTIONAL LEARNING PROMPTS

"Research shows that SEL not only improves achievement by an average of 11 percentile points but also increases prosocial behaviors, improves student attitudes toward school, and reduces depression and stress among students" (Durlak et al., 2011). SEL creates a more inclusive and supportive school environment for all.

1. PURPOSE AND IDENTITY
- Do you feel you were born for a purpose? What is your purpose?
- Is your ethnicity, gender, culture, or hobbies an important part of your identity? How so?

2. SELF-REFLECTION AND PERSONAL GROWTH

- Beautiful with a short life or physically unattractive with a long life . . .? What would you choose and why?
- How has reading changed you?
- What is the difference between your real life and the way you represent yourself on social media?
- What is your unfair advantage in life—the thing you can do better than anyone else?
- If you were braver, what actions would you take to accomplish a secret, big ambition?

3. SOCIAL INTERACTIONS

- What motivates bullying?
- Have you personally experienced or witnessed discrimination? In what form?
- How do we combat discrimination?
- What would your friends say is your best quality?
- Think about your five favorite peers. What qualities do they all have in common?

4. GOALS AND ASPIRATIONS

- What are your biggest physical, emotional, intellectual, and spiritual strengths and weaknesses?
- What are your biggest obstacles to future greatness? How can you overcome them?

Workbook: Reflecting on Chapter 15 Topics

1. What are some early signs of compassion fatigue that educators should be aware of?
2. What strategies can be employed to maintain healthy boundaries?
3. How does maintaining a regular sleep schedule contribute to emotional resilience? How is your sleep hygiene?
4. Discuss the benefits of incorporating mindfulness practices such as box breathing and meditation into a daily routine.
5. How can one effectively steer clear of chronic complainers in the workplace?
6. What types of midweek treats and activities would contribute to overall mental health and resilience?
7. Examine the role of physical exercise in managing stress and enhancing emotional resilience. What types of exercises are most effective?
8. Consider the concept of reframing negative thoughts. How can this practice change one's perspective and improve emotional health?
9. How do ancillary materials like posters and handouts assist in managing stage fright?

Going Deeper—Advanced Questions

1. How can the absence of boundaries affect professional and personal relationships, and what are the psychological implications?
2. How can educators leverage both personal and environmental resources to cultivate resilience in themselves and their students?
3. How can teachers create a trauma-informed classroom that supports all students?
4. How can educators balance the demands of their profession with the need for self-care to prevent burnout and maintain long-term effectiveness?

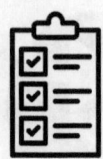

Checklist of Activities and Strategies to Try (Pick 2)

❏ Incorporate humor with jokes and funny videos to enhance engagement and retention.
❏ Notice and respond to students' emotions with simple acknowledgments.
❏ Foster a sense of belonging with class rituals, group activities, and inclusive language.
❏ Combine text with relevant images to improve memory retention.
❏ Allow students to revise work after feedback to promote a growth mindset.
❏ Highlight former students' success stories to motivate current students.
❏ Show a video at the start of the year highlighting fun moments from past classes to build excitement.
❏ Practice sleep hygiene by tracking sleep, maintaining a regular bedtime, and turning off electronics 30 minutes before bed.
❏ Laugh regularly, finding reasons to laugh daily, as it lowers blood pressure and cortisol levels.
❏ Walk and talk, combining brisk walking with talking to a friend to release endorphins and reduce stress.
❏ Try box-breathing by inhaling, holding, exhaling, and holding for four seconds each to reduce stress.
❏ Other: _____.

Describe Your Progress

1. What activities were most successful?

2. What challenges did you face?

3. How can you improve for next time?

 **References for Chapter 15**

American Psychological Association. (2013). How to help in an emotional crisis. https://www.apa.org/topics/mental-health/help-emotional-crisis

Barnett, J. E., & Cooper, N. (2009). Creating a culture of self-care. *Clinical Psychology: Science and Practice*, 16(1), 16–20. https://doi.org/10.1111/j.1468-2850.2009.01138.x

Batchelor, S., Stoyanov, S., Pirkis, J., & Kõlves, K. (2021). Use of Kids Helpline by children and young people in Australia during the COVID-19 pandemic. *Journal of Adolescent Health*, 68(6), 1067–74. https://doi.org/10.1016/j.jadohealth.2021.03.015

Bram, M. H. (2024, October 15). How to establish classroom routines for productive learning. Edutopia. https://www.edutopia.org/article/establish-classroom-routines-productive-learning/

Center for Healthy Minds, University of Wisconsin-Madison. (n.d.). Try the 5-3-1 practice. https://centerhealthyminds.org/join-the-movement/try-the-5-3-1-practice

Center on the Developing Child, Harvard University. (2017, August 25). Building the skills adults need for life: A guide for practitioners. https://developingchild.harvard.edu/resources/handouts-tools/building-skills-adults-need-life-guide-practitioners/

Centers for Disease Control and Prevention. (2021). Preventing adverse childhood experiences. Retrieved from https://www.cdc.gov/violenceprevention/aces/index.html

Desautels, L. (2016, September 16). Energy and calm: Brain breaks and focused-attention practices. Edutopia. https://www.edutopia.org/article/blog-brain-breaks-focused-attention-practices-lori-desautels/

Durlak, J. A., Weissberg, R. P., Dymnicki, A. B., Taylor, R. D., & Schellinger, K. B. (2011). The impact of enhancing students' social and emotional learning: A meta-analysis of school-based universal interventions. *Child Development*, 82(1), 405–32. https://doi.org/10.1111/j.1467-8624.2010.01564.x

Ergas, O. (2014). Mindfulness in education at the intersection of science, religion, and healing. *Critical Studies in Education*, 55(1), 58–72. https://doi.org/10.1080/17508487.2014.858643

Hanover Research. (2011, March). School structures that support 21st-century learning. District Administration Practice. https://www.sas.edu.sg/uploaded/Perspectives_Blog_Categories/Hanover_Research_%281%29.pdf

Herman, J. L. (1992). *Trauma and recovery: The aftermath of violence—from domestic abuse to political terror*. Basic Books.

Holden, R. (1993). *Laughter: The best medicine*. Thorsons. https://archive.org/details/laughterbestmedi00robe

Imad, M. (2021, May 25). How to make mental health a top priority this fall and beyond. The Chronicle of Higher Education. https://www.chronicle.com/article/how-to-make-mental-health-a-top-priority-this-fall-and-beyond

Kuban, C., & Steele, W. (2011). Restoring safety and hope: From victim to survivor. *Reclaiming Children and Youth*, 20(1), 41–4. https://eric.ed.gov/?id=EJ932137

Leiterland. (n.d.). Anthology assignment directions for 30 literary works. http://t.ly/4IUY

Martinelli, K. (n.d.). How can we help kids with transitions? Child Mind Institute. https://childmind.org/article/how-can-we-help-kids-with-transitions/

Minahan, J. (2019, October). Trauma-informed teaching strategies. *Educational Leadership*, 77(2), 30–5. https://www.ascd.org/publications/educational_leadership/oct19/vol77/num02/Trauma-Informed_Teaching_Strategies.aspx

NAEYC. (2015). Creating trauma-sensitive classrooms. *Young Children*, 70(2), 56–61. https://www.naeyc.org/resources/pubs/yc/may2015/trauma-sensitive-classrooms

National Sleep Foundation. (2023, December 21). How much sleep does a teenager need? https://www.sleepfoundation.org/teens-and-sleep/how-much-sleep-does-a-teenager-need

NovoPsych. (2021). The professional quality of life scale—5 (ProQOL). https://novopsych.com/assessments/clinician-self-assessment/the-professional-quality-of-life-scale-5-proqol/

Peixoto, F., Silva, J. C., Pipa, J., Wosnitza, M., & Mansfield, C. F. (2020). The multidimensional teachers' resilience scale: Validation for Portuguese teachers. *Journal of Psychoeducational Assessment*, 38(3), 402–8. https://doi.org/10.1177/

Rajendran, K., & Videka, L. (2006). Relational and academic components of resilience in maltreated adolescents. *Annals of the New York Academy of Sciences*, 1094, 345–9. https://doi.org/10.1196/annals.1376.047

Spencer, E. (2022, January 17). The 10 things I say to my teens when they are stressed out. Grown & Flown. https://grownandflown.com/10-things-say-teens-stressed-out/

Spencer, J. (2022). Making rest a priority in the summer. Medium. https://medium.com/@spencerideas/making-rest-a-priority-in-the-summer-52e5dc99746c

Tawwab, N. (2021). *Set boundaries, find peace: A guide to reclaiming yourself*. Atria Books.

Washington State Department of Social and Health Services. (n.d.). Types and signs of abuse. https://www.dshs.wa.gov/altsa/home-and-community-services/types-and-signs-abuse

Willsey, P. S. (2020, January 16). 7 ways to help teens manage stress. *Psychology Today*. https://www.psychologytoday.com/us/blog/packing-success/202001/7-ways-help-teens-manage-stress

Chapter 16

Beyond the Classroom

Beyond the Classroom

Because teaching is a lifestyle, what we do in our personal lives and the broader community impacts our instruction. Classroom professionals are often the first line of communication between the school and families. Handling interactions with parents, especially in challenging situations, requires a delicate balance of empathy, professionalism, and effective communication skills. This chapter discusses how to manage these interactions.

Self-care and efficient time management outside of school hours also affect instruction. Hence, this chapter shares practical suggestions to streamline your daily routines and prioritize your well-being.

The following pages also highlight the significance of teacher activism and community engagement. Whether it's advocating for more instructional autonomy, fair educator compensation, or standing against inequities, your voice is vital.

However, if you want to go fast, go alone but if you want to go far, go together. Writes Randi Weingarten in TeachThought, "Where educators are raising and combining their voices, the seeds of positive change have emerged. Collective voice, exercised through the union, is power—the power to drive real change for our kids, families, and communities" (2023).

Key Chapter 16 Strategies

1. Show that you value parents' concerns by actively listening and taking notes. Ask follow-up questions to fully understand their worries.
2. Update parents on actions taken after the meeting with guardians to reinforce your commitment to resolving their concerns.
3. Prepare pancakes or waffles ahead of time, freeze them, and pop them in the toaster for quick breakfast options.
4. Cook multiple variations of chicken at once using aluminum foil dividers in your pan to save time without boring your taste buds.
5. Refrigerate uncooked slow cooker food the night before and start the cooker in the morning before leaving home.
6. Identify how your state is addressing salary inequity, share relevant myths and facts, and support or start petitions for teacher salary increases on platforms like Change.org.
7. Contact your state's senator or representative to discuss the benefits of increased teacher pay and invite them to visit your school.
8. Partner with local businesses and organizations to support campaigns for raising teacher pay.
9. Provide all students with feelings of efficacy by showing authentic evidence of their academic success and reinforcing their value and contributions.
10. Provide authentic evidence of students' academic success, show they are valued, reinforce their contributions to the community and make them feel empowered.

Memory Device for this Chapter
Visualization Mnemonic

Imagine Meeting an Aggravated Parent—Do the Following

1. Request that a supportive administrator attend the meeting (Secure Backup).
2. Listen carefully to the parent (Listen and Take Notes).
3. Maintain calm by breathing deeply (Manage Your Emotions).
4. Solve problems through actionable steps (Offer a Solution).
5. Follow up with parents (Follow-Up Promptly).
6. Gather feedback for improvement (Seek Feedback).

HOW TO DEFUSE ANGRY PARENTS

"With the right framework in place, you can turn a volatile situation into an opportunity to build trust, respect, and stronger home-school relationships" (Connex Education Partnership, n.d.). Embrace every challenge as a chance to engage in meaningful dialogue.

1. LISTEN AND TAKE NOTES

Signal to the parent that what they have to say is important. Take notes and listen intensively. Ask, "What else is worrying you? What else should I understand?"

2. SECURE BACKUP

If you anticipate a belligerent parent, ask an administrator to join you. But if a parent yells, the meeting is over.

3. MANAGE YOUR EMOTIONS

Breathe slower than the parent. Keep your fingers, toes, and jaw loose.

4. IF YOU WERE IN THE WRONG . . .

Take responsibility. State what you'll do differently. Ask, "How else can I make this right?"

5. OFFER A SOLUTION

Instead of just acknowledging the problem, offer actionable solutions and timelines. This shows you are proactive and committed to resolving the issue.

6. FOLLOW-UP PROMPTLY

After the meeting, follow up with the parents to update them on the actions taken. This reinforces your commitment to addressing their concerns.

7. SEEK FEEDBACK

Ask the parent for feedback on how the situation was handled and what could be done better in the future. This can help improve future interactions.

MEAL PREP TIPS FOR TEACHERS

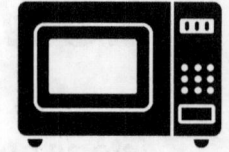

"Amidst hectic weekday schedules, meal prep or meal planning is a great tool to help keep us on a healthy eating track. Although any type of meal prep requires planning, there is no one correct method, as it can differ based on food preferences, cooking ability, schedules, and personal goals" (Harvard T.H. Chan School of Public Health, 2017). Transform the challenge of a busy week into an opportunity for creative self-care.

1. BATCH PANCAKES
Make pancakes or waffles ahead of time and freeze them. In the morning, pop them in the toaster.

2. 3 BIRDS, 1 PAN
"Save time without boring your taste buds by preparing two or three variations of chicken at once, using aluminum foil dividers in your pan. Sriracha, BBQ, honey mustard—you can have it all" (Fit Men Cook, n.d.).

3. EGG MUFFINS
Make several egg muffins with a muffin tin. Add turkey bacon, chopped onion, bell peppers, and baby spinach. Recipe: bit.ly/3qnRePz (Delish, n.d.).

4. SLOW COOKER TIP
Refrigerate uncooked slow cooker food the night before. Then start the cooker the next morning before leaving home.

5. WAKE UP TO COFFEE
Set a brewing timer on an automatic coffee pot so you can caffeinate while dressing.

6. SALAD DRESSING IN YOUR CLASS
Store a bottle of salad dressing in your classroom and drizzle it over your mason jar salad at lunch. No one enjoys soggy lettuce!

INTERVIEW QUESTIONS

Preparation is everything in an interview. Be ready to discuss your expertise in supporting the whole child, addressing their academic, social, and emotional growth. Be prepared to explain how you integrate these elements seamlessly in your approach.

1. What's your philosophy of teaching?
2. Describe your most successful lesson.
3. Describe a challenge you overcame.
4. How do you handle feedback? Give an example.
5. What questions do you have for us?
6. What activities would you consider coaching or advising?
7. Describe your classroom management approach.
8. What aspect of your teaching are you working on right now?
9. Why do you want to work with children/adolescents?
10. What can you bring to our school that makes you unique?
11. Give an example of how you might differentiate instruction.
12. How do you incorporate UDL?
13. What is your teaching style?
14. What are your professional strengths and weaknesses?
15. What would you do if . . . . . . a student stood at your classroom door and refused to come inside at the bell? . . . a parent complained about your teaching methods? . . . a colleague you were co-planning with had an inferior idea?
16. How do you motivate students?
17. What educational experts do you most admire?
18. How do you develop a strong classroom community?
19. How have you used data to change your teaching?
20. What will you do if you have students with widely different learning abilities?
21. What kind of homework will you give?
22. What processes have you modeled?
23. What's the best teaching idea you've learned in the last year?
24. What technologies do you have students use most often?
25. How do you engage resistant learners?
26. Do you teach to the test?
27. What does an inclusive classroom look like?
28. Why would we choose you for this job over someone with more experience?
29. Give an example of how you are student-centered.
30. What questions do you have for us?

HOW TO RAISE TEACHER PAY

Investing in fair compensation is more cost effective than repeatedly training new teachers. Providing competitive pay helps retain experienced educators, ensuring stability and expertise in schools.

1. LEARN WHAT YOUR STATE IS DOING
The Teacher Salary Project identifies the most promising ways that every state is addressing salary inequity: https://www.teachersalaryproject.org/

2. SHARE PAY MYTHS AND FACTS
See the NEA's definitive list of myths and facts about teacher pay. Example: "almost 20% of teachers leave the profession because of low pay" (NEA, 2018).

3. CALL YOUR REPRESENTATIVE
Call the Capitol switchboard to be connected to your state's senator or representative: 202–224–3121. Invite them to visit your school and watch you teach.

4. SHARE BENEFITS WITH LEGISLATORS
The National Center for Analysis of Longitudinal Data in Ed. Research (2019) reported that increasing teacher salaries by $4,000 reduced turnover by 3%.

5. SIGN PETITIONS
Support teacher salary petitions on Change.org or start one.

6. MEDIA OUTREACH
Write op-eds and letters to local newspapers and online platforms highlighting the benefits of increased teacher pay.

7. COLLABORATIVE CAMPAIGNS
Partner with local businesses and organizations to create campaigns supporting teacher pay raises.

WHAT TEACHERS SHOULD STAND FOR

"Teachers naturally become role models, influencing academic growth and shaping the values and character of their students. Society often looks up to teachers, mirroring their behavior and attitudes. For instance, a teacher who is resilient to challenges can inspire children to adopt a positive mindset and pursue teaching roles" (Teachers of Tomorrow, 2024). By embodying qualities such as empathy, perseverance, and a lifelong passion for learning, teachers can spark a transformative ripple effect, inspiring students to cultivate a positive mindset and become influential, resilient leaders in their own communities.

1. CALLING OUT INEQUITY

The Government Accountability Office (2018) found that Black kids are 3.2 times more likely to be suspended or expelled than White students, despite no evidence showing more misbehavior compared to their White counterparts.

2. COMMUNITY BUILDING

Freire (1996) and Maslow (1987) showed that kids are motivated by teachers who make them feel like they belong.

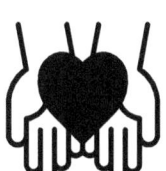

3. RADICAL GENEROSITY

Five teachers at Whitney Achievement Elementary School walked students home daily to ensure their safety and build relationships. Examples of radical generosity:

- Linda Joseph secured free water safety lessons for kids with special needs.
- Jen Scully gave a student her kidney.
- Bennie Berry adopted a student in foster care.

4. REJECT DEFICIT THINKING

Provide all students with feelings of efficacy by:

- Providing authentic evidence of academic success (competence).
- Showing they're valued (belonging).
- Reinforcing that they've contributed to their community (usefulness).
- Making them feel empowered (potency) (Sagor, 2000).

Workbook: Reflecting on Chapter 16 Topics

1. How does active listening enhance communication with parents and students?
2. Why is it important to have administrative support during challenging parent meetings?
3. What techniques can be used to manage emotions during stressful interactions with parents or colleagues?
4. How can reflecting on your teaching philosophy help you prepare for a teaching job interview?
5. What are some effective ways to advocate for better teacher pay and benefits?
6. How can teachers build a sense of community within their classrooms and the broader school environment?
7. How can educators actively work to call out and address inequities in the school system?

Going Deeper—Advanced Questions

1. How can educators develop and apply emotional intelligence to foster stronger home-school relationships and mitigate conflicts effectively? Consider the implications of emotional regulation, empathy, and social skills within the educational context.
2. How can consistent, constructive feedback loops enhance educational outcomes, parent–teacher relationships, and overall school culture?
3. Explore the intersection of mindfulness practices and teacher resilience. How can incorporating mindfulness techniques such as meditation, box breathing, and reflective journaling into daily routines influence teacher stress levels, job satisfaction, and instructional effectiveness?
4. Investigate teacher-led movements for fair compensation; how did those movements affect teacher retention, student achievement, and community support for schools?
5. Propose recommendations for best practices in teacher self-care and time management.

Checklist of Activities and Strategies to Try (Pick 2)

- ❏ How does active listening enhance communication with parents and students?
- ❏ Why is it important to have administrative support during a challenging parent meeting?
- ❏ What techniques can be used to manage emotions during stressful interactions with parents or colleagues?
- ❏ How can reflecting on your teaching philosophy help you prepare for a teaching job interview?
- ❏ What are some effective ways to advocate for better teacher pay and benefits?
- ❏ How can teachers build a sense of community within their classrooms and the broader school environment?
- ❏ How can educators actively work to call out and address inequities in the school system?
- ❏ Other: _____.

Describe Your Progress

1. What activities were most successful?

2. What challenges did you face?

3. How can you improve for next time?

 **References for Chapter 16**

Connex Education Partnership. (n.d.). How to handle an angry parent. https://connex-education.com/how-to-handle-an-angry-parent/

Delish. (n.d.). Egg muffins [Recipe]. https://www.delish.com/cooking/recipe-ideas/a25563943/egg-muffins-recipe/

Fit Men Cook. (n.d.). 3 birds, 1 pan [Recipe]. https://fitmencook.com/

Freire, P. (1996). *Pedagogy of the oppressed* (30th anniversary ed.). Continuum.

Government Accountability Office. (2018). Discipline disparities for Black students, boys, and students with disabilities. U.S. Government Accountability Office. https://www.gao.gov/products/gao-18-258

Harvard T.H. Chan School of Public Health. (2017). Healthy living guide. The Nutrition Source. https://www.hsph.harvard.edu/nutritionsource/

Maslow, A. H. (1987). *Motivation and personality* (3rd ed.). Harper & Row.

National Center for Analysis of Longitudinal Data in Education Research. (2019). The effects of school finance reforms on teacher salary and student achievement. *Educational Researcher*, 48(6), 324–37.

National Education Association. (2018, September 1). Teacher compensation: Fact vs. fiction. NEA. https://www.nea.org/resource-library/teacher-compensation-fact-vs-fiction

Sagor, R. (2000). *Guiding school improvement with action research*. Association for Supervision and Curriculum Development.

Teachers of Tomorrow. (2024). 12 reasons why teachers play a crucial role in society 2024. https://www.teachersoftomorrow.org/blog/insights/reasons-why-teachers-play-a-crucial-role-in-society/

TeachThought. (2023). 50 of the best education quotes for teachers. https://www.teachthought.com/education/best-education-quotes/

Appendices

Appendix A

Index of Foundational Instructional Strategies

This index highlights Cheat Codes from this guide that have been specifically curated for preservice and new teachers, featuring essential strategies to boost their teaching effectiveness.

Classroom Management and Organization

First-Week Activities	5
Ice Breakers	6
Plan Lessons Faster	35
Set Strong Norms	8
Rapport Builders!	9
The Organized Teacher	33
Tips for Managing Student Paperwork	36
Reduce Classroom Commotion	19
Resistant Classes	20
Classroom Conflict	21
A Child Refuses Classwork. Now What?	22
Sub Tub Components	37
I Finished Early—Now What?	142

Instructional Strategies

Lesson Starters	45
Schema Activation Strategies	46
Metacognition	47
To Clarify Something Complex	48
Engaging Text-Based Lessons	50
Powerful PowerPoint	90
Make Thinking Visible	91
Timeline Learning Activities	94

Professional Development and Advice

I Wish My Education Profs Had Told Me . . .	10
Interview Questions	253

Teaching Techniques

How to Scaffold Texts to Unlock Meaning	113
Scaffolding English Language Arts	114
Effective Use of Text Evidence . . . Remember C.A.S.E.	115
Post-Reading Journal Alternatives	116
Book Report Alternatives	117
Vocabulary Instruction	118
How Students Conceal Reading Struggles	119
Where to Find Free Readings	120
Stage Fright	236
Poem Analysis Activities	121
Techniques for Helping Kids Summarize	122
Writing Tips	123
Writing to Learn Strategies	124
Low-Stakes Writing	125
Revising and Editing Checklists	126

Listening Activities 127
Public Speaking Formats 128

Classroom Interaction
Helping Introverts Participate in Discussions 143
How to Increase Participation in Whole Class Discussion 153

Teacher Habits and Confidence
Eight Habits of Successful Teachers 102
Boost Your Teaching Confidence 103
Effective Teacher Nonverbals 104

Appendix B

Index of Advanced Instructional Strategies

This index highlights *Cheat Codes* specifically curated for experienced teachers who wish to push the boundaries of traditional teaching methods.

Classroom Management and Student Behavior

Indicators That a Child Might Become Violent 23
Supporting a Child Who Might Become Violent 24
Tips for Dealing with Hate Speech 25
Handling a Big Class 7
Decrease Task Difficulty 56
Classroom Stations 59
Year-Enders 60
Unsung Duties 62
How to Facilitate Difficult Discussions 158
A Discussion Goes Off-Topic. What Do You Say? 156
When Students Can't Answer 157
Make Class Discussions Constructive 154

Instructional Strategies and Advanced Techniques

How to Engage in Deliberate Practice 52
Upgrade Presentation Handouts 53
Alliterative Weekday Activity Themes 51
Boost Classroom Rigor 54
The Science of Chunking 49
Upgrade Reading Homework 55
Study Tips 58
How to Reduce Cognitive Overload 79
Pair Visual with Critical Thinking 92
Video Viewing Tips 93
Formative Assessment Tech 174
Creative Ways to Promote Learning When Testing 175
Final Exam Alternatives 171
Exam Prep Activities 170
Exit Ticket Prompts 176
They Bombed the Test, Now What? 177
Advice for Kids with Test Anxiety 178
Teaching to the Test: The Issues 179

Teacher Well-being and Emotional Support

Compassion Fatigue 232
Withstand that Tough Tuesday 233
How to Maintain Healthy Boundaries 235
Mindfulness Tips 237
How to Help Traumatized Students 239
Ways to Help Stressed Teens 240
Helplines for Kids 241

Teaching Diverse Learners and Equity

Inclusion 137
Supporting Students with Executive Function 138
Gender Equity Strategies for Faculty 139
Poverty Deficit Myths 140
Micro-Aggressions 141
Indicators of Bulimia 144
Trauma-Informed Teaching 238
Talking About Race: Ground Rules 159
Debunk Conspiracy Theories 160

Assessment and Feedback

Test Construction Errors 173
Efficient Grading Part 1 188
Efficient Grading Part 2 189
Ways to Solicit Student Feedback 190
CAT (Classroom Assessment Techniques) 172

Technology Integration

ChatGPT Time-Savers 198
What Can You Do with Google Docs? 200
Using Social Media for Education 201
Classroom YouTube Tips 199
HyperDoc Templates 204
Improve Remote Instruction 202
Teacher Presence During Remote Instruction 203

Motivation and Engagement

How to Motivate Me 213
Teacher-Student Relationship Building 215
Trigger Students' Happy Brain Chemicals 216
Leverage Social Proof to Motivate Students 217
Classroom Rewards! 218
Ways to Say, "Good Job!" 219
Give Activities Engaging Names 220
Personality Characteristics of Most Liked Teachers 221
Make Students Feel Heard 222
Why Lessons Fail 223
Research on Student Engagement 214

Professional Growth and Beyond

How to Raise Teacher Pay 254
What Teachers Should Stand For 255
Meal Prep Tips for Teachers 252
How to Defuse Angry Parents 251

Appendix C

Glossary

Adaptive Testing: A method of assessment where the test is calibrated to the student's abilities.

Advanced Organizers: Instructional tools used to introduce the lesson and illustrate the relationship between what students are about to learn and the information they have already learned.

Annotate the Text: Making notes on important points in the text to enhance understanding and retention.

Brain Blast: Infographics packed with practical, tactical, evidence-based, and creative teaching methods.

Chunking: The process of grouping individual pieces of information into larger units to improve memory and understanding.

Claim, Answer, Support, Explain (CASE): A writing strategy that helps students structure their responses by making a claim, answering a question, supporting it with evidence, and explaining their reasoning.

Classroom Norms: Shared expectations and rules established by teachers and students to guide behavior, promote respect, and create a positive and productive learning environment.

Cloze: An assessment where students fill in the blanks of a passage, outline, or slides with the correct terms.

Cognitive Load: The total amount of mental effort being used in the working memory.

Cognitive Overload: A state where the amount of information being processed exceeds the capacity of the working memory, leading to decreased learning effectiveness.

Cooperative Learning: An instructional approach where students work together in small groups to achieve learning goals, promoting socialization and collaborative skills.

Constructive Feedback: Information provided to students to help them improve their performance and understanding.

Deliberate Practice: A highly structured activity aimed at improving performance through specific tasks designed to address weaknesses, with careful monitoring and adjustment.

Differentiation: Tailoring instruction to meet the individual needs of students based on their abilities, interests, and learning styles.

Discussion Prompt: Questions used to facilitate whole-class discussions on various topics.

E-Portfolio: A collection of learner artifacts and reflections demonstrating learning over time.

Exam Wrappers: Sheets with reflection prompts that help students learn from their mistakes.

Exit Ticket: A formative assessment tool where students write down their understanding or questions at the end of a lesson. Various prompts that allow students to reflect on what they learned and provide feedback.

Fishbowl Discussion: A discussion format where a small group discusses a topic while others observe, followed by a class-wide discussion.

Formative Assessment: Ongoing assessments used to monitor student learning and provide feedback that can be used to improve their performance.

Free Writes: Unrestricted writing time for students to explore topics creatively and expressively.

Frontloading Vocabulary: Teaching difficult vocabulary before reading to improve comprehension.

Gamification: The application of game-design elements and principles in non-game contexts to increase engagement and motivation.

Genre Conventions: Typical features and structures that define a particular genre of text, helping students make predictions about texts.

Graphic Organizer: Visual tools such as charts or diagrams used to organize information and illustrate relationships between concepts.

Guided Reading Questions: Questions provided during reading to help students focus on key concepts and ideas.
Higher Order Thinking: Cognitive processes that involve analysis, evaluation, synthesis, and creation, as opposed to merely remembering facts.
HyperDoc: Digital documents that integrate all elements of a lesson plan into one cohesive, interactive learning experience.
Icebreaker: An activity or game used at the beginning of a session or class to help participants get to know each other and feel more comfortable.
Inquiry Projects: Projects that involve students in investigating questions, problems, or scenarios, promoting active learning and critical thinking.
Interactive Lecture: A teaching method where the instructor periodically engages students in activities that let them interact with the material, enhancing understanding and participation.
Learning Objective: Specific goals that outline what students should know or be able to do after a lesson.
Metacognition: Awareness and understanding of one's own thought processes, often involving self- regulation and reflection on learning strategies.
Mind Mapping: Text and graphics that visually organize concepts.
Mnemonic Device: Memory aids such as acronyms, rhymes, or narratives used to help recall information.
Paraphrase: Rewriting text in one's own words to enhance understanding and retention.
Peer Review: An assessment method where students evaluate each other's work and provide constructive feedback.
Post-Reading Activities: Tasks that reinforce and extend students' comprehension and engagement with the text after reading.
Pre-Reading Activities: Tasks that prepare students for reading by building background knowledge and setting a purpose for reading.
Productive Struggle: The concept that struggling through challenging tasks is essential for deep learning and growth.
Quiz Circuit: A relay race where each leg involves a quiz question and physical challenge.
Reflective Listening: Techniques for actively listening and responding to group members to enhance communication and understanding.
Scaffold or Scaffolding: A temporary support structure provided to students to help them achieve learning goals, which is gradually removed as students become more proficient.
Schema Activation Strategies: Techniques used to help students connect new information to existing knowledge, enhancing understanding and retention.
Self-Assessment: A process where students evaluate their own work and learning progress.
Simulation: Students make choices based on a real-life scenario.
Socratic Seminar: A method of teaching through structured group discussion, where students explore and articulate their thoughts on a topic, guided by open-ended questions.
Socrative: Kids use computers or smartphones to answer quiz questions, which are automatically scored and reported.
Structured Talks: Guided and purposeful discussions that allow students to explore various interpretations and perspectives.
Task Tree: A visual strategy that provides step-by-step instructions for students to follow, helping them manage and complete tasks effectively.
Teaching to the Test: The practice of drilling students on specific test content rather than on a broader and richer curriculum.

Test Anxiety: The stress and fear associated with taking exams, which can impact academic performance.
Think-Aloud: A teaching method where the instructor verbalizes their thought process to model metacognition for students.
Think-Pair-Share: A collaborative learning strategy where students think about a question, discuss it with a partner, and then share their ideas with the larger group.
Timeline Learning Activities: Activities that involve creating timelines to help students identify patterns, make comparisons, and develop historical perspectives.
Trashketball: Kids answer review questions in teams, with correct answers earning a chance to shoot a paper ball into a trash can for extra points.
Universal Design for Learning (UDL): An educational framework that provides all students with equal opportunities to learn through multiple means of engagement, representation, and action/expression.
Visual Thinking Strategies (VTS): Techniques involving visual aids and images to help students think critically and understand complex concepts.
Visuals: Images, graphic organizers, or videos used to enhance understanding before reading a text.
Word Sorts: Activities where students categorize vocabulary words to enhance understanding.
Word Walls: Classroom displays of key vocabulary and concepts to support vocabulary development.

Appendix D

Final Words

Dear Reader,

If you regard the classroom as a sacred space and greet students every morning with curiosity, joy, and humility, then you, my inspiring friend, are walking the same path cleared by Confucius, Freire, Al Hroub, MacDonnell, Montessori, Sullivan, and Pierson. They all led lives of significance and service. As you continue to forge new trails, please share them with me on social media and via email. I'd love to hear about your adventures. Below, I've included one last resource to energize your determination—an affirmation to post next to your toothbrush. -Todd

Daily Affirmation for Teachers

"Today, I embrace the power of my influence. I am a beacon of inspiration, compassion, and knowledge. Every interaction with my students is an opportunity to make a positive impact and foster a love of learning. I am committed to creating an inclusive and empowering environment where every student feels valued and capable. I believe in my ability to overcome challenges and grow as an educator. I am shaping the future, one word at a time. I rock."

For Product Safety Concerns and Information please contact our EU representative GPSR@taylorandfrancis.com
Taylor & Francis Verlag GmbH, Kaufingerstraße 24, 80331 München, Germany

www.ingramcontent.com/pod-product-compliance
Lightning Source LLC
Chambersburg PA
CBHW060509300426
44112CB00017B/2601